On Care
for Our Common Home
Laudato Si'

Ecology and Justice

An Orbis Series on Integral Ecology

The Orbis Series on Integral Ecology publishes books seeking to integrate an understanding of Earth's interconnected life systems with sustainable social, political, and economic systems that enhance the Earth community. Books in the series concentrate on ways to:

- reexamine human–Earth relations in light of contemporary cosmological and ecological science
- develop visions of common life marked by ecological integrity and social justice
- expand on the work of those exploring such fields as integral ecology, climate justice, Earth law, eco-feminism, and animal protection
- promote inclusive participatory strategies that enhance the struggle of Earth's poor and oppressed for ecological justice
- deepen appreciation for dialogue within and among religious traditions on issues of ecology and justice
- encourage spiritual discipline, social engagement, and the transformation of religion and society towards these ends.

Viewing the present moment as a time for fresh creativity and inspired by the encyclical *Laudato Si'*, the series seeks authors who speak to eco-justice concerns and who bring into this dialogue perspectives from the Christian communities, from the world's religions, from secular and scientific circles, or from new paradigms of thought and action.

On Care
for Our Common Home
Laudato Si'

The Encyclical of Pope Francis
on the Environment

with commentary by

SEAN MCDONAGH

ORBIS BOOKS

Maryknoll, New York 10545

ORBIS BOOKS
Maryknoll, New York 10545

Fathers and Brothers
MARYKNOLL™
TOGETHER IN GOD'S MISSION OF MERCY

Founded in 1970, Orbis Books endeavors to publish works that enlighten the mind, nourish the spirit, and challenge the conscience. The publishing arm of the Maryknoll Fathers and Brothers, Orbis seeks to explore the global dimensions of the Christian faith and mission, to invite dialogue with diverse cultures and religious traditions, and to serve the cause of reconciliation and peace. The books published reflect the views of their authors and do not represent the official position of the Maryknoll Society. To learn more about Maryknoll and Orbis Books, please visit our website at www.maryknollsociety.org.

Library of Congress Cataloging-in-Publication Data

Catholic Church. Pope (2013– : Francis)
[Laudato si'. English]
    Our common home : the encyclical of Pope Francis on the environment, Laudato Si' / with commentary by Sean McDonagh.
      pages cm
    Includes index.
    ISBN 978-1-62698-173-7 (pbk.)
    1. Human ecology—Religious aspects—Catholic Church. 2. Ecotheology. 3. Climatic changes—Effect of human beings on. 4. Christian sociology—Catholic Church. 5. Catholic Church—Doctrines. I. McDonagh, Sean, 1935– commentator. II. Title.
BX1795.H82C38313 2016
261.8'8—dc23
                                                                 2015033670

For lifelong friends
Thomas O'Domnaill and
Liam and Mary B. Reddan

Contents

Preface

The encyclical letter of Pope Francis, *Laudato Si': On Care for Our Common Home,* was published in Rome on June 18, 2015. It is certainly one of the most important documents from the Holy See in recent decades. In this short document Pope Francis has moved the Catholic Church from the periphery of global engagement with ecology right to the very heart of the debate. The full text of *Laudato Si'* is included as Part II of this volume.

Laudato Si' has two related focal points. The first of these is the call to all human beings to respect, cherish, and stop exploiting planet earth—the home for all creation. The language is very challenging and often emotional. In the words of St. Francis of Assisi, the earth is our sister. But today, according to Pope Francis, "this sister cries out to us because of the harm we have inflicted on her by our irresponsible use and abuse of the goods with which God has endowed her" (no. 2). Later in the document, while reflecting on the damage that humans are causing to the fabric of the planet, he writes that "the earth is beginning to look more and more like an immense pile of filth" (no. 21).

The second focus of *Laudato Si'* is on the poor of the world and those who are excluded from reaching their true potential. The pope is adamant that "the deterioration of the environment and of society affects the most vulnerable people on the planet" (no. 48). For him, it is crucial that all humanity hear both the cry of the earth and the cry of the poor.

To those familiar with the life and work of the pope, formerly known as Jorge Mario Bergoglio, *Laudato Si'* did not come as a complete surprise because of his work among the poor in Buenos Aires and the growing concern of Latin American bishops for environmental degradation, especially in the Amazon region. From the time Bergoglio became archbishop of Buenos Aires in 1996, he had prolonged experience of ministering to poor people living on the margins of society. He was particularly concerned about the lives and well-being of the 300,000 people, or 10 percent of the population of the city, who lived in extreme poverty in areas known as villas. He constantly visited these communities, listened respectfully to the concerns of those living there, and did everything in his power to support the individuals and organizations that were dedicated to alleviating poverty and promoting community in these areas.

During the Fifth General Conference of the Bishops of Latin America and the Caribbean, which was held at Aparecida, Brazil, in May 2007, he was chosen to chair the important committee assigned the task of drafting the final document. That document speaks of the church's commitment to the poor and to those on the periphery of society. It also deals extensively with the fact that the beauty and fruitfulness of the natural world, particularly in the Amazon area, is being exploited in so many different ways.

On being elected pope on March 13, 2013, he opted to be called Francis—the first time any pope had chosen that name. Three days later he explained that choice to an assembly of six thousand journalists gathered in Rome: "Francis was a man of poverty, who loved and protected creation." From the outset, he made it clear that concern for the poor and for creation would be central themes of his pontificate.

He elaborated further on these themes on a number of occasions. For example, in a homily on March 19, 2013, the feast of St. Joseph, during a mass marking his inauguration as bishop of Rome, he called St. Joseph "protector of Jesus and his mother." He expanded the notion of protector to include concern for creation. He continued:

> The vocation of being a "protector" also has a prior dimension . . . involving everyone. It means protecting all creation, the beauty of the created world, as the Book of Genesis tells us and as Saint Francis of Assisi showed us. . . . Everything has been entrusted to our protection, and all of us are

responsible for it. Be protectors of God's gifts! To all those who have positions of responsibility in economic, political and social life, and all men and women of goodwill: let us be "protectors" of creation, protectors of God's plan inscribed in nature, protectors of one another and of the environment!

In his message on World Environment Day in 2013, Pope Francis warned that "consumerism and a culture of waste" have led some of us to tolerate the waste of precious resources, including food, while others are literally wasting away from hunger. I ask all of you to reflect on this grave ethical problem in a spirit of solidarity grounded in our common responsibility for the earth and for all our brothers and sisters in the human family."[1] The same themes emerged in his address to the Diplomatic Corps on March 22, 2013:

Fighting poverty, both material and spiritual, building peace and constructing bridges . . . are the reference points for a journey that I want to invite each of the countries here represented to take up. But it is a difficult journey, if we do not learn to grow in love for this world of ours. Here too, it helps me to think of the name of Francis, who teaches us profound respect for the whole of creation and the protection of our environment, which all too often, instead of using it for the good, we exploit greedily, to one another's detriment.[2]

In *Urbi et Orbi (To the City and the World)* on Easter Sunday, 2013, Pope Francis said, "Let us be renewed by God's mercy, let us be loved by Jesus, let us enable the power of his love to transform our lives too; and let us become agents of this mercy, channels through which God can water the earth, protect all creation and make justice and peace flourish."

---

[1] Pope Francis, "Pope at Audience: Counter Culture of Waste with Solidarity," Vatican Radio, June 5, 2013.

[2] Pope Francis, Address to the Diplomatic Corps, Sala Regia, March 22, 2013.

Many people saw his apostolic exhortation *Evangelii Gaudium* as a statement of the priorities and agenda for his pontificate. This document includes a trenchant criticism of unfettered free-market economics, which sidelines tens of millions of poor people globally. But concern for the environment was also stressed:

> Thanks to our bodies, God has joined us so closely to the world around us that we can feel the desertification of the soil almost as a physical ailment and the extinction of species as a painful disfigurement. Let us not leave in our wake a swath of destruction and death which affect our lives and those of future generations. (no. 4)

He went on to quote from the 1988 pastoral letter of the Philippine bishops, *What Is Happening to Our Beautiful Land,* the first pastoral letter exclusively devoted to the environment from any conference of bishops:

> God intended this land for us, his special creatures, but not so that we might destroy it and turn it into a wasteland. . . . After a single night's rain, look at the chocolate brown rivers in your locality and remember that they are carrying the life blood of the land into the sea. . . . As Christians we are called to watch over and protect the fragile world in which we live and all its peoples. (no. 5)

Given this history, it was quite logical that Pope Francis would write an encyclical encompassing his critique of global poverty and his concern for what is happening to the earth.

Given the prominence of the pope and the high stakes, both political and economic, involved with questions regarding climate change, energy production, and the global economic system, anticipation of Pope Francis's encyclical was keen—for some a matter of apprehension, for many a source of hope. One of the questions was whether Pope Francis would clearly recognize the role of human actions in affecting climate change. (He does.) But the encyclical went far beyond the question of climate change to evaluate the scientific, ethical, and religious implications of biodiversity; the pollution of the waters of the world; and the current operation of global capitalism, whereby many of the world's resources are controlled by a few, while so many people are excluded and forced to live in poverty. Significantly, he addressed the encyclical not only to Catholics and other Christians, but to all humanity. Quoting the bishops of Southern Africa, he notes that "everyone's talents and involvement are needed to redress the damage caused by human abuse of God's creation" (no. 14). The timing of the encyclical was also significant, coming prior to a major UN summit on climate scheduled in Paris for December 2015.

Among those long committed to promoting global action on the environment the significance of this timing was clear. Their response was generally enthusiastic. They included Ban Ki-moon, the secretary-general of the United Nations, whose spokesperson said, "The Secretary-General welcomes the papal encyclical released today by His Holiness Pope Francis which highlights that climate change is one of the principal challenges facing humanity, and that it is a moral issue requiring respectful dialogue with all parts of society." He also hoped that this initiative would encourage governments "to place the global common good above national interests and to adopt an ambitious, universal climate agreement in Paris this year."[3]

Christiana Figueres, a Costa Rican diplomat who shoulders a heavy responsibility as the executive secretary of the United Nations' Framework Convention on Climate Change, praised the encyclical while also noting the coming meetings in Paris.

Pope Francis' encyclical underscores the moral imperative for urgent action on climate change to lift the planet's most vulnerable populations, protect development, and spur responsible growth. This clarion call should guide the world

---

[3] "Pope Francis Releases Encyclical on Climate and Environment: UN Leaders React," UN Climate Change Newsroom, n.d.

towards a strong and durable universal climate agreement in Paris at the end of this year.[4]

President Barack Obama, too, in praising the encyclical, expressed his hope that "world leaders will consider Pope Francis's plea for bold action to curb climate change, ahead of the United Nations climate talks in December 2015 in Paris."[5] Lord Nicholas Stern, an English economist and chair of the Grantham Research Institute on Climate Change and the Environment, noted that

> publication of the Pope's encyclical is of enormous significance. He has shown great wisdom and leadership. Pope Francis is surely absolutely right that climate change raises vital moral and ethical issues. . . . Moral leadership on climate change from the Pope is particularly important because of the failure of many heads of state and government around the world to show political leadership.[6]

Needless to say, not everyone's reaction was positive. Leading figures in the Republican Party in the United States, the heads of the fossil-fuel industries, and conservative foundations such as the Heartland Institute have challenged the encyclical's teaching, especially the section on climate change. Senator James Inhofe, a veteran climate-change denier and chair of the Senate Environment and Public Works Committee, said that "the pope ought to stay with his job, and we'll stay with ours."[7] Rick Santorum, a devout

---

[4] Ibid.

[5] See "The Latest: Obama Welcomes Pope's Call for Climate Action," Associated Press, June 18, 2015.

[6] "Nicholas Stern Welcomes the Pope's Encyclical on the Environment as Being of 'Enormous Significance,'" London School of Economics and Political Science, June 18, 2015.

[7] Quoted in Suzanne Goldenberg, "Angry US Republicans Tell Francis to 'Stay with His Job and We Will Stay with Ours,'" *The Observer,* June 14, 2015.

Catholic and a contender for the Republican nomination for the 2016 presidential election, told a Philadelphia radio station: "The Church has gotten it wrong a few times on science, and I think we are probably better off leaving science to scientists and focusing on what we're good at, which is theology and morality."[8]

Fossil-fuel companies such as Arch Coal, an American coal-mining and processing company, did not accept Pope Francis's arguments on climate change. Arch Coal operates thirty-two active coal mines and controls approximately 5.5 billion tons of proven and probable coal reserves. Its mines are located in Central Appalachia, as well as Colorado, Utah, and Wyoming. Much of the coal mined in these sites is destined to generate electric power. A lobbyist from Arch Coal sent an email to Republican lawmakers stating that the pope "does not appear to address the tragedy of global energy poverty." The lobbyist argued that Pope Francis, if he really cares about the poor, should promote fossil fuels. The email suggested "talking points" to the legislators for defending the coal industry and rejecting the arguments of the pope. The lobbyist wrote: "Billions of people around the globe are living without electrification and suffering through untold poverty and disease as a result."[9]

While the majority of Catholic clergy support the encyclical, there are some deniers within the church, as well. Australian Cardinal George Pell, while agreeing that there are many beautiful elements in the encyclical *Laudato Si'*, told the *Financial Times* that the church has no mandate from the Lord to pronounce on scientific matters. Nevertheless, he admitted that the encyclical has been "very well received" and that it "beautifully set out our obligations to future generations and our obligations to the environment."[10]

---

[8] Quoted in ibid.

[9] "Climate Deniers Say Nope to 'Red Pope,'" *The New Republic*, June 17, 2015.

[10] Rosie Scammell, "Cardinal George Pell Takes a Swing at Pope Francis' Environmental Encyclical," *Crux: Covering All Things Catholic,* July 17, 2015.

Overview of *Laudato Si'*

Pope Francis provides his own outline for the structure of his encyclical:

> I will begin by briefly reviewing several aspects of the present ecological crisis, with the aim of drawing on the results of the best scientific research available today, letting them touch us deeply and provide a concrete foundation for the ethical and spiritual itinerary that follows. I will then consider some principles drawn from the Judeo-Christian tradition which can render our commitment to the environment more coherent. I will then attempt to get to the roots of the present situation, so as to consider not only its symptoms but also its deepest causes. This will help to provide an approach to ecology which respects our unique place as human beings in this world and our relationship to our surroundings. In light of this reflection, I will advance some broader proposals for dialogue and action which would involve each of us as individuals, and also affect international policy. Finally, convinced as I am that change is impossible without motivation and a process of education, I will offer some inspired guidelines for human development to be found in the treasury of Christian spiritual experience. (no. 15)

The introduction begins with the Canticle of St. Francis of Assisi, which praises "Our Sister, Mother Earth." However, Pope Francis is aware that Sister Earth is being exploited in many parts of the world. The pope associates the encyclical with St. Francis because "he was particularly concerned for God's creation and for the poor and outcast" (no. 10).

To show that there is continuity between the teaching on ecology and justice in *Laudato Si'* and earlier teaching, Pope Francis quotes Pope John XXIII, Pope Paul VI, Pope John Paul II, and Pope Benedict XVI. In particular, he develops and sharpens Pope John Paul II's teaching on "ecological conversion." But naturally, since it is the first encyclical to address ecology in an extensive way, there is much that is new and refreshing in *Laudato Si'*. Francis's way of communicating is also quite different from the earlier popes. Previous encyclicals tended to refer mostly to the scriptures, the fathers of the church, and eminent theologians. Pope Francis, reflecting a more collegial vision of the church, also includes quotations from twenty-one episcopal conferences from all over the world. Pope Francis widens the circle further by giving a place of honor to the teachings on ecology of the Ecumenical Patriarch Bartholomew, who is the spiritual leader of Orthodox Christians (nos. 7, 8).

In Chapter 1, entitled "What Is Happening to Our Common Home" (nos. 17–61), Pope Francis presents many of the environmental problems facing our planet. These include climate change (nos. 23–26), water (nos. 27–31), and the loss of biodiversity (nos. 32–42). The chapter ends with reflections entitled "Decline in the Quality of Human Life and the Breakdown of Society" (nos. 43–47) and "Global Inequality" (nos. 48–52). The final section of Chapter 1 reflects on efforts at the international level to protect the environment (nos. 53–59). The chapter ends with a reflection, "A Variety of Opinions" (nos. 60–61). Throughout the chapter the pope highlights the interconnectedness of all creation and cautions that human flourishing cannot happen if the environment is exploited and polluted. He is particularly critical of the modern "throw-away" culture (no. 22).

Having diagnosed the problem, the pope focuses on ways to address and cure it. Chapter 2 sets out the wealth of understanding and insight that the Bible and the Judeo-Christian tradition offer to those engaged with these issues. He deals in some length with the Genesis account of creation and insists on the correct interpretation of Genesis 1:28. As we will see in the next chapter, the "dominion" given to humans in Genesis 1:28 is not a license for humans to control and destroy the earth (nos. 65–70). God is concerned about the well-being of all creation, so that the laws directing rest on the Sabbath day apply not just to humans but to all creation (no. 71). The psalms invite the sun and moon and all creation to praise God (no. 72). He reminds us that God created the universe out of love and that "every creature has its own value and significance" (no. 76). And he also reminds us that the "universe speaks of God's love, his boundless affection for us" (no. 84). Furthermore, the universe also "shows forth the inexhaustible riches of God" (no. 86).

Motivated by this rich, religious understanding of creation, Pope Francis examines the "human roots of the ecological crisis" in Chapter 3. His focus is primarily on the ecological damage that began with the invention of the steam engine in the middle of the eighteenth century, and its roots in the "dominant technocratic paradigm" that began 250 years ago with the scientific and technological revolutions (nos. 101–14). He is particularly concerned with "excessive anthropocentricism" that sets out to completely control and dominate nature (nos. 115–21). He challenges the "culture of relativism" (no. 123) and underlines the importance of work for everyone (nos. 124–29). The last section in this chapter is on biotechnology and genetic engineering (nos. 130–35).

Chapter 4, "Integral Ecology," includes environmental, economic, and social ecology (no. 138). *Interconnectedness* is the key word here (no. 138). He cautions against theories of economic growth that do not respect ecology and highlights the danger of a consumerist vision of humankind (nos. 141–44). He calls for a preferential option for the poor since those with the least are most harmed by ecological degradation (no. 158) and underscores the importance of thinking about the well-being of future generations (no. 159).

Chapter 5, "Lines of Approach and Action," assesses the success of various efforts at the international and local levels to protect the environment (nos. 164–81). Unfortunately, except in a few situations, progress has been very slow. "World Summits on the environment have not lived up to expectations because, due to lack of political will, they were unable to reach truly meaningful and effective global agreements on the environment" (no. 166).

In Chapter 6, "Ecological Education and Spirituality," Pope Francis begins by saying that "many things have to change course, but it is we human beings above all who need to change" (no. 202). We need to educate ourselves for a covenant between humanity and the environment (no. 209). He talks about creating an "ecological citizenship" that curbs bad behavior and promotes ecological virtues (no. 211). Ecological education in the family and in the church is needed to lead to a profound "ecological conversion" (nos. 213–16). This means that we must "examine our lives and acknowledge the ways in which we have harmed God's creation through our actions or our failure to act" (no. 218). The pope ends Chapter 6 with reflections on the sacraments, especially the Eucharist in which "the whole cosmos gives thanks to God. Indeed the Eucharist is itself an act of cosmic love: 'Yes, cosmic! Because even when it is celebrated on the humble altar of a country church, the Eucharist is always in some way celebrated on the altar of the world'" (no. 236). He reminds us that the sacraments and the Sabbath help Christians develop a proper relationship with all creation (nos. 233–37). His final reflections are on the relationship of the Trinity, Mary, and Joseph to all creation. The encyclical ends with a prayer for the earth and a Christian prayer in union with creation (nos. 238–46).

In Part 1 of this volume, "Catholic Teaching and the Environment," I elaborate on some of the issues of ecology and justice that are highlighted in the encyclical. In Chapter 1, I outline some of the historical and theological underpinnings of the encyclical. Chapter 2 deals with climate change, while the focus of Chapter 3 is the destruction of biodiversity. In Chapter 4 I discuss the difficulties people face in accessing fresh water. Chapter 5 focuses on the well-being of the oceans, which have been polluted and over-fished for decades. Chapter 6 draws attention to the need to feed the projected nine to ten billion people who will be living on planet earth by the year 2050. Chapter 7 looks to the future and suggests that a three-year synod, beginning at the parish and diocesan levels and culminating two years later with an international synod, might be an excellent way of communicating the message of *Laudato Si'* within the Catholic Church and to the world at large.

PART I

CATHOLIC TEACHING
AND THE ENVIRONMENT

SEAN MCDONAGH

1

Theological and Historical Background of *Laudato Si'*

The title of *Laudato Si' (Care for Our Common Home)*, Pope Francis's encyclical letter on environmental and economic issues, is drawn from the opening words: "Praised be to you." These words, in the Umbrian dialect of St. Francis of Assisi, are also the opening words of Francis's wonderful "Canticle of the Creatures," in which the saint gives thanks to God for the different creatures and other elements of creation: "Brother Fire," "Sister Moon," and "Mother Earth."

Pope Francis's *Laudato Si'* is one of the most important documents to come from a pope in the past 120 years—the era of modern Catholic social teaching. In this encyclical the pope wishes to address every person on the planet about the condition of our common home (no. 3). He states quite bluntly that "due to an ill-considered exploitation of nature, humanity runs the risk of destroying it and becoming in turn a victim of this degradation" (no. 4). He uses quite startling language when he writes that "the earth, our home, is beginning to look more and more like an immense pile of filth" (no. 21). He then goes on to remind Christians "that their responsibility within creation and their duties towards nature and the Creator are an essential part of their faith" (no. 64). But he is adamant that there is "an intimate relationship between the poor and the fragile planet" (no. 16). He is convinced that "a deep communion with the rest of nature cannot be real if our hearts lack tenderness, compassion and concern for fellow human beings. . . . Concern for the environment thus needs to be joined to a sincere love for our fellow human beings and an unwavering commitment to resolving the problems of society" (no. 91). Pope Francis wishes that this document, "which is now added to the Church's social teaching, can help us to acknowledge the appeal, immensity and urgency of the challenge we face" (no. 15).

Laudato Si' can be compared with three other crucially important social encyclicals. One dealt with the rights of workers, the second with the threat of nuclear war, and the third with the right to development of poor people.

Rerum Novarum (New Things) by Pope Leo XIII in 1891 essentially inaugurated the era of modern Catholic social teaching. The teaching in this encyclical criticized the exploitation of workers (RN, no. 2), called for a living wage, and stated that workers had the right to form unions (RN, no. 49). According to Donal Dorr, the encyclical contradicted the central thesis of liberal capitalism that "labor is a commodity to be bought at market prices determined by the laws of supply and demand rather than by the human needs of the workers."[1]

In *Laudato Si'* Pope Francis refers to another historic encyclical, Pope John XXIII's *Pacem in Terris (Peace on Earth)* written in 1963 "when the world was teetering on the brink of the nuclear crisis" (PT, no. 3). That encyclical not only rejected war but provided a path to lasting peace.

Populorum Progressio (The Development of Peoples), written in 1967 by Pope Paul VI, created a framework for evaluating what kind of development could be called authentic human development. In the post–World War II era there was significant economic growth in many countries in Europe, North America, Japan, and elsewhere. However, *Populorum Progressio* did not give priority to economic development. Rather, it favored development that "will guarantee man's authentic development—his transition from less than human conditions to truly human ones" (PP, no. 20).

---

[1] Donal Dorr, *Option for the Poor and the Earth: Catholic Social Teaching* (Maryknoll, NY: Orbis Books, 2012), 19.

Previous Papal Teaching on the Environment

In *Laudato Si'* the Catholic Church takes an even wider perspective to embrace not only workers and the poor, but all creation as well. While he offers many new insights in *Laudato Si'*, Francis also links his concern for the plight of the poor and the devastation of the earth to the teachings of his predecessors. In *Laudato Si'* he recalls the warning Pope Paul VI gave in a talk to the UN Food and Agriculture Organization

> about the potential for an 'ecological catastrophe under the effective explosion of industrial civilization,' and stressed the urgent need for a radical change in the conduct of humanity, in as much as the most extraordinary scientific advances, the most amazing technical abilities, the most astonishing economic growth, unless they are accompanied by authentic social and moral progress, will definitely turn against man. (no. 4)

In his first encyclical, *Redemptor Hominis*, Pope John Paul II made the point that human beings frequently seem to "see no other meaning in their natural environment than what serves immediate use and consumption." In the same paragraph he called for "a global ecological conversion" and declared that action "to improve our world entails profound changes in lifestyles, models of production and consumption, and the established structures of power which today govern society" (no. 5). He also issued an important document on ecology entitled *Peace with God the Creator, Peace with All Creation* on January 1, 1990. In this document he stated that "the ecological crisis is a moral issue." Ecological concerns appear in many of his encyclicals, especially in *Sollicitudo Rei Socialis (On Social Concerns),* written in 1987.

In *Laudato Si'* Pope Francis also calls to mind the work of his predecessor, Pope Benedict XVI, who, in his social encyclical *Caritas in Veritate,* asked people to "recognize that the natural environment has been greatly damaged by our irresponsible behaviour and that the social environment has also suffered damage" (no. 6).

While these documents are insightful on social and economic issues, they remain decidedly human centered, as if all the goods of the planet are meant only for human beings. *Laudato Si'* attempts to avoid this anthropocentric focus.

Other Voices

One major change in Pope Francis's style as bishop of Rome is that he is willing to include other voices, as he does in both his apostolic exhortation *Evangelii Gaudium (The Joy of the Gospel)* and in *Laudato Si'*.

The first voice in *Laudato Si'* comes from the Ecumenical Patriarch Bartholomew, who has constantly focused on protecting God's creation, especially the water bodies of the world, since his election as patriarch in 1991. The patriarch focuses on the moral responsibility to protect creation when he writes that "for human beings . . . to destroy biological diversity of God's creation; for human beings to degrade the integrity of the earth by causing changes in its climate, by stripping the earth of its natural forests or destroying its wetlands and its life—these are sins" (quoted in LS, no. 8). Subsequent to the publication of *Laudato Si'*, on August 6, 2015, the feast of the Transfiguration, Pope Francis announced that he was designating September 1, 2015, as a World Day of Peace for the Care of Creation. He called attention to the fact that the Orthodox Church, under the leadership of the Ecumenical Patriarch Bartholomew, already celebrated and prayed for creation on that day. The pope believes that Christians from every tradition are now being called upon to offer their own contributions to overcoming the ecological crisis facing planet earth today. This is both a new spirituality and a new moral teaching that previous generations of Christians did not have to deal with. For most of the two-thousand-year history of the Christian faith, moral teaching was focused on human relationships with God and other human beings. Christians knew it was wrong to worship false gods, to kill, to steal, to commit adultery, to lie. However, the majority of Christians never thought it was wrong to devastate forests or to drain marshes. Those who plowed the prairies of North

America, or cut down the forests of Ireland, or used mercury for mining purposes in Australia, or devastated the tropical forests in the Philippines did not think of what they were doing as morally wrong. It is only during the past few decades that such actions have been considered sins. And still, the majority of Catholics would not think of including such behavior in their celebration of the sacrament of penance. So, if *Laudato Si'* is to have a profound, long-lasting influence on Catholic social and ecological teaching, it needs to be followed up with systematic and extensive moral catechesis aimed at bringing about the serious changes envisaged in *Laudato Si'*.

St. Francis of Assisi

Early on, Pope Francis acknowledges his devotion to St. Francis, noting, "I do not want to write this Encyclical without turning to that attractive and compelling figure, whose name I took as my guide and inspiration when I was elected Bishop of Rome" (no. 10). The pope believes that "Saint Francis is the example par excellence of care for the vulnerable and of an integral ecology lived out joyfully and authentically" (no. 10). In the document he constantly emphasizes the inseparable bonds among concern for nature, justice for the poor, commitment to society, and interior peace (no. 11), bonds exemplified by St. Francis, who "communed with all creation, even preaching to the flowers, inviting them 'to praise the Lord,' just as if they were endowed with reason" (no. 11).

Anti-Body and Anti-Creature Sentiments

It would be nice to suppose that the vision of St. Francis, especially his fraternal relationship with all creation, continued and blossomed during the centuries after his death. Unfortunately, this did not happen. In fact, the opposite occurred; the creation-centered focus of Francis's vision was lost, even among the Franciscans. The reason for this was the anti-body/anti-creature bias that dominated the spiritual literature circulated in religious houses of formation until the time of the Second Vatican Council in the 1960s. Spirituality gave priority to the salvation of one's soul and future life in heaven rather than being involved in the affairs of the world. Christians were warned not to be seduced by the allure of the world.

Some aspects of the classic fifteenth-century text the *Imitation of Christ* illustrate this tendency. In a reflection "On Acknowledging Our Own Infirmities and the Miseries of This Life," Thomas à Kempis writes: "How, then, can this life be love, which is so full of bitterness and subject to so many trials? How can it be even called life since it brings forth so many deaths and spiritual plagues? Yet it is love and many seek all their pleasure in it."[2] Sulpician Adolphe Alfred Tanquerey, an early-twentieth-century spiritual writer, encouraged the novice to pray: "May I know Thee, O Lord, and may I love Thee; May I know myself, that I may despise myself."[3]

The negative attitude to creation was also present in the missal of Pius V, which was used until the Second Vatican Council. The Post-Communion Prayer during Advent read: "Domine, doceas nos terrena despicere, et amare celestia" (Lord, teach us to despise the things of earth, and to love the things of heaven). The same lack of appreciation for the beauty and value of creation is expressed in the prayer *Salve Regina,* which refers to the condition of human beings in this life, "mourning and weeping in this valley of tears." If our true home is in heaven and this world is just a valley of tears, all our energies need to be devoted to our interior life.

Many people believe that this pessimistic, anti-world mood of the late medieval period was strengthened by the trauma of the Black Death in Europe, one of the most devastating pandemics in human history. It claimed the lives of between 75 and 200 million people—30 to 60 percent of Europe's population. Because of the speed of its transmission and the vast numbers of people affected,

---

[2] Thomas à Kempis, *The Imitation of Christ*, ed. Clare L. Fitzpatrick (New York: Catholic Book Publishing Co., 1977), 141.

[3] Quoted in Matthew Fox, *Original Blessing* (Santa Fe: Bear and Company, 1983), 59.

it sparked a series of religious, social, and economic upheavals that had a profound effect on the course of European history. Clerical sermons in the wake of the plague interpreted it as a punishment from God. The only protection was to embrace a spirituality based on prayer, asceticism, mortification, and a withdrawal from engagement with the world. This spiritual attitude continued right up to Vatican II. Its prevalence is reflected in the fact that, as recently as 1961, Pope John XXIII had to remind Catholics in his encyclical *Mater et Magistra* that "the laity must not suppose they would be acting prudently to lessen their Christian commitment to this passing world. On the contrary, we insist they must intensify it and increase it continually. . . . Let no one suppose that a life of activity in the world is incompatible with spiritual perfection" (MM, no. 254).

Of course, not everyone viewed creation in a negative way. There were saints such as John of the Cross who felt that "mountains have heights and they are plentiful, vast, beautiful, graceful, bright and fragrant. The mountains are what my Beloved is to me."[4]

But such voices were exceptions. Many Christians, especially in the second millennium, had a much more jaundiced view and did not always respect the earth. Pope Francis acknowledges this: "If a mistaken understanding of our own principles has at times led us to justify mistreating nature, to exercise tyranny over creation, to engage in war, injustice and acts of violence, we believers should acknowledge that by so doing we were not faithful to the treasures of wisdom which we have been called to protect and preserve" (no. 200).

The Book of Genesis

In Chapter 2 of *Laudato Si'* Pope Francis develops his own theology of creation. Many of the quotations are taken from the Bible, and Pope Francis believes that "our faith convictions can offer

---

[4] Taken from Cardinal Cahal Daly, *The Minding of the Planet* (Dublin: Veritas, 2004), 55.

Christians, and some other believers as well, ample motivations to care for nature and the most vulnerable of brothers and sisters" (no. 64). He begins by reviewing the creation stories from Genesis, finding there an affirmation of the goodness of the world while also countering interpretations that are commonly invoked to justify a spirit of domination over nature.

The first chapter of the book of Genesis tells us that the world was created by a loving, personal God. "In the beginning God created the heavens and the earth" (Gen 1:1). The world is good in itself; God contemplates what he has done and finds that "it was good" (Gen 1:10, 13, 18, 21, 26). "After the creation of man and woman, 'God saw everything that he had made, and behold it was *very good*' (Gen 1:31)" (no. 65). Repeating the clauses—good and very good—is important because the Jewish faith evolved with cultures that maintained that the spirit world was created by a good spirit and that matter came from an evil spirit. The Genesis story rejects this radical dualism.

The creation account in Genesis 1:1—2:4a comes from a liturgical source. The text has a ritual cadence and structure, finely tuned by decades of use in temple worship. Even in translation one can sense the majesty and rhythm, "God said, let there be light. . . . God said, let there be a vault in the waters," building up to a climax in Genesis 2:3, "God blessed the seventh day and made it holy, because on that day he had rested after all his work of creating."

In reading the text it is obvious that the author did not set out to give a scientific account of creation in either an ancient or modern sense. While the text builds on the cosmology of the day, it was written to answer the more basic questions: Who created the world? Why? The answers were clear and emphatic. God created the world and sustains it by his power. There is nothing hidden from God's domain. God's creative outpouring reaches its zenith in the creation of man and woman.

> "Let us make man in our own image, in the likeness of ourselves, and let them be masters of the fish of the sea, the birds of heaven, the cattle, all the wild beasts and the reptiles

that crawl upon the earth. . . . God blessed them, saying to them, 'Be fruitful, multiply, fill the earth and conquer it.'" (Gen 1:26–28)

The repercussions of this command "to fill the earth and conquer it" have had a profound impact on the way Jews and Christians have related to the natural world. The *New Jerusalem Bible* uses the phrase "subdue it," while other translations say "have dominion over it." Pope Francis is aware that "the Genesis account which grants man 'dominion' over the earth has encouraged the unbridled exploitation of nature by painting him as domineering and destructive by nature" (no. 67). The pope is adamant that "this is not a correct interpretation of the Bible as understood by the Church" (no. 67).

In the second account of creation the pope points out that in Genesis 2:15, God commands Adam and Eve to "'till and keep' the garden of the world." "'Tilling' refers to cultivating, ploughing or working, while 'keeping' means, caring, protecting, overseeing and protecting" (no. 67). As far as the pope is concerned, this text calls on humans to be thoughtful and careful in the way they relate to creation, stating, "Although it is true that we Christians have at times incorrectly interpreted the Scriptures, nowadays we must forcefully reject the notion that being created in God's image and given dominion over the earth justifies absolute dominion over other creatures" (no. 67).

Pope Francis joins with modern biblical scholars who insist that the divine command in Genesis 1:28 cannot be interpreted as a license for humans to change and transform the natural world according to any human whim or fancy. The dominion given in Genesis 1:28 is, in fact, a challenge to human beings to imitate God's loving kindness and faithfulness and to act as his viceroy in relationship with the nonhuman component of the earth.

Like viceroys of the ruler, men and women were expected to be just and honest and to render real service. They were forbidden to exploit the people or the earth. Furthermore, exegetes remind us that the first account of creation does not end at Genesis 1:31 with the creation of humans. It ends, rather, in Genesis 2:3 with the Sabbath rest of God. The Sabbath was a very important institution for the people of Israel, both for the well-being of humans and other creatures. Pope Francis highlights the importance of the Sabbath as a time of rest for everyone, and of the Jubilee as a way of distributing the goods of creation (no. 71).

Genesis Understood from the Sixteenth to the Nineteenth Centuries

The pope rejects any understanding of world dominion that would devalue creation and give humans tyrannical control over it. Although contemporary scripture scholars agree with the pope, this argument faces an uphill battle against centuries of interpretation to the contrary. In Tudor and Stuart England, for example, the biblical teaching on dominion over creation was interpreted in just this way. As Keith Thomas notes, the Bible taught that

> the world had been created for man's sake and that other species were meant to be subordinate to his wishes and needs. . . . Those theologians and intellectuals who felt the need to justify it could readily appeal to the classical philosophers and the Bible. Nature made nothing in vain, said Aristotle, and everything had a purpose. Plants were created for the sake of animals and animals for the sake of man. Domestic animals were there to labor, and wild ones to be hunted. The Stoics had taught the same: nature existed solely to serve man's interests.[5]

This anthropocentric vision of creation, of course, was not confined to Britain. The French philosopher René Descartes believed that "man stood to animal as did heaven to earth, soil to body, culture to nature. There was a total qualitative difference between man and nature."[6]

---

[5] Keith Thomas, *Man and the Natural World: A History of the Modern Sensibility* (New York: Pantheon Books, 1983), 17.

[6] Quoted in ibid., 35.

Aware of this history Pope Francis points out that "unhealthy dualism, nonetheless, left a mark on certain Christian thinkers in the course of history and [as a result] disfigured the Gospel" (no. 98). The tragedy for the world is that this human-centered and dualistic approach to nature was firmly in place at the beginning of the scientific and technological era when James Watt was experimenting with his steam engine in 1750. Robin McKie, science editor of the *Observer,* argues:

Today, many scientists believe that the processes unleashed by Watt have begun to alter the physical makeup of our planet. After two-and-a-half centuries of spewing out carbon dioxide from plants and factories built in the wake of the condenser's invention, the atmosphere and crust of the earth are beginning to be transformed. Watt truly changed the world.[7]

Pope Francis gives a comprehensive list of the technological revolutions during the past 250 years. They include steam engines, the railways, the telegraph, electricity, automobiles, airplanes, chemical industries, modern medicine, information technology and the digital revolution, robotics, biotechnologies, and nano-technologies (no. 102). While he rejoices in the God-given human creativity which was responsible for all these inventions, he is also aware that "our immense technological development has not been accompanied by a development in human responsibility, values and conscience" (no. 195). He regrets that "humanity has taken up technology and its development *according to an undifferentiated and one-dimensional paradigm*". . . in which the relationship between humans and technology "has become confrontational" (no. 106). Furthermore, the pope claims that "the technocratic paradigm also tends to dominate economic and political life. The economy accepts every advance in technology with a view to

---

[7] Robin McKie, "Water, Steam, and the Sabbath Stroll That Sparked the Industrial Revolution," *Observer,* May 24, 2015.

profit, without concern for its potential negative impact on human beings" (no. 109).

As we will see in the chapter on climate change, some of these technologies have changed the chemical composition of the air. I also discuss how humans have polluted the water in our rivers and oceans, and have caused the extinction of many of our fellow creatures. Pope Francis knows that the human community will have to make radical changes in the way we treat the earth if future generations of all creatures are to inherit a planet as healthy, beautiful, and fruitful as the one this generation has inherited. Achieving this goal of living in a sustainable way on planet earth will define the nature of Christian mission for decades if not centuries to come.

The Second Vatican Council's Domination Theology

In the Catholic world, 2012 marked the fiftieth anniversary of the opening of the Second Vatican Council. This council transformed our understanding of what it meant to be a Catholic in the twentieth century and changed the ways Catholics viewed many aspects of Church life and practice. It viewed the Church not primarily as a highly structured, hierarchical organization but as the mystery of God's saving love present in our world. It emphasized the equality of believers based on our common baptism and membership in the people of God. Other changes involved the introduction of vernacular languages for the celebration of the liturgy and a serious effort to reach out to other Christians and other faiths through ecumenism and respect for other religions. This was evident especially in the *Decree on Ecumenism (Unitatis Redintegratio), the Declaration of the Relationship of the Church to Non-Christian Religions (Nostra Aetate),* and the *Pastoral Constitution of the Church in the Modern World (Gaudium et Spes).*

Though some people have attempted to downplay or even decry the achievements of Vatican II, there is no doubting its revolutionary impact. Yet, despite its great achievements, the perspective of Vatican II remained quite anthropocentric. This can be seen in *Gaudium et Spes* (no. 12), which claims almost universal agreement for the teaching that, "according to the unanimous opinion of believers and unbelievers alike, all things on earth should be related to man as their center and crown." This reflects the hubris of *man the transformer,* which we readily associate with the name of Francis Bacon (1561–1626). In his classic work *Novum Organum,* Bacon dismissed much of the metaphysical speculation that had preoccupied Western thought for almost two thousand years. He considered that human thought would be much more productively used inquiring into how things work and how they might be made into things to serve humans. For him, knowledge was not about insight into the nature of things but rather about power. This power should be used to transform the earth's resources.

Bacon himself wrote, "The end of our Foundation [technical school] is the knowledge of causes and the secret motion of things, and the enlarging of the bounds of the human empire, to the effecting of all things possible."[8] Bacon set two important waves in motion in the Western world which have continued to gather power and momentum ever since. First, there was what Pope Francis calls "the Promethean vision of mastery over the world" (no. 116), which released enormous psychic energies to study, record, and correlate the secrets of the Earth, no matter what the cost to living beings. Second, his ideas legitimized the pursuit of knowledge for its own sake, irrespective of the meaning of the knowledge and how it might be used.

As one phase of the industrial revolution followed another, the dark side of technology began to appear. This included climate change, the depletion of the ozone region, the destruction of biodiversity, acid rain, soil erosion, pollution of oceans and rivers, and nuclear waste. Pope Francis devotes a separate section in *Laudato Si'* to technology (nos. 106–14) in which he attacks the belief in unlimited growth. He believes it is built on the lie that "there is an infinite supply of the earth's goods, and this leads to the planet being squeezed dry beyond every limit" (no. 106). He reminds us that natural biological systems are circular, while modern technologies are not. He states:

---

[8] Quoted in Stephen Mason, *A History of the Sciences* (New York: Collier Books, 1962), 255.

It is hard for us to accept that the way natural ecosystems work is exemplary: plants synthesize nutrients which feed herbivores; these in turn become food for carnivores, which produce significant quantities of organic waste which gives rise to a new generation of plants. But our industrial system, at the end of its cycle of production and consumption, has not developed the capacity to absorb and reuse waste and by-products. (no. 22)

Redefining Relationships

In many ways *Laudato Si'* is an attempt to redefine the relationship between humans and the rest of creation, so that we can soon reach a point where the basic needs of all humans will be met in a way that does not endanger the rest of creation or irreversibly damage it. But Pope Francis has his own engaging style of writing. He presents earth as a sister "who now cries out to us because of the harm we have inflicted on her by our irresponsible use and abuse of the goods with which God has endowed her. We have come to see ourselves as her lords and masters, entitled to plunder her at will" (no. 2).

In the document Pope Francis asserts that "the urgent challenge to protect our common home includes a concern to bring the whole human family together to seek a sustainable and integral development, for we know that things can change" (no. 13). He challenges those who think that the ecological crisis is not so extensive: "Superficially, apart from a few obvious signs of pollution and deterioration, things do not look that serious, and the planet could continue as it is for some time. Such evasiveness serves as a license to carrying on with our present lifestyles and models of production and consumption" (no. 59). Later in the encyclical the pope says that the "gravity of the ecological crisis demands that we all look to the common good, embarking on a path of dialogue which demands patience, self-discipline and generosity, always keeping in mind that 'realities are greater than ideas'" (no. 201).

Linking the Poor and the Earth

Pope Francis constantly links ecological devastation and human impoverishment. "We are faced not with two separate crises, one environmental and the other social, but rather with one complex crisis which is both social and environmental" (no. 139). He reminds us that there is scientific evidence to support the claim that "everyday experience and scientific research show that the gravest effects of all attacks on the environment are suffered by the poorest" (no. 48). Throughout *Laudato Si'* Pope Francis attempts to listen to both the cry of the earth and the cry of the poor (no. 49). He claims that "whatever is fragile, like the environment, is defenseless before the interests of a deified market, which become the only rule" (no. 56). This challenges "the modern myth of unlimited progress. A fragile world, entrusted by God to human care, challenges us to devise intelligent ways of directing, developing and limiting our power" (no. 78).

In a section entitled "Global Inequality," the pope links human impoverishment with the degradation of the planet. "The human environment and the natural environment deteriorate together: we cannot adequately combat environmental degradation unless we attend to the causes related to human and social degradation" (no. 48). In fact, as Pope Francis pointed out in *Evangelii Gaudium*, published in 2013, the global economic system is dysfunctional when it comes to alleviating poverty. "Just as the commandment 'Thou shalt not kill' sets a clear limit in order to safeguard the value of human life, today we also have to say 'thou shalt not' to an economy of exclusion and inequality. Such an economy kills" (EG, no. 53). It is in this context that we can understand Pope Francis's attack in that encyclical on the "idolatry of money." He has said that unchecked capitalism is a "new tyranny" and that trickle-down economics does not help the poor. He also calls attention to the fact that "while the earnings of a minority are growing exponentially, so too is the gap separating the majority from the prosperity enjoyed by the happy few" (EG, no. 56). Research in June 2015 found that chief executives in the top Financial Times

Stock Exchange (FTSE) 100 companies are now paid 150 times more than the average worker, and that the gap is growing. In 1998 it was forty-seven times the pay of the average worker in a company.[9] This imbalance is the result of ideologies that defend the absolute autonomy of the marketplace and financial speculation.

Pope Francis is aware that the poor suffer most from environmental damage. Africa, for example, has done least to cause climate change through the emission of greenhouse gases, and yet it suffers most in terms of the impact of extreme weather on the environment and on people. Severe weather does enormous damage to crops in African countries where population levels are rising dramatically.

Laudato Si' is the first encyclical to capture the extent of the modern ecological crisis—across the land, the air, and the oceans in every part of the globe. It also emphasizes the urgent need to respond to the environmental crisis immediately, before humans do more irreversible damage to the life systems of the world. "Doomsday predictions can no longer be met with irony or disdain. We may well be leaving to coming generations debris, desolation and filth" (no. 161). These are certainly very strong words from a pope. Hopefully, they will arouse Catholics, people of other faiths, and people of none to begin the daunting task of protecting our planet and caring for the poor.

Excessive Anthropocentrism

Pope Francis also criticizes "the excessive anthropocentrism which today, under another guise, continues to stand in the way of shared understanding and of any effort to strengthen social bonds" (no. 116). He tells us that other creatures have "intrinsic value independent of their usefulness" (no. 139); that "each creature has its own purpose. None is superfluous" (no. 84); and, that "because all creatures are connected, each must be cherished with love

---

[9] David Oakley, "Top Executives' Wage Gap Stretches to 150 Times That of the Average Worker," *Financial Times,* June 13, 2015.

and respect, for all of us as living creatures are dependent on one another" (no. 41). It must be noted that the pope does not entirely follow through on the implications of what he has written. When discussing the principle of the common good, he writes: "God gave the earth to the whole human race for the sustenance of all its members, without excluding or favoring anyone" (no. 93). What about all the other species? Despite all the great breakthroughs in science during the past 250 years, we have little knowledge of how many species share this planet with us. Scientists in research centers such as Kew Gardens in Britain have some data on roughly two million species. Yet biologists tell us that there might be six million, or even thirty million. The reality is we do not know. Do they and their offspring have rights to their particular habitat on planet earth? Or is everything that swims in the seas, that flies through the air, or walks on the land primarily meant for humans? Pope Francis is certain that "there can be no ecology without an adequate anthropology" (no. 118). But it must be remembered that throughout hundreds of millions of years there were superbly functioning ecosystems operating efficiently across our world, long before humankind arrived a mere two million years ago. We cannot have a properly functioning anthropology without a proper biology and cosmology. Part of the reason why we have a global ecological crisis is that humans did not know their proper place in the biosphere and, in recent times, with the help of powerful technologies, they have begun to make more and more demands on the resources of the earth for their own exclusive use, often to the detriment of other species. In terms of belief systems, until very recently humans thought that everything in the world was made for them and no other creatures had any rights to their habitat. We need to begin to reinsert ourselves in the biosphere while respecting human dignity. Pope Francis rejects "biocentrism" in his encyclical (no. 118), but maybe we should examine ways of reducing the human footprint on the planet that is having such a devastating impact on other creatures. Educational Resources, published by *National Geographic,* tells us that "humans have influenced 83 percent of Earth's surface." The statistics claim that US citizens own 30 percent of the cars of the world and use 25 percent of the world's energy even though they only make up 5 percent of the world population. By his or her first birthday the average American child will be responsible for more carbon dioxide emissions than a person in Tanzania will generate in a lifetime.[10]

In the end the pope is aware that bringing about ecological change will not be easy, "not only because of powerful opposition but also because of a more general lack of interest. . . . As the bishops of Southern Africa have stated: everyone's talents and involvement are needed to redress the damage caused by human abuse of God's creation." He is aware that "obstructionist attitudes, even on the part of believers, can range from denial of the problem to indifference, nonchalant resignation or blind confidence in technical solutions" (no. 14). Later in the encyclical he laments the fact that "Christians have not always appropriated and developed the spiritual treasures bestowed by God upon the Church, where the life of the spirit is not dissociated from the body or from nature or from worldly realities, but lived in and with them, in communion with all that surrounds us" (no. 216).

In sum, this is an important encyclical letter with serious insights into one of the most urgent contemporary challenges facing our planet: the task of creating a dignified life for all human beings while, at the same time, protecting our planet. It is the task of this generation to bring about creative and just solutions to major challenges, because if this generation does not respond generously, no future generation will be able to reverse the negative impact on planet earth. We will be creating a new geological epoch, called the Anthropocene, which will make the world less habitable for our own and many other species.

In the following chapters I assess some of the issues that the pope raises in *Laudato Si'*. These include climate change, the destruction of biodiversity, the state of the world's rivers and oceans, and the quest for sustainable food production.

---

[10] "Human Footsteps," *National Geographic*, Educational Resources PDF (2008).

Bibliography

Boff, Leonardo, *Cry of the Earth, Cry of the Poor* (Maryknoll, NY: Orbis Books, 1997).

Dorr, Donal, *The Option for the Poor and for The Earth: Catholic Social Teaching* (Maryknoll, NY: Orbis Books, 2012).

Deane-Drummond, Celia, *Eco-Theology* (London: Darton, Longman and Todd, 2008).

Edwards, Denis, *Jesus the Wisdom of God: An Ecological Theology* (Maryknoll, NY: Orbis Books, 1995).

————, Ecology at the Heart of Christian Faith (Maryknoll, NY: Orbis Books, 2004).

Hallman, David, ed., *Ecotheology: Voices from the South and North* (Maryknoll, NY: Orbis Books, 1994).

Hill, Brennan R., *Christian Faith and the Environment: Making Vital Connections* (Maryknoll, NY: Orbis Books, 1998).

LaChance, Albert J., and John E. Carroll, eds., Embracing Earth: Catholic Approaches to Ecology (Maryknoll, NY: Orbis Books, 1995).

McDonagh, Seán, *To Care for the Earth: A Call to a New Theology* (London: Chapman, *1986).*

————, *The Greening of the Church* (Maryknoll, NY: Orbis Books, 1990).

Toolan, David, *At Home in the Cosmos* (Maryknoll, NY: Orbis Books, 2001).

Wessels, Cletus, *Jesus in the New Universe Story* (Maryknoll, NY: Orbis Books, 2003).

2

Climate Change

When *Laudato Si'* was published on June 18, 2015, many people immediately turned to what the document had to say about climate change. Pope Francis was clear and unambiguous: "A very solid scientific consensus indicates that we are presently witnessing a disturbing warming of the climate system" (no. 23). Further down in that paragraph he claims that humans are mainly responsible for releasing the greenhouse gases in the atmosphere that cause climate change. So, in one paragraph Pope Francis makes it clear that he accepts the scientific consensus that climate change is happening and that humans are generating the greenhouse gases that are causing the change. The focus on climate change led some people to think that that was the only theme discussed in the encyclical. In fact, the encyclical also deals with poverty, the destruction of biodiversity, the pollution of fresh water and the oceans, sustainable food, extractive industries, and the waste created by the global economy.

The Catholic Church has not always spoken out emphatically on the issue of climate change; during the 1980s and 1990s the voice of the World Council of Churches (WCC), for example, was much louder. In 1994, the WCC published an excellent document on the climate called *Sign of Peril, Test of Faith*.[1] In 1993, researchers accepted scientific evidence for climate change and

---

[1] World Council of Churches, *Sign of Peril, Test of Faith: Accelerated Climate Change* (Geneva: WCC, 1994). I was part of a group that included other Catholics who worked with the committee that drew up this document.

attempted to predict what the consequence would be. Recommendations were made in the document to countries, corporations, and individuals to reduce their greenhouse gas emissions. Christians began to develop a theological and ethical framework to help them understand the implications of climate change for their faith. *Sign of Peril, Test of Faith* examined the potential role of the churches in addressing the crisis of human-induced climate change. The document focused on the prophetic vocation of the churches to denounce evil and to seek ways to reduce greenhouse gas emissions and to work creatively with secular organizations such as the Friends of the Earth.

Pope Francis is not the first pope to write about climate change. Pope John Paul II, in *Peace with God the Creator, Peace with All Creation,* his World Day of Peace Message for 1990, writes: "The gradual depletion of the ozone layer and the related 'greenhouse' effect have now reached crisis proportion as a consequence of industrial growth, massive urban concentrations and vastly increased energy needs" (no. 6).

But the church's general reticence on climate changed dramatically with the publication of *Laudato Si'*. Pope Francis states:

> The climate is a common good, belonging to all and meant for all. . . . A very solid scientific consensus indicates that we are presently witnessing a disturbing warming of the climatic system. In recent decades this warming has been accompanied by a constant rise in the sea level, and it would appear, by the increase of extreme weather events, even if a scientifically determinable cause cannot be assigned to each particular phenomenon. (no. 23)

The pope specifically names the gases involved in climate change: "Scientific studies indicate that most global warming in recent decades is due to the great concentration of greenhouse gases (carbon dioxide, methane, nitrogen oxides and others)" (no. 23). He then links this to the "model of development based on the intensive use of fossil fuel" (no. 23). A major theme of the encyclical that links the plight of the poor and the care of earth is taken up here as well when he claims that the "worst impact [of climate change] will probably be felt by developing countries in coming decades" (no. 25). The pope states that "the [global] warming caused by huge consumption on the part of some rich countries has repercussions on the poorest areas of the world, especially Africa where a rise in temperature, together with drought, has proved devastating for farming" (no. 51). Pope Francis reminds us that we have obligations to the poor and to future generations when he writes that "twenty percent of the world's population consumes resources at a rate that robs the poor nations and future generations of what they need to survive" (no. 96). Pope Francis is also convinced that fossil-fuel products—coal, oil, and gas—cannot continue to be the dominant sources of energy for our global economy.

What Causes Climate Change?

During the past two centuries human activity has changed the chemistry of the air. The projected impact of this on humans and other creatures is devastating. The atmosphere of planet earth is composed of a thin layer of gases. The principal gases nitrogen and oxygen, are responsible for 78 percent and 21 percent of the atmosphere respectively. There are also minute amounts of other gases such as carbon dioxide, methane, nitrous oxide, and chlorofluorocarbons. These gases, sometimes called greenhouse gases, trap infrared radiation from the sun that otherwise would pass back into space. In the climate debate in recent years greenhouse gases are often seen in a negative way, but it is important to remember that if these gases did not exist, the average global temperature would be -18 degrees Celsius (-4 degrees Fahrenheit), which would mean that the earth would be too cold to sustain complex life forms. The presence of these gases in our atmosphere means that the average global temperature is +15 degrees Celsius (59 degrees Fahrenheit), which allows life to flourish in almost every part of the globe.

The number of these gases and their concentration in the atmosphere have changed dramatically during the five-billion-year history of planet earth. Prior to 3.5 billion years ago, the atmosphere probably consisted of gases similar to those emitted from modern volcanoes: carbon dioxide, sulphur dioxide, carbon monoxide, water, and nitrogen. But they did not include free oxygen. One billion years ago marine organisms called blue-green algae began using energy from the sun to split the molecules of water and carbon dioxide and recombine them into organic compounds and molecular oxygen in a process called photosynthesis. This process released oxygen into the atmosphere. The average temperature of the earth during the past five hundred million years has changed enormously, both because of the composition of the gases in the atmosphere itself and the configuration of the continents due to the movement of the earth's plates. At times the earth was almost a ball of ice; at other times there was no ice on the planet and tropical creatures swam in both the Arctic and Antarctic oceans.

For eighty-five thousand of the past one hundred thousand years, glaciers covered much of the Northern Hemisphere. Ice cores taken from the Arctic and Antarctic confirm that from the end of the last ice age, ten thousand years ago, until the beginning of the Industrial Revolution in the mid-eighteenth century, there were 280 ppm (parts per million) of carbon dioxide in the atmosphere. That is why, despite some regional variations, the global climate was relatively stable during much of this time. However, since the beginning of the Industrial Revolution, and especially since World War II, humans have been releasing vast amounts of carbon dioxide into the atmosphere due to the burning of fossil fuels, beginning with coal and followed after the 1860s with the burning of petroleum and natural gas. On May 10, 2013, measurements taken at the Mauna Loa Observatory in Hawaii indicated that the concentration of carbon dioxide in the atmosphere had passed 400 ppm. The last time this happened was about fifty-six million years ago. At that time the earth was 3 to 5 degrees Celsius warmer and sea levels were 131 feet higher than today—and Homo sapiens had not yet evolved.[2]

---

[2] Paul Gillespie, "Saving the Planet and Saving Ourselves," *Irish Times,* August 24, 2013.

Fourth and Fifth Assessment Reports of the Intergovernmental Panel on Climate Change (IPCC)

The Fourth Assessment of the IPCC was published in April 2007, while the Fifth Assessment Report was finalized in 2014. The predictions of the Fourth Assessment Report about how climate change would affect both human beings and the whole biosphere were based on scientific data and computer models that are being constantly revised in order to improve their accuracy. Almost three thousand scientists were involved. The report makes grim reading. It states that climate change will give rise to increased heat waves, like the one that killed thirty-five thousand people in Europe in 2003. It will also increase the frequency and intensity of storms in both the Caribbean and Pacific. This will bring pain, suffering, and death to between two hundred million and six hundred million people by the year 2060.

If nothing is done to stabilize the level of greenhouse gases in the atmosphere, especially carbon dioxide, between 1.1 and 3.2 billion people will face water shortages by 2080. Droughts may well affect areas of the world, such as the US Midwest, which currently play a very important role in global food production. With rising sea levels caused by thermal expansion of the oceans and melting of glaciers in both Greenland and the Western Antarctic, flood waters could claim between two and seven million people in New York and Tokyo alone. A rise of a single meter (3.3 feet) would make life impossible for the thirty-five million people who live in the delta area of Bangladesh. Glaciers retreating in the Himalayas and the Andes will affect vast numbers of people in Asia and Latin America.

The Fifth Assessment Report of the IPCC made it clear that the oceans were becoming more acidic due to increased levels of carbon dioxide (CO_2) (no. 24). The current rate of carbon release stands at thirty gigatons (Gt) of CO_2 per year. This is ten times that which preceded the last major species extinction. The increased acidification of the oceans is leading to a loss of calcium carbonate, a substance that is critical for forming coral reefs and sustaining crustaceans, mollusks, and other planktonic species.

The combined warming and acidification will likely lead to further decline of tropical coral reefs by 2050. A rise of just two degrees Celsius could bring about the extinction of 30 percent of the species on the planet. Plant life will be particularly vulnerable, since plants cannot migrate to a new, more suitable ecological niche in such a short period. Marine ecosystems, especially coral reefs, which are the "rainforests of the oceans," are also being destroyed by climate change. Tim Flannery, the director of the South Australian Museum in Adelaide and author of *Weather Makers,* states that "visitors travelling to Queensland by 2050 may see the Great Stump Reef."[3]

Most of the damage from climate change will be inflicted on the poor of the world in Asia, Latin America, and Africa who did little to cause the problem. Africa, for example, has been responsible for a mere 3 percent of greenhouse gases since 1900. And yet the African continent has suffered from long droughts and severe floods associated with climate change.

Given what in an earlier era would have constituted an apocalyptic claim, it is understandable that scientists such as Sir David King, the chief scientist to the British government, considers that climate change is the most serious at problem facing humankind and the earth. It has the potential to do enormous, and often irreversible damage, to human beings and to the fabric of life that supports them on this planet. The timeframe in which we might expect these predictions to become a reality is not within two hundred to three hundred years, but rather within the lifetime of people living today.

Apart from comments in *Peace with God the Creator, Peace with All Creation* in 1990, there was very little comment from Rome on climate change, even though the IPCC issued five reports on the subject from 1988 onward. Each report signaled that we are facing a crisis of enormous proportions and came closer and closer to saying that human activity, especially the growing level of greenhouse gas emissions, was responsible for the crisis. The reports underscored the fact that we cannot postpone indefinitely

---

[3] Tim Flannery, *Weather Makers: The History and Future Impact of Climate Change* (London: Allen Lane/Penguin, 2006), 103.

the need for drastic action to reduce greenhouse gases. We have, at the most, twenty years to take action before we reach a "tipping point" that will set in motion a series of events like the melting of the Greenland ice sheet, which will make the planet a more inhospitable place to live for succeeding generations of human beings and other creatures.

Pontifical Council for Justice and Peace Conference on Climate Change

In May 2007, the Pontifical Council for Justice and Peace organized a two-day seminar on climate change. More than eighty people attended. While there were excellent presentations from credible scientists, whose writings have been peer reviewed, the organizers also gave a platform to at least four participants who are either in denial about climate change or believe it is a good thing. One of these was Professor Craig Idso, adjunct professor at the Office of Climatology at Arizona State University. He is chairman of the Center for the Study of Carbon Dioxide and Global Change, an institute whose stated mission is to "separate reality from rhetoric in the emotionally charged debate that swirls around the subject of carbon dioxide and global change." Together with his father, Sherwood, and his brother, Keith, he co-authored a report entitled "Enhanced or Impaired? Human Health in a CO_2–Enriched World." The report argues that global warming and an increase in atmospheric CO_2 would be beneficial to humanity.

Why did the Pontifical Council for Justice and Peace give a platform to these skeptics? Did the council think that there is still significant doubt about the science underpinning climate change? Naomi Oreskes, now a scientist at Harvard, analyzed 923 articles in scientific journals written between 1993 and 2003. She published the results of her findings in *Science* in December 2004. Not a single scientific article disputed that human activity was causing a rise in global temperatures. These conclusions have also been endorsed by leading scientific organizations around the world, including the science academies of Brazil, India, and China.

A paragraph on climate change did appear in the *Compendium of the Social Doctrine of the Church* (no. 470). The reference occurs in Chapter 10, entitled "Safeguarding the Environment," which is the weakest chapter in the document. It shows little understanding of environmental issues like climate change, the destruction of biodiversity, and modern developments in creation theology. In contrast to *Laudato Si'*, the single paragraph in the *Compendium* failed to capture either the magnitude of the climate-change problem or the urgency with which it must be faced.

The *Compendium* does state that climate is a good that must be protected. Concern for the common good has traditionally been at the heart of Catholic moral and social teaching. In an extensive reflection on the common good the *Compendium* states: "The common good that people seek and attain in the formation of social communities is the guarantee of their personal, familial and associative good" (no. 61; see also nos. 164, 165, 168, 170). But what the *Compendium* (with the exception of no. 170) and almost all Catholic social teaching overlook is that life-giving human social relations are always embedded in vibrant and sustainable ecosystems. Anything that negatively affects ecosystems or alters the equilibrium of the biosphere, such as global warming, is a disruption of the common good in a most fundamental way—especially if it creates negative irreversible changes. In contrast, *Laudato Si'* begins its treatment of climate change by stating that the climate "is a common good, belonging to all and meant for all" (no. 23). Pope Francis, quoting Vatican II's *Gaudium et Spes,* tells us that "common good is the sum of those conditions of social life which allow social groups and their individual members relatively thorough and ready access to their own fulfillment" (no. 156).

Bishops' Conferences and Climate Change

Bishops' conferences in a number of countries have written documents on climate change. In November 2005, Catholic Earthcare Australia organized an international conference on climate change in Canberra. Bishop Christopher, chair of Catholic Earthcare Australia, spoke on our responsibility to sustain God's earth.

He said that "rapid climate change as a result of human activity is now recognized by the global scientific community as a reality." He went on to make the point that the well-being of the human community and the well-being of the earth are intertwined:

> The web of life on earth is under threat from accelerated climate change. The web compares to a seamless garment and it needs the application of a consistent ethic to protect it, one that considers life now and in the future, and ranges from the protection of the unborn child to cherishing the diversity of species. Life is one, and human well-being is at its base interwoven with all life on earth and the rhythms of its systems. The suffering of one part means that all creation groans and rapid global climate change dramatically displays that suffering.[4]

In September 2006, the German Bishops Commission for Society and Social Action published a document entitled "Climate Change: A Focal Point for Global, Intergenerational, and Ecological Justice." The document states that "coming generations will be victims of our present-day actions. This is why climate change is also a problem of intergenerational justice." It goes on to discuss how climate change affects other creatures: "Climate change fundamentally changes the living conditions for non-human nature. Habitats and environments for plant and animal species are disappearing, which in turn reduces biological diversity on earth. Hence, climate change is also a problem for justice for creation."[5]

The Irish bishops also published a pastoral reflection on climate change entitled *The Cry of the Earth*. The bishops state that "every action taken in favour of a just and more sustainable environment, no matter how small, has an intrinsic value. Action at a global level,

---

[4] Catholic Earthcare Australia, *Climate Change: Our Responsibility to Sustain God's Earth* (2005), 4, 7.

[5] The German Bishops Commission for Society and Social Affairs, Commission for International Church Affairs, "Climate Change: A Focal Point of Global, Intergenerational and Ecological Justice" (2006), 7.

as well as every individual action that contributes to integral human development and global solidarity, helps to construct a more sustainable environment and, therefore, a better world."[6]

Shaping a Theology and Morality around Climate Change

Intergenerational Justice

Concern for intergenerational justice is another reason the churches are shaping a theology and morality around the issue of climate change. Traditional ethical concerns normally dealt with the impact of our behavior on individuals or communities in the here and now or in the immediate future. This is no longer an adequate framework because this generation, through its powerful technologies, is bringing about massive changes to the fabric of the earth that will affect in a negative way every succeeding generation of humans and other creatures. The basic principle from this ethical concern is that future generations have the right to inherit a world as fertile and as beautiful as the one which we inhabit. This new moral context is recognized in the *Compendium of the Social Doctrine of the Church:* "From a moral perspective based on equity and intergenerational solidarity, it will be necessary to continue, through the contribution of the scientific community, to identify new sources of energy, develop alternative sources and increase the security level of nuclear energy" (no. 470).

Laudato Si' gives extensive treatment to intergenerational justice. Pope Francis realizes that intergenerational solidarity is not optional, but rather a basic question of justice, since the world we have received also belongs to those who will follow us. "Once we start to think about the kind of world we are leaving to future generations, we look at things differently; we realize that the world is a gift which we have freely received and must pass on to others" (no. 159). "Leaving an inhabitable planet to future generations is,

---

[6] Irish Catholic Bishops' Conference, *The Cry of the Earth: A Pastoral Reflection on Climate Change from the Irish Catholic Bishops' Conference* (2009), 27.

first and foremost, up to us. The issue is one which dramatically affects us, for it has to do with the ultimate meaning of our earthly sojourn" (no. 160).

The concept of intergenerational justice might help counteract a tendency I have noticed among bureaucrats in the civil service and among some religious leaders. I have often heard them say that something such as climate change is "not going to happen on my watch." They choose to leave it to their successor to deal with it, even though they know what they are doing will exacerbate the problem and maybe create a situation that will be irreversible. The pope hopes that "once we think about the kind of world we are leaving to future generations, we look at things differently, we realize that the world is a gift which we have freely received and must share with others" (no. 159). But the pope is aware of what the poor today are suffering, indicating that "in addition to a fairer sense of intergenerational solidarity there is also an urgent moral need for a renewed sense of intragenerational solidarity" (no. 162).

Sustainable Living

The church needs to develop its teaching on sustainability. Here Pope Francis mentions the statement of the 1992 Earth Summit in Rio de Janeiro, which proclaimed that "human beings are at the centre of concerns for sustainable development" (no. 167). This statement came at the end of a decade of reflection on sustainable development by those involved in researching the Brundtland Report for the United Nations. The report was published in *Our Common Future* in 1987. It defined sustainable development as seeking "to meet the needs and aspirations of the present without compromising the ability to meet those of the future." Then it went on to affirm "that far from requiring the cessation of economic growth, it recognizes that the problems of poverty and underdevelopment cannot be solved unless we have a new era of growth in which developing countries play a large role and reap large benefits."[7]

---

[7] *Report of the World Commission on Environment and Development: Our Common Future* (Brundtland Report) (Oxford: Oxford University Press, 1987), 40.

Almost twenty years later, any ecological evaluation of the impact of economic growth in the Celtic Tiger economy of Ireland makes it absolutely clear that the Western, oil-dependent growth that both China and India are now pursuing are socially and environmentally unsustainable. Pope Francis constantly reminds us that "the environment is one of those goods that cannot be adequately safeguarded or promoted by market forces" (no. 190). We need to be reminded that the earth is finite and that we must live in a way that is fair and just toward future generations of humans and other creatures. Pope Francis is also convinced that oil-dependent growth is not the way into a sustainable future. He points out that he agrees with the bishops of Bolivia, who have stated that "the countries which have benefited from a high degree of industrialization, at the cost of enormous emissions of greenhouse gases, have a greater responsibility for providing solutions to the problems they have caused" (no. 170).[8]

The Precautionary Principle

The precautionary principle is another moral principle mentioned in the *Compendium of the Social Teachings of the Church* (no. 469). Pope Francis also invokes this principle and spells out how it might be used to protect the environment. He writes:

The precautionary principle makes it possible to protect those who are most vulnerable and whose ability to defend their interest to assemble incontrovertible evidence is limited. If objective information suggests that serious and irreversible damage may result, a project should be halted or modified, even in the absence of indisputable proof. Here the burden of proof is effectively reversed, since in such cases objective and conclusive demonstrations will have to be brought forward to demonstrate that the proposed activity

---

[8] The source of the quotation in no. 170 is the Bolivian Bishops' Conference, *Pastoral Letter on the Environment and Human Development in Bolivia, El universo, don de Dios para la vida* (March 2012), 86.

will not cause serious harm to the environment or to those who inhabit it. (no. 186)

This understanding of the precautionary principle, which actually reverses how it is normally articulated, is one of the most important claims in the encyclical. I foresee it being used in litigation in many countries in the years to come.

We also need to understand the nature of irreversible ecological damage and its implications for future generations. The potential damage from global warming to the earth and its peoples is enormous. Unless this generation stabilizes the emissions of global-warming gases, the consequences are inevitable and will be irreversible in geological time. It is an extraordinary and awesome moment in human and earth affairs that the behavior of one or two generations can have such profound and irreversible impact, not just on human history, but on the planet as well.

Preferential Option for the Poor

Another principle that is helpful in the search for an ecological theology is the preferential option for the poor. This relatively recent moral principle emerged, especially, from the struggles of poor people in Latin America during the second part of the twentieth century. Stated in the *Compendium of the Social Doctrine of the Church* (no. 59), it is now enshrined in Catholic social teaching. It challenges individuals and societies to examine ethical and economic choices from the point of view of how they will affect poor people, not just in their locality, but globally as well. *Laudato Si'* describes the preferential option for the poorest of our brothers and sisters "as an ethical imperative essential for effectively attaining the common good" (no. 158). Global warming will have a devastating impact on the poor. *Laudato Si'* calls attention to the fact that "the worst impact [of climate change] will probably be felt by developing countries in coming decades. Many of the poor live in areas particularly affected by phenomena related to warming, and their means of subsistence are largely dependent on natural reserves and ecosystemic services such as agriculture, fishing and forestry" (no. 25). Later in the encyclical the pope writes that "the warming caused by huge consumption on the part of some rich countries has repercussions on the poorest areas of the world, especially Africa, where a rise in temperature, together with droughts has proved devastating for farming" (no. 51).

Financially rich countries may have the resources to adapt to the problems that climate change will pose. Economically poor countries do not have the resources to adapt to severe climate events and should not be asked to carry this burden. In a speech delivered on the south lawn of the White House on September 23, 2015, Pope Francis called for urgent action on climate change. Invoking the memory of Martin Luther King Jr., he identified action to protect our "common home" as a moral issue, especially as it serves to protect the underprivileged of the world, those most at risk from the effects of global warming.[9]

Solidarity

The church community and all humankind need to respond to the plight of the poor. Solidarity is a concept much beloved of Pope John Paul II. In his 1987 encyclical *Sollicitudo Rei Socialis (On Social Concern)* he describes solidarity "not [as] a feeling of vague compassion or shallow distress at the misfortunes of so many people, both near and far. On the contrary, it is a firm and persevering determination to commit oneself to the common good; that is to say the good of all and of each individual, because we are all really responsible for all" (SRS, no. 38). Solidarity will mean making available resources to economically poorer countries to help them adapt to the changes that severe weather, lack of water, and a significant rise in sea levels will bring.

In the context of the deepening ecological crisis, solidarity acknowledges that we are increasingly bound together as members of the earth community. In her overview of the statement on ecology

---

[9] Dan Roberts and Stephanie Kirchgaessner, "Pope Francis Calls for Urgent Action on Climate Change in White House Speech," *Guardian*, September 23, 2015.

from the Holy See, Sister Marjorie Keenan writes that the "concept of solidarity also extends to nature."[10] We are responsible for the well-being of the poor and of all creation. Their destinies are intertwined. We will either bequeath to the next generation of all creatures a fruitful, beautiful, and vibrant planet, or alternatively, all future generations will inherit a planet diminished in beauty and biodiversity. On such a barren and polluted world future generations would be forced to live amid the ruins, not merely of the technological world, but of the natural world itself.

There is a growing consensus on what needs to be done. Both the UN Framework Conference on Climate Change (UNFCCC) and the authors of *Fate of Mountain Glaciers in the Anthropocene* insist that it is necessary to reduce significantly carbon-dioxide emission without delay, using all means possible. Obviously rich countries, which for decades have been emitting carbon dioxide, have the primary obligation to set ambitious and legally binding targets to reduce carbon-dioxide emissions. In 2009, the UNFCCC stated that every effort must be made to keep the average global temperature below a 2-degree Celsius rise in order to protect the planet against the worst effects of climate change. Unfortunately, the meeting could not agree on an ambitious, legally binding treaty.

Climate Change in the United States

Denial

Before discussing the response of the US bishops to climate change, it is important to be sensitive to the wider context of climate change in the United States. In ways that are not true in Europe, many people in the United States are in denial about climate change. The pope recognizes that there are rich people and powerful institutions closely linked to the fossil-fuel and transport industries who are funding "climate skeptic" campaigns. Sowing

---

[10] Sister Marjorie Keenan, RSHM, *From Stockholm to Johannesburg* (Vatican City: Pontifical Council for Justice and Peace, 2002), 38.

the seeds of doubt makes it more difficult for politicians to take the difficult decisions to curb carbon emissions. The encyclical states that "many of those who possess more resources and economic or political power seem mostly to be concerned with masking the problems or concealing their symptoms, simply making efforts to reduce some of the negative impacts of climate change" (no. 26). Given that major climate disruption will happen as a result of global warming, the activities of these groups are irresponsible and immoral, particularly when the Fifth Assessment Report of the IPCC states that "it is at least 95% likely that human activities—chiefly the burning of fossil fuels—are the main cause of warming since the 1950s." The Republican Party in the United States has increasingly taken a skeptical stance regarding global warming.

Politicians and Climate Change

A report on the impact of climate change on the United States was undertaken by the National Climate Group. This included scientists and representatives from a large cross section of US society, including representatives from two oil companies. The report was overseen by the government and finally approved at a meeting in Washington DC on May 6, 2014.[11]

At the launch of the report in the White House, President Obama spent much of the day highlighting the findings. The Obama administration hoped to use the findings of the report to garner public support for the president's climate policies as he sought to put new regulations in place to limit carbon emissions. Many believe there will be a major political battle between those favoring President Obama's climate policy and the one being pursued by Republicans in Congress.

The trouble for the Republicans who continue to support the fossil-fuel industry is that the National Climate Assessment report makes it clear that the effects of human-induced climate change are being felt in every corner of the United States, especially in

---

[11] Justin Gillis, "Climate Change Study Finds US Is Already Widely Affected," *New York Times,* May 6, 2014.

California. Some areas are becoming drier, while other areas are experiencing torrential rain. Heat waves are becoming more common, and there are more severe droughts. This, in turn, is leading to more wildfires and to forests being attacked by heat-loving insects.

The report claims that such major changes have been caused by an average warming of less than 2 degrees Fahrenheit over most land areas of the country in the past century. The fear is that if the emissions of carbon dioxide and methane continue to escalate, warming could conceivably exceed 10 degrees Fahrenheit by the end of this century.

Until very recently many people in the United States considered climate change to be an issue for the next generation. This scientific report claims that it has moved firmly into the present. "Summers are longer and hotter, and extended periods of unusual heat last longer than any living American has ever experienced." The report continues, "Winters are generally shorter and warmer. Rain comes in heavier downpours. People are seeing changes in the length and severity of seasonal allergies, the plant varieties that thrive in their gardens, and the kinds of birds they see in any particular month in their gardens." Jerry M. Mellilo, chairman of the scientific panel that produced the report, said at the briefing in the White House that "we are all bearing the costs of increases in extreme heat, heavy downpours and higher coastal storm surges."[12]

Despite the overwhelming scientific evidence in support of climate change, some members of Congress still believe that the science of global warming is a hoax perpetrated by a global conspiracy of climate scientists. "The Center for American Progress Action Fund estimates that 169 members of the 114th Congress (or 56 percent) have expressed doubts about the science behind climate change, 35 of whom identify as Catholic."[13]

President Obama dismissed the skeptics, comparing them to those who still believe the earth is flat. There is another group

---

[12] Ibid.

[13] Jack Jenkins, "Vatican Announces Major Summit on Climate Change," April 15, 2015.

that, while conceding that climate change is happening, fear that implementing the president's climate-change strategy will lead to mine closures, with an effect on the broader US economy. The authors of the report were surprised at data on the rising frequency of torrential rains. It makes sense that more water evaporates from a warming ocean surface and that the warmer atmosphere can hold the excess vapor, which then falls as rain or snow. The statistics are quite startling. Over the past fifty years the proportion of precipitation that fell in very heavy rain events has jumped by 71 percent in the Northeast, by 37 percent in the Midwest, and by 27 percent in the Southeast of the United States.

In recent years intense rain has caused extensive damage to infrastructures and crops. The devastating floods in Nashville in 2010 were caused by two days of torrential rain that produced twenty inches of rain. In 2013, parts of Colorado had as much rain in a week as normally falls in a year. In March 2014, a storm killed dozens after heavy rains in Washington State. In the last week of April 2014, widespread flooding occurred in the Florida Panhandle as a result of very heavy rain over a period of two days. In the past few years the United States has had numerous incidences of severe weather.

In March 2015, President Obama unveiled details of the pledges he and President Xi Jinping of China made in Beijing, in November 2014, that the United States would cut greenhouse gas emissions by 28 percent by 2025 and China's emissions would drop by 2030. Included in President Obama's plan are domestic initiatives. These include the freezing of new coal-fired power plants and increasing the fuel-economy requirement for vehicles. The plan relies on the executive authority of the president being exercised through the Environmental Protection Agency, since it is clear that a Republican-controlled Congress will block climate-related legislation.

On August 3, 2015, the US Environmental Protection Agency (EPA) published its Clean-Power Plan. The plan, which took two years to complete, involved EPA discussions with states and electricity providers. The plan stipulates that electricity providers must lower their carbon emissions by 32 percent below the 2005 levels by 2030. It is estimated that investment in renewable forms of energy and carbon-capture technologies will cost the electricity industry $8.4 billion. On the positive side, the EPA points out that doing so will benefit the environment by between $34 and $54 billion over the long term.[14] The plan is expected to run into opposition from those who claim that it will be costly, will lead to the closure of many coal-fired power stations, and will destroy the coal industry.

As details of the Clean-Power Plan were being launched, the Republican candidates for the presidency in 2016 were promising to undo President Obama's plans if elected. Leading the campaign against the president is Senate Majority Leader Mitch McConnell from Kentucky, who claims the so-called clean-power regulation is "unfair and probably illegal." Senator McConnell is urging state governors to fight the Obama regulations by refusing to disclose their state plans and targets to the Federal Government.[15] While environmental groups approve of President Obama's program, Lou Leonard, the vice president for climate-change policy with the World Wildlife Fund, says it doesn't go far enough: "In fact, the US must do more than just deliver on this pledge—the 28 percent domestic target can and must be the floor, not a ceiling."[16]

US Catholic Church and Climate Change

What about the record of the US Catholic Church in relation to climate change? The fact that the United States, with only 5 percent of the world's population, is responsible for 25 percent of greenhouse gas emissions should raise moral issues for US Catholics. If one adds to that the disruptive behavior of the US delegation at the annual UNFCCC and the policies of President George W. Bush, one has to question whether the response has

---

[14] Dan Roberts, "Campaigners Hail Obama's Carbon Cuts," *Guardian,* August 4, 2015, 1, 14.

[15] Mitch McConnell, "States Should Reject Obama Mandate for Clean-Power Regulations," *Lexington Herald Leader,* March 3, 2015.

[16] Quoted in Coral Davenport, "Obama's Strategy on Climate Change, Part of Global Deal, Is Revealed," *New York Times,* March 31, 2015.

been very insightful or prophetic. In June 2002, the United States Conference of Catholic Bishops (USCCB) published a document entitled *Climate Change: A Plea for Dialogue, Prudence, and the Common Good.* The bishops were very clear that prudence is not meant to inhibit action or promote a business-as-usual approach. It challenges people, especially those in authority, to reflect on the current scientific data on climate change and take the appropriate action.

Climate change is killing people, and it will kill millions more in the decades to come as the warming increases. *Laudato Si'* congratulates the US bishops for continuing to focus on the differentiated responsibilities for various groups. "As the United States bishops have said, greater attention must be given to 'the needs of the poor, the weak and the vulnerable, in a debate often dominated by more powerful interests'" (no. 52).

Another document from the USCCB appeared in March 2007. *Faithful Stewards of God's Creation: A Catholic Resource for Environmental Justice and Climate Change* is weak in its analysis of climate-change data. The document states: "We enter this debate not to embrace a particular treaty, nor to urge particular technical solutions, but to call for a different kind of national discussion," and it makes clear that there is near unanimity among the scientific community about the causes of climate change. Then the document reflects on the debate about climate change. It focuses in four pages on how climate change will affect the poor; this is very much to be welcomed. Yet the document does not have an adequate contemporary theology of creation, which would include an admission from the Catholic Church that it has been ambivalent about the natural world down through the centuries. The document relies extensively on the notion of stewardship. While this captures certain elements in the human-earth relationship, it also has many problems. Some might ask for whom we are stewarding? Is it an absent God? Or is it for future generations or other creatures? Many might say that our stewardship has been poor on all of these grounds.

This document calls on "our people and government to recognize the seriousness of the global threat and develop effective policies that will diminish the possible consequences of global climate change," but it fails to be specific. In April 2007, the US Supreme Court showed more courage when it handed down a decision declaring that the Federal Government has the authority to regulate greenhouse gas emissions.

Climate Change and Economics

The Economics of Climate Change was released in October 2006, before the UNFCCC Convention in Nairobi. This excellent book attempts to bring together what we know about climate change from an economic perspective. In the seven-hundred-page document the author, Nicholas Stern, claims that climate change is the greatest and most wide-ranging market failure ever, and therefore presents a huge challenge to economics. Stern's main conclusion is that early action on climate change would benefit everyone and far outweighs not taking any action. If no action is taken now, the overall costs of climate change could reach 5 percent of global domestic product (GDP) each year into the indefinite future.[17] According to the report, lack of action could lead to a 4- to 5-degree Celsius rise before the end of the twenty-first century. In an interview given in Davos in 2013, Stern admitted the effects of climate change will be much worse than those he had predicted in the 2006 report.[18]

Stranded Assets

In June 2013, the International Energy Agency reported that a business-as-usual approach to fossil fuels could lead to a mean global temperature increase of 5.3 degrees Celsius by the end of the century.[19] Michael Greenstone has calculated that the total is

---

[17] Nicholas Stern, *The Economics of Climate Change: The Stern Review* (Cambridge, UK: Cambridge University Press, 2007).

[18] Heather Steward and Larry Elliot, "Nicholas Stern: 'I got it wrong on climate change—it's far, far worse,'" *Guardian,* January 26, 2013.

[19] Bryan Walsh, "Power Surge: The US Is Undergoing an Energy Revolution in Oil, Gas, Wind, Solar, and Efficiency," *Time* (October 28, 2013), 31.

16.2 degrees Fahrenheit above preindustrial levels.[20] To put the argument in another way, climate activist Bill McKibben says that scientists reckon that humans can emit 565 gigatons of carbon dioxide into the atmosphere and still have some reasonable hope of keeping the average global temperature less than 2 degrees Celsius above preindustrial levels. However, the proven reserves of fossil fuel that we are planning to extract and burn stands at more than 2,795 gigatons. This means that there are more than 2,000 gigatons, worth billions of dollars, which we cannot burn if we want our children to live in a tolerable world.[21] It is now estimated that 80 percent of the known coal reserves, 50 percent of gas, and 30 percent of oil will have to stay underground if we are to meet the two degrees Celsius mark.[22]

Even Ben van Beurden, the chief executive of Shell, accepts that all the fossil fuel cannot be burned unless a way is found to capture the carbon. He is of the opinion that "the global energy system will become 'zero carbon' by the end of the century, with his group obtaining a 'very, very large segment' of its earnings from renewable power."[23] But the article states that "the company claims to be one of the largest renewable energy companies in the world despite spending annually less than $1bn on green schemes out of a total $33bn capital expenditure budget."[24] In this new scenario whether it is possible to take such a leap given the current economic and political realities is questionable.

However, many commentators, including the authors of the Pontifical Academy of Sciences' *Fate of Mountain Glaciers in the Anthropocene* believe that an average 2-degree Celsius rise in global temperature above the preindustrial age is too high. They

---

[20] Michael Greenstone, "If We Dig Out All Our Fossil Fuels, Here Is How Hot We Can Expect It to Get," *New York Times,* April 8, 2015.

[21] Alan Rusbridger, "Why We Put the Climate on the Cover," *Guardian,* March 7, 2015.

[22] Alan Rusbridger, "The Argument for Divesting from Fossil Fuels Is Becoming Overwhelming," *Guardian,* March 17, 2015.

[23] Terry Macalister and Damian Carrington, "Shell Boss Endorses Warnings About Fossil Fuels and Climate Change," *Guardian,* May 22, 2015.

[24] Ibid.

claim that the level for avoiding "dangerous anthropogenic inter-ference" should be reduced to 1.5 degrees Celsius. This would mean reducing the concentration of carbon dioxide in the atmo-sphere to 350 ppm. Regrettably, in July 2013, it was discovered that there is 400 ppm of carbon dioxide in the atmosphere and that this figure is rising by between 2 ppm and 3 ppm annually. That is why an ambitious, legally binding global treaty on curbing greenhouse gas emissions must be negotiated within the next two years. Otherwise future generations will pay a terrible price for the negligence of this generation. On November 6, 2013, Michel Jarraud, secretary-general of the World Meteorological Organisa-tion, stated: "We need to act now, otherwise we will jeopardise the future of our children, grandchildren and many future generations. Time is not on our side."[25]

With regular extreme climate events such as Hurricane Sandy or Typhoon Haiyan, the world is beginning to appreciate that adapting to climate change will be very costly. This is why the UN Conference on Climate Change set up a fund called the Adaptation Fund to help economically poor countries adapt to climate change. Severe weather, a rise in the level of the ocean, melting glaciers, and droughts will have a devastating impact on many poor coun-tries. The Holy See has constantly stated that the Adaptation Fund needs to be at least $200 billion each year.

Divestments

In *Laudato Si'* Pope Francis writes about what consumer groups can achieve by boycotting certain products (no. 206). I think the Catholic Church should join with the Anglican Church and the WCC and divest from fossil-fuel companies. In April 2015, sev-enteen bishops and archbishops from the Anglican Communion Environmental Network (ACEN) said that "investments in fossil fuel companies were incompatible with a just and sustainable future." They called "for a review of our churches' investment

---

[25] Quoted in Dick Ahlstrom, "Greenhouse Gas Build-up Continues in Earth's Atmosphere," *Irish Times,* November 7, 2013.

practices with a view to supporting environmental sustainability and justice by divesting from industries involved primarily in the extraction and distribution of fossil fuels."[26] The authors are aware that the Church of England is currently debating whether to dump fossil fuels from its £6.1 billion fund. One of the leaders in the divestment movement in the Anglican Communion is Archbishop Desmond Tutu. "Archbishop Tutu told the *Guardian* in 2014 that 'people of conscience need to break their ties with corporations financing the injustice of climate change.'" His successor in Cape Town, Archbishop Thabo Makgoba, says that the ACEN "accepts the science of climate change and identified climate action as a spiritual imperative for all Anglicans."[27] For religious people the aim of divestment is to bankrupt the fossil-fuel industry morally, not financially. Hopefully, because of their duty to manage their resources, these companies will invest in renewable forms of energy.

Norway Dumps Coal Stocks

The most dramatic decision in terms of divestment thus far was made by Norway in June 2015. It decided to dump all coal-focused investments from its $900 billion sovereign wealth fund. The decision will cost between $9 billion and $10 billion, according to the Norwegian government. This will involve removing funds from energy companies such as RWE in Germany, Shenhua in China, Duke Energy in the United States, AGL Energy in Australia, Reliance Power in India, and Electric Power Development in Japan. It is hoped that because of the amount involved, other countries and pension funds and investment-portfolio organizations will do the same and that businesses will also join the divestment movement.

The insurance group AXA has removed its $500 million investment in coal. Instead, it is investing $3 billion in renewable energy initiatives, because both "the World Bank and the Bank of England have said that fossil fuel reserves will be worthless if the

---

[26] Karl Mathiesen, "Bishops Urge Churches to Divest from Fossil Fuel Industry," *Guardian*, March 2015.

[27] Damian Carrington, "Fossil Fuel Divestment Gives Earth a Prayer of a Change," *Guardian,* May 2, 2015.

action needed to cut carbon emissions kicks in."[28] Tom Sanzillo, a former comptroller of New York State who managed a $156 billion pension fund, believes that many countries and funds will follow the example of Norway. According to him, "No investment policy that I am familiar with can keep holding stocks in an industry with catastrophic losses and with no realistic case for an upside."[29] Clearly, the challenge to divest from the fossil-fuel-industry holdings is both moral and pragmatic.

The *Guardian* supported a campaign to encourage the Welcome Trust and the Bill and Melinda Gates Foundation to divest from fossil-fuel companies. The Welcome Trust has a portfolio of £18 billion, while the Bill and Melinda Gates Foundation has an endowment of £43.5 billion. Both currently have investments in fossil fuels. The Bill and Melinda Gates Foundation has $372 million invested in BP and $5.5 million in Shell.[30] The divestment campaign reminds them that, while their organizations have made a huge contribution to human progress and equality by supporting scientific research and development projects, their investments in fossil fuels are putting all of this at risk in the long term. That is why these companies are being asked to withdraw their investments in fossil-fuel companies.[31]

Changes Need to Be Made Now

We need to make bold decisions now because, despite the public focus on climate change since 1998, emissions are continuing to increase. In 1990, for example, emissions were increasing at 0.1 percent per annum. By the year 2000, with growing economies such as China and India, emissions had jumped to 3 and 4 percent. The only time that growth dipped was during 2009, at the

---

[28] Damian Carrington, "Norway's Decision to Dump Coal Stocks Expected to Prompt More Divestments," *Guardian,* May 25, 2015.

[29] Quoted in ibid.

[30] David Smith, "Gates Could Have His Legacy Doing the Right Things, But Fossil Fuels Destroy African Lives," *Guardian,* May 27, 2015.

[31] Rusbridger, "The Argument for Divesting from Fossil Fuels Is Becoming Overwhelming."

height of the financial crisis.[32] We must act quickly because the International Energy Agency (IEA) insists that our emissions need to be under control by 2017; if not, we will lock in to our climate system extremely dangerous global warming. Faith Birol, the chief economist of IEA, is clear: "The door to reach two degrees is about to close. In 2017 it will be closed forever."[33]

Stop Subsidizing Fossil Fuel

On May 19, 2015, the *Guardian* reported that global fossil-fuel corporations were receiving massive subsidies. The report estimates that the global subsidy in the previous year reached $5.3 trillion. The *Guardian* found the revelation shocking, because that is more than all the governments of the world spend on health care. "Nicholas Stern, an eminent climate economist at the London School of Economics, said: 'This very important analysis shatters the myth that fossil fuels are cheap by showing just how huge their real costs are. There is no justification for these enormous subsidies for fossil fuels, which distort markets and damage economics, particularly in poorer countries.'" The IMF report says that cutting these subsidies would cut carbon emissions by 20 percent. A $2.3 trillion subsidy goes to the coal industry in China. The Chinese are very dependent on large coal-fired power stations. Fossil-fuel subsidies in other countries are also huge: in the United States, $700 billion; in Russia, $335 billion; in India, $277 billion; and in Japan, $157 billion. In the European Union subsidies run to $330 billion.[34]

Renewables

Laudato Si' applauds the current efforts to "substitute fossil fuel and develop sources of renewable energy . . . and to develop

---

[32] Naomi Klein, "Introduction to Climate Change," *Guardian,* March 9, 2015.

[33] Quoted in ibid.

[34] Damian Carrington, "IMF Uncovers the Fossil Fuel Industry's $5.3tn Dirty Secret," *Guardian,* May 19, 2015.

adequate storage capacity" (no. 26). Thankfully, the production of renewable energy is growing. Global investment in clean energy jumped by 16 percent in 2014 to £205 billion, with the cost of producing solar energy dropping two-thirds between 2009 and 2014.[35] By 2016, green energy will provide double the electricity of nuclear plants and outstrip every other source of electricity except coal.[36] Unfortunately, the growth in renewable energy is not sufficient to stop dangerous climate change because our appetite for energy across the globe is also growing. This is why new gas- and coal-fired power stations are planned in a number of countries, especially China and India. Still, Pope Francis is encouraged by the efforts being made. Pope Francis believes that even poor countries must

> develop less polluting forms of energy production, but to do so they require the help of countries which have experienced great growth at the cost of the ongoing pollution of the planet. Taking advantage of abundant solar energy will require the establishment of mechanism and subsidies that allow developing countries access to technology transfer, technical assistance and financial resources. (no. 172)

The pope points out that "in some places, cooperatives are being developed to exploit renewable sources of energy which ensure local self-sufficiency and even the sale of surplus energy" (no. 179).

At a local level individuals, parishes, and dioceses could conduct an energy audit to ascertain how much fossil fuel they use. Better insulation of church buildings would help reduce the amount of fossil fuel used in heating. Using public transport would also cut use of fossil fuels. Catholic institutions should look at their investment portfolios to ensure that financial resources are not invested in fossil-fuel companies, but rather in renewable energy initiatives.

---

[35] Rusbridger, "The Argument for Divesting From Fossil Fuels Is Becoming Overwhelming."

[36] Michael Marshall and Peter Aldhous, "Our Green Future Starts Now," *New Scientist* (July 6, 2013), 6.

Young Catholics in parishes and dioceses could be involved in ongoing monitoring of these green initiatives. The church also needs to encourage local and national governments to enact robust climate-change legislation. It should also support the efforts of the UNFCCC meeting to have a robust, ambitious, legally binding, and fair treaty on climate change signed at the UNFCCC meeting in Paris in 2015. Pope Francis recognizes that this might not be easy because "recent World Summits on the environment have not lived up to the expectations, due to the lack of political will, and they were unable to reach meaningful and effective global agreements on the environment" (no. 166). But critics of the Catholic Church would argue that the church has not taken a prominent position in these talks, unlike the WCC, which has always sent a delegation of experts to the UNFCCC meetings. One hopes that this will change and that there will be a well-prepared delegation at the 2015 meeting. Many commentators believe it is crucial that the conference achieve significant success to begin the process of decarbonizing our industry and culture.

With the publication of *Laudato Si'*, no one can accuse the leadership of the Catholic Church of not taking a stand on climate change. Pope Francis has shown himself to be the true "watchman," sensitive to the dangers facing everyone (see Ezek 33:6). He has also challenged and emboldened us to take the necessary steps to avoid this catastrophe.

Bibliography

Flannery, Tim, *Weather Makers: The History and Future Impact of Climate Change* (London: Allen Lane/Penguin, 2006).

Intergovernmental Panel on Climate Change (IPCC), *Climate Change 2014 Synthesis Report: Fifth Assessment Report*, http://ar5-syr.ipcc.ch/.

Klein, Naomi, *This Changes Everything: Capitalism vs. Climate* (London: Penguin Random House UK, 2015).

McDonagh, Sean, *Climate Change; A Challenge to Us All* (Dublin: Columba Press, 2006).

McKibben, Bill, *Eaarth: Making a Life on a Tough New Planet* (New York: Times Books, 2010).

Northcott, Michael S., A Moral Climate: The Ethics of Global Warming (Maryknoll, NY: Orbis Books, 2007).

3

Biodiversity

According to many scientists the earth is experiencing the sixth greatest extinction of life since life began 3.8 billion years ago.[1] Pope Francis puts it more graphically: "The earth's resources are being plundered because of short-sighted approaches to the economy, commerce and production" (no. 34). What is now happening is comparable to the extinction event that wiped out the dinosaurs as well as almost half the species of the world sixty-five million years ago. Though there is still some uncertainty among paleontologists as to the cause of the extinction, the major factor in this event was a ten-kilometer-wide asteroid that struck what is now the Yucatán peninsula in Mexico. The effect was global. Forest fires burned around the world. The smoke blocked sunlight and led to a cold period.

Pope Francis realizes that the current mass extinction is a direct result of human activity on the planet (no. 33). The extinction rate in the twentieth century is up to 100 times higher than it would have been without human activity.[2] Dr. Gerardo Ceballos of the National Autonomous University of Mexico says that this is a conservative estimate "which only looked at species that had been declared extinct."[3]

---

[1] Adam Vaughan, "Earth Heading for Sixth Mass Extinction, Study Says," *Guardian,* June 20, 2015.

[2] Ibid.

[3] Ibid.

This is why Dr. Edward Wilson, emeritus professor of biology at Harvard University, wrote in 2000 that the "quenching of life's exuberance will be more consequential to humanity than all present-day warming, ozone depletion, and pollution combined."[4] He is not the only person sounding the alarm. A study by the International Union for the Conservation of Nature (IUCN), conducted in 2010, estimates that one in five mammals, one in four plants, one in three amphibians, and one in eight birds are in danger of being pushed over the precipice of extinction.[5] David Roberts, from the Durrell Institute of Conservation and Ecology at the University of Kent, one of the co-authors of the study, says: "If we take the number of species that are known to be threatened, and add to that those that are yet to be discovered, we can estimate that between 27% and 33% of all flowering plants will be threatened with extinction."[6] In *Laudato Si'* Pope Francis laments the fact that "the loss of forests and woodlands entail the loss of species which may constitute extremely important resources in the future, not only for food but also for curing disease and other uses. Different species contain genes which could be key resources in years ahead for meeting human needs and regulating environmental problems" (no. 32).

David Roberts makes the same point when he writes: "Plants are the basis of much of life on Earth, with virtually all other species depending on them. If you get rid of those you get rid of a lot of the things above them."[7]

The IUCN believes that of the estimated 634 primate species in the world, 48 percent are now facing extinction. The mountain gorilla is critically endangered, with only 720 left in the wild in the Congo, Rwanda, and Uganda. Poachers have devastated their numbers. However, the major threat to the gorillas is the

---

[4] Edward O. Wilson, "Vanishing before Our Eyes," *Time Special Edition,* April/May 2000.

[5] Juliette Jowit, "At Least a Quarter of Flowers May Face Extinction," *Guardian,* July 7, 2010.

[6] Ibid.

[7] Ibid.

continuing destruction of forests, mainly to make charcoal for people to cook their meals.[8]

A quick search online reveals that orangutans, like other great apes, are close relatives to humans. They live only in Indonesia and Malaysia. At one time there were hundreds of thousands of orangutans living in the wild. However, the destruction of their habitat by illegal loggers and the clearance of the tropical forests to make way for palm oil plantations have decimated their numbers. Even the estimated twenty-five hundred found in Gunung Palung National Park in Indonesia are under threat from poachers. Many people now fear that orangutans in the wild could be extinct within ten to fifteen years.

Websites show that other primates are also on the brink of extinction. There are only between fifty and seventy golden-headed langurs *(Trachypithecus poliocephalus)* on the island of Ca Ba and fewer than 110 eastern black-crested gibbons *(Nomascus nasutus)* in northeastern Vietnam. On the island of Madagascar there are fewer than 100 northern sportive lemurs *(Lepilemur septentionalis).* It is not a coincidence that primates on the Island of Madagascar are endangered. After the coup in March 2009, Madagascar's world-renowned national parks were infiltrated by illegal loggers. Tens of thousands of hectares have been affected, and the resulting instability has caused a boom in lemur bushmeat hunting, with these animals killed and then sold as meat in restaurants.

In September 2010, before the UN Convention on Biological Diversity in Nagoya, Japan, scientists from the Royal Botanic Gardens at Kew, the Natural History Museum in London, and the IUCN released a study that reported that one in five of the world's species of plants, estimated to be around 380,000, is threatened with extinction within this century because of human activity. This study ought to have received extensive news coverage; in fact, it was almost ignored by the media.

---

[8] David Smith, "After the Killings: New Hope for Rescued Gorillas," *Guardian,* March 9, 2010.

One of the reasons for this indifference is that many people do not know what biodiversity means and how crucial it is to the well-being of life on earth, including human life. But whether people realize it or not, plant diversity is extremely important and needs to be protected. According to Stephen Hopper, the director of Kew Gardens in London, "plants are the basis of all life on earth, providing clean air, water, food and fuel. All animal and bird life depends on them and so do we."[9] Humans have lived for tens of thousands of years without money, for example, but we cannot live without biodiversity. Other creatures fertilize and pollinate our crops, provide oxygen, and recycle water. We depend on biodiversity for our food, fabrics, fibers, and pharmaceuticals, to mention but a few. For example, in the 1960s people who suffered from leukemia, Hodgkin's disease, and other cancers had a 20 percent chance of surviving. Today they have an 80 percent chance of long-term survival because of drugs that are derived from the rose periwinkle plant, which is only found in Madagascar.[10]

Biodiversity Hotspots

It is important to point out that countries in the tropics, which are often poor in economic terms, are very rich in biodiversity. Possibly one-half to three-quarters of the world's biological diversity is to be found in the tropical rainforests of South America, Asia, and Africa. Taken together, these areas make up only 7 percent of the earth's surface. Countries in the Northern Hemisphere, which are economically rich, are poor in biodiversity. "The hills around a small volcano in the Philippines possess more tree species than does Canada, and a 15 hectare plot in Borneo has more tree species than does the entire United States."[11] The tragedy is that much of the biodiversity found in tropical countries is disappearing at an alarming rate.

---

9 "A Fifth of World's Plant Species at Risk of Extinction," *Irish Times,* Reuters, September 30, 2010.

10 "Biodiversity: What's at Stake?" (London: Catholic Institute for International Relations, 1993), 5, 6.

11 Ibid., 9.

And yet, the threats to biodiversity are not really appreciated by many people. Few people would lose any sleep at the thought that in 2015 the extinction of species is taking place one thousand times faster than at the end of the Ice Age. When one factors in a projected nine to ten billion people on the planet by 2050, extinction rates are expected to speed up even further.[12]

The WWF prepared a report for the UN Convention on Biological Diversity: *Living Planet Report 2010: Biodiversity, Biocapacity, and Development.* It too makes sobering reading. Nearly a quarter of all mammal species, one-third of amphibians, and one-third of flowering species are threatened with extinction within this century, unless radical remedial action is taken in the next five to ten years. The report uses the ecological footprint indicator, which calculates the biologically productive land and water required to provide the renewable resources that people need. Based on data from 2007, the human ecological footprint overshot the biologically regenerative capacity of the earth by 50 percent.

The destruction of biodiversity by human beings ignores the fact that all these creatures have, as Pope Francis points out in his encyclical, "intrinsic value in themselves independent of their usefulness. Each organism, as a creature of God, is good and admirable in itself; the same is true of the harmonious ensemble of organisms existing in a defined space and functioning as a system" (no. 140).

This is certainly new teaching, and it has enormous implications for Christians living in our world today. If each species has intrinsic value, we humans are challenged to be attentive to them and their habitat, so that they can thrive on earth. Oftentimes in the past century humans have had an almost autistic relationship with the rest of creation. We pay little attention to trees or flowers around us, and we seldom allow nature to evoke any type of emotional response from us. Seldom do modern humans show the kind of empathy with nature that was so typical of St. Francis of Assisi.

More and more modern technology has helped to widen the gap between ourselves and the rest of creation. This is partly because

---

[12] "Biodiversity: Boundless, Priceless, and Threatened," *Guardian,* January 1, 2011.

so few of us work in the rural world to plant and harvest the food we eat. Just think of the amount of time people spend on their iPads or mobile phones instead of getting to know, appreciate, and love creation.

If we took the intrinsic value of creation seriously, we would be imitating what Adam did in the Garden of Eden. He was asked by God to name all the creatures in his world (Gen 2:19–20). We should be as knowledgeable about our world as he was about his world. This would mean learning the names of the birds, the insects, the trees, the creatures of the oceans, the wildflowers and mosses and grasses in our locality. This kind of attentiveness to creation would become the foundation stone of our creation spirituality.

Since nature moves much more slowly than our ever more complex technologies, this kind of active rootedness in our local place would slow us down from what Pope Francis calls "rapidification" and allow us to enter into a fuller relationship with creation and God (no. 18).

From this perspective, protecting biodiversity should be one of the primary goals of human life, the central human vocation. Later in the document Pope Francis tells us that ecological conversion "also entails a loving awareness that we are not disconnected from the rest of creatures, but joined in a splendid communion" (no. 220).

The Conference of the Parties to the UN Convention on Biological Diversity, which Pope Francis mentions in the encyclical (no. 167), has received very little media coverage over the years, unlike the similar convention for climate change. In 2010, at the opening ceremony, Ahmed Djoghlaf, executive secretary of the Convention on Biological Diversity, told the sixteen thousand participants who had gathered from across the world that they are called to address seriously the unprecedented loss of biodiversity that is compounded by global warming. He stated: "The report predicts that if we allow current trends to continue we shall soon reach a tipping point with irreversible and irreparable damage to the capacity of the planet to sustain life on Earth. The report warns that the status of biodiversity for the next million years will be determined by the action or inaction, of one specie, we human being of mankind in the coming decades" [*sic*].[13] The Catholic Church, which presents itself as a pro-life church, should take a special interest in the UN Convention on Biological Diversity.

At the Earth Summit in Rio in 1992, 150 countries signed the Convention on Biological Diversity. The object of this convention is to protect biodiversity and to ensure that there is a fair and equitable distribution of any financial benefits derived from these biological and genetic resources. Yet, "while the Convention has legally binding status, it is couched in vague and confusing language."[14] This has created loopholes that allow large multinational corporations to obtain easy access to the biological diversity of poor countries for a pittance.

As part of the Convention on Biological Diversity each country, state, and local area is expected to draw up a biodiversity data base and a plan to protect any species that might be threatened. The church should give ethical and religious underpinning to the work of the Convention on Biological Diversity globally, nationally, and locally.

Extinction of Species and Faith

The extinction of species is not treated formally in the scriptures. Yet appreciation for life, gratitude to God for the gift of life, and a strong belief that God cares for life and wishes humans to emulate this care are central features of both the Hebrew and Christian scriptures.

The book of Genesis tells us that human sin destroys our relationship with God, severs human bonds, and disfigures creation. The good news of the gospel is about restoring all these fractured relationships. Protecting and restoring creation must be at the heart of promoting the reign of God in our contemporary world.

---

[13] UNEP, Convention on Biological Diversity, "Statement by Ahmed Djoghlaf Executive Secretary of the Convention on Biological Diversity at the Opening Session of the Tenth Meeting of the Conference of the Parties to the Convention on Biological Diversity," Nagoya (October 16, 2010).

[14] "Biodiversity: What's at Stake?" 17.

The present mega-extinction of species is not only sterilizing the planet, undermining its diversity, and grieving the Spirit of Life, but it is also seriously compromising our ability to develop new insights into the nature of God. As one species after another is jostled over the abyss of extinction, the unique way in which that species reflected God's goodness is lost forever. St. Bonaventure used the image of the stained-glass window to capture the difference. "As a ray of light entering through a window is colored in different ways, according to the different colors of the various parts, so the divine ray shines forth in each and every creature in different ways in different properties."[15]

Pope Francis quotes St. Thomas Aquinas, who is even more explicit about the ability of each creature to image God in a particular way. He argues that God created a magnificent variety of creatures so that God's goodness might be communicated to them and reflected by them. Pope Francis writes:

> Multiplicity and variety "come from the intention of the first agent" who willed that "what was wanting to one in the representation of the divine goodness might be supplied by another", inasmuch as God's goodness "could not be represented fittingly by any one creature". Hence we need to grasp the variety of things in their multiple relationships. We understand better the importance and meaning of each creature if we contemplate it within the entirety of God's plan. (no. 86)[16]

In his reflections on the relationship of humans with other species the pope reminds us that "the Church does not simply state that other creatures are completely subordinated to the God of human beings, as if they have no worth in themselves and can be treated as we wish" (no. 65).

In *Laudato Si'* Pope Francis quotes the Canadian bishops, "who rightly point out that no creature is excluded from this

---

[15] Quoted in Denis Edwards, "Theological Foundations for Ecological Praxis," *Ecotheology* 5–6 (1998): 130.

[16] See Thomas Aquinas, *Summa Theologiae* I, q. 47, art. 1; art. 2, ad. 1; art. 3.

manifestation of God: 'From panoramic vistas to the tiniest living form, nature is a constant source of wonder and awe'" (no. 85). In the same paragraph the pope also quotes a statement from the Japanese bishops that "to sense each creature singing the hymn of its existence is to live joyfully in God's love and hope." Further on in the encyclical Pope Francis states that we must respect others creatures because "they have intrinsic value independent of their usefulness" to humans (no. 140).

In order to address biodiversity loss effectively, we must first realize that we are living on a finite planet. Lifestyles of high material consumption must yield to the provision of greater sufficiency for all. For the rest of the world to reach US, Australian, Japanese, or European levels of consumption with existing technologies would require four more planets like our present one. Such lifestyles would lead to the further destruction of planet earth.

Another element in the moral framework is a concern for the wider earth community, which encompasses all life. This perspective on life has only begun to emerge in recent times. Today, moral theologians are arguing that other creatures have more than just instrumental value for human beings as sources of food, clothing, and medicine. Pope Francis recognizes that the wider earth community is not recognized as having intrinsic value in itself (no. 33). Anyone who studies nature knows that God has taken as much care in creating other species as in creating human beings. After all, we only emerged over two million years ago, a mere flicker of an eyelid in the 3.8 billion years of life on earth. God loves other creatures, and we are linked to them through close biological and genetic bonding. Given our present ecological challenges, either the whole biosphere will prosper or we will all go down together.[17]

Extinction and the Resurrection of Jesus

In reflecting on extinction, it is important to remember that every living creature on earth has a profound relationship with the resurrected

---

[17] Edwards, "Theological Foundations for Ecological Praxis," 130.

Lord. His loving touch heals our brokenness and fulfills all creation. In Acts 3:15 Peter speaks of Jesus as the Prince of Life. In this text commentators interpret the role of Jesus as the one who leads his people to the fullness of life, even though it cost him his own life. Through his death Jesus has reconciled all reality to God. So, to destroy any aspect of creation or to banish species forever from their place in the community of life is to deface the image of Christ that is radiated throughout our world. Christ still suffers, not only when people are denied their rights and exploited, but when seas, rivers, and forests are desecrated and biocide is perpetrated. It would be wonderful if the churches could promote a devotion to Christ, the Prince of Life. The royal title does not imply control or any effort to force others to serve his interests. Rather, it is the proclamation of God's love and care for those who need it most, the poor and exploited. But today, in the light of environmental destruction, Jesus's preferential option for the poor includes the plundered earth. As Australian theologian Norman Habel puts it, "God is found in weakness, in suffering, and in servant earth."[18] This aspect of extinction is developed in *Laudato Si'* (no. 100). The church should also develop liturgies to mourn the extinction of particular species.

Levels of Human Population

In the context of preaching a gospel of life, it is important to revisit the question of human population levels on this planet. *Populorum Progressio* admits:

> There is no denying that the accelerated rate of population growth brings many added difficulties to the problems of development where the size of the population grows more rapidly than the quantity of available resources to such a degree that things seem to have reached an impasse. In such

---

[18] Norman Habel, "Key Ecojustice Principles: A Theologia Crucis Perspective," *Ecotheology* 5–6 (1998): 120.

circumstances people are inclined to apply drastic remedies to reduce the birth rate. (PP, no. 37)

There is no doubt that public authorities can intervene in this matter, within the bounds of their competence. They can instruct citizens on this subject and adopt appropriate measures, so long as these are in conformity with the dictates of the moral law and the rightful freedom of married couples is preserved completely intact. When the inalienable rights of marriage and of procreation are taken away, so is human dignity.

Finally, it is for parents to take a thorough look at the matter and decide on the number of their children. This is an obligation they take on themselves, before their children already born, and before the community to which they belong—following the dictates of their own consciences informed by God's law authentically interpreted and bolstered by their trust in God.

When the encyclical appeared, some commentators felt that it might signal a change in the Catholic Church's position on artificial methods of birth control as articulated by Pope Pius XI in *Casti Connubi* in 1931.

This did not happen. In July 1968, Pope Paul VI published the encyclical *Humanae Vitae.* It reaffirmed the traditional teaching that each and every marriage act must remain open to the transmission of life (HV, no. 14). In *The Greening of the Church* I explored the population issue in greater detail, noting that the earth's carrying capacity for different levels of population was not addressed in *Humanae Vitae.*[19] Today, when measuring tools such as the human ecological footprint index are available both in bioregions and globally, there is an urgent need to revisit the population issue. It is important to state that a fall in population levels will not, of itself, reduce the stress on the planet unless it is accompanied by a drop in our consumption patterns. Pope Francis makes this point in *Laudato Si'* when he states, "To blame population growth instead

[19] Sean McDonagh, *The Greening of the Church* (Maryknoll, NY: Orbis Books, 1990), 8–74.

of extreme and selective consumerism on the part of some, is one way of refusing to face the issue." However, to claim, as he does, that "it must nonetheless be recognized that demographic growth is fully compatible with an integral and shared development" is a questionable generalization. Pope Francis seems to qualify this generalization later in the paragraph when he states,

> still, attention needs to be paid to imbalances in population density, on both the national and global levels, since a rise in consumption would lead to complex regional situations, as a result of the interplay between problems linked to environmental pollution, transport, waste treatment, loss of resources and quality of life. (no. 50)

In June 2013, the United Nations published a report entitled "World Population Prospects: The 2012 Revision." It estimated that the world's population in 2012 was 7.2 billion people. By 2025, it is expected to reach 8.1 billion, and 11 billion by the end of the twenty-first century.[20]

Take the situation in Africa today, where birthrates are still very high. According to estimates in the UN report, the population of Nigeria will surpass that of the United States by the year 2050. If these figures are realized, it will become the third-most-populous country by the end of the twenty-first century. But population growth is also very serious in other African countries. The UN report predicts that more than half of the global population growth will take place in Africa. The current African population is 1.1 billion. This is expected to reach 2.4 billion by 2050. "The populations of Mali, Niger, Somalia, Tanzania and Zambia are expected to increase at least fivefold by 2100."[21]

In 2012, India had the second-largest population in the world. But because of its demographic profile, its population is expected to reach 1.45 billion by 2028, when it will have the same population as China. After 2028, the Chinese population is expected to

---

[20] See Claire Provost, "Nigeria Expected to Have Larger Population than US by 2050," *Guardian,* June 13, 2013.

[21] Ibid.

begin to fall, while India's will increase and reach 1.5 billion by the end of the twenty-first century.

Other countries where population growth will be significant are the Philippines, Indonesia, and Pakistan. I worked in the Philippines and saw the impact of population growth on the T'boli people, who live on the southern island of Mindanao. Population increase has been very rapid in the Philippines during the last century. In the year 1900 there were six million Filipinos. By 1949, the figure had jumped to 19.2 million. By 1970 it had increased further to 38.5 million people. In 1989, the number was 63.8 million.[22] The Philippines' "symbolic 100 millionth Filipino baby" was born to great acclaim on Sunday, July 27, 2014.[23] The problem for the Philippines is that in 1900, when there were six million people in the country, almost all the ecosystems were thriving. Now, in 2015, almost all of the tropical forests have been destroyed. Tens of millions of tons of top soil have been eroded from hillsides and deposited in the sea. This affects marine environments such as corals and mangroves. Biodiversity has also been decimated, so that the ability to produce food for the growing population has been seriously compromised.

It would be fallacious to point the finger exclusively at population growth as the main cause of environmental degradation, because much of the damage has been done by people and corporations who represent only a minute fraction of the population. Still, it would also be incorrect to discount population growth as a contributing factor. The activities of landless people who burn down the tropical forests in order to grow food or to make charcoal in order to earn money to buy food have left huge scars on the surface of the earth. Similarly, the cumulative effect of many small fishermen using dynamite or poison to increase their catch is also devastating.

Despite the above predictions for population growth around the world, in forty-three countries population levels are expected to

---

[22] Gareth Porter and Delfin Galapin, Jr., "Resources, Population, and the Philippines' Future," paper no. 4 (Washington DC: World Resources Institute, 1988), 2.

[23] "Philippines Welcomes 100 Millionth Baby," Inquirer.net, July 27, 2014.

fall by 15 percent by 2050. These countries include Belarus, Bulgaria, Cuba, Romania, Russia, and Ukraine. Many other countries in the North will depend on an estimated 2.4 million people from the South who, each year from 2013 to 2050, will migrate to the North. Without this, the populations of many European and other developed countries would decline significantly.

The increase in global population, but especially the rapid increase in population levels in countries that cannot currently feed themselves, raises the question of accessible family planning methods. In 2015, UN figures show that "22 percent of women of reproductive age who were married or in unions in the least-developed countries had an unmet need for family planning, despite a stated desire to avoid or delay childbearing."[24] The concentration of population growth in the poorest countries makes it very difficult to eradicate poverty and inequality.

In the face of this demographic crisis I think that the time is now ripe for the Catholic Church to revisit its teaching on birth control.[25] The basis of that teaching is that each act of sexual intercourse must be open to achieving conception. But if this leads, as it inevitably must, to larger families, then there will be increased stress on global ecosystems within four or five decades. Such a breakdown, especially in the area of food production, will lead to a dramatic fall in human population levels that may well be permanent because the damage done to the earth's fertility could be irreversible.

The irony then would be that a strict adherence to *Humanae Vitae*, which sets out to promote respect for life, will in the longer term undermine the conditions that are necessary for human life in the future. An ecological ethical perspective must focus on reality in a holistic way rather than on the interaction of individual entities or actors. As has been seen in this chapter, we and all other creatures are now living through a mega-extinction spasm, mainly because of human activity. This will get much worse unless hu-

---

[24] Sam Jones and Mark Anderson, "World Population Heading to 10bn by 2050," *Guardian,* July 30, 2015.

[25] See McDonagh, *The Greening of the Church,* chap. 2.

mans show greater willingness to share the global commons with other species. Today, our economic and political culture assumes that all the global space—on land, in the air, and in the seas—primarily belongs to humans. This assumption is also found in both *Populorum Progressio* and *Humanae Vitae*. This assumption will have to change dramatically if other creatures are going to survive in the world.

Pope Francis sums up the new understanding of other creatures on our planet:

> In our time, the Church does not simply state that other creatures are completely subordinated to the good of human beings, as if they have no worth in themselves and can be treated as we wish. The German bishops have taught that where other creatures are concerned, "we can speak of the priority of *being* over that of being *useful*". The Catechism clearly and forcefully criticizes a distorted anthropocentrism: "Each creature possesses its own particular goodness and perfection. . . . Each of the various creatures, willed in its own being, reflects in its own way a ray of God's infinite wisdom and goodness. Man must therefore respect the particular goodness of every creature, to avoid any disordered use of things." (no. 69)

Bibliography

McDonagh, Sean, *The Death of Life, the Horror of Extinction* (Dublin: Columba Press, 2004).

White, Lynn, "The Historical Roots of Our Ecologic Crisis," *Science* (1967).

Wilson, Edward O., *Biophilia: The Human Bond with Other Species* (Cambridge, MA: Harvard University Press, 1984).

———, *The Future of Life* (New York: Little Brown, 2001).

———, *The Meaning of Human Existence* (New York: Liveright Publishing Corporation, 2014).

World Wildlife Fund, *Living Planet Report 2012: Biodiversity, Biocapacity, and Better Choices*, http://www.worldwildlife.org.

4

Fresh Water

Without water there would be no life on Earth; 97.5 percent of the world's water is in the oceans. Yet only 3 percent of the world's water is fresh water, and much of that is locked up in ice and snow in Antarctica, Greenland, the Arctic, the Himalayas, and the Andes. As Pope Francis notes, "Fresh drinking water is an issue of primary importance since it is indispensable for human life and supporting terrestrial and aquatic ecosystems" (no. 28).

Every living being on earth needs water. The basic amount of water needed by each person is approximately 13 gallons a day. Of this total a little over 1 gallon is needed for drinking and cooking. Another 6.5 gallons are needed for personal hygiene, such as washing and sewage. The remainder goes into producing food.[1] The average person in the United States uses 158.5 gallons of domestic urban water per day. Europeans use about 65 to 80 gallons a day, while people in sub-Saharan Africa use only 2.5 to 5 gallons a day.[2]

During the twentieth century the human population tripled. Water consumption jumped sevenfold. Worldwide the demand for water is doubling every twenty-one years. By 2020, water use is expected to grow by 40 percent. It is no surprise then that the global demand for fresh water is currently overtaking its ready supply in many parts of the world. Writing in *Scientific American,* Peter Rogers states that "scientists expect water scarcity to become

---

[1] "Needing and Getting," *New Internationalist* (March 2003).

[2] Patrick Smith, "The Great Water Divide," *Irish Times,* March 22, 2003.

more common in large part because the world's population is rising and many people are getting richer (thus expanding demand) and because climate change is exacerbating aridity and reducing supply in many regions."[3]

Water Shortages

In 2008, the United Nations estimated that between eight hundred million and nine hundred million people experienced water shortages. In the contribution to the Sixth World Water Forum in Marseille, France, held March 12–17, 2012, the Holy See pointed out that "by adopting a broad definition of *access to water*—a regular, continuous access to drinking water that is economically, legally and truly accessible and acceptable from the viewpoint of usability—the reality described by some studies is even more worrying; 1.9 billion people have only unhealthy water at their disposal, while 3.4 billion periodically use water of unsafe quality."[4]

The situation may deteriorate further in the next two decades. The United Nations predicts that by the year 2025, two-thirds of the world's population will experience water shortages, with severe lack of water blighting the lives and livelihoods of 1.8 billion people. This also means that there will not be sufficient water for the flora and fauna in particular ecosystems. The looming water crisis is the reason UN Secretary-General Ban Ki-moon told the Budapest Water Summit on October 8, 2013, that water scarcity should be at the top of the international agenda.

To date, in order to meet the human demand for water, over 60 percent of the world's largest 227 rivers have been dammed. As a result, rivers such as the Nile, the Jordan, the Murray-Darling, the Yangtze, and the Colorado are overtaxed and for parts of the year dry up altogether. The major factors that account for the

---

[3] Peter Rogers, "Facing Freshwater Crisis," *Scientific American* (August 2008), 28.

[4] Pontifical Council for Justice and Peace, *Water: An Essential Element for Life: Designing Sustainable Solutions: An Update* (Vatican City: 2012), 15.

increased use of water are population growth, industrialization, and, especially, irrigation for agriculture.

According to the UK's Institution of Mechanical Engineers, approximately 3.8 trillion cubic meters of water are used by humans annually, with 70 percent being consumed by the global agriculture sector. The institution predicts that by the year 2050 between 10 and 13 trillion cubic meters will be needed to meet the food needs of humanity. This is approximately three times current use.[5]

Water Pollution

Pope Francis is aware that "the quality of available water is constantly diminishing" (no. 30). Many of the industrial and agricultural processes pollute water and thus make it toxic for humans and other creatures. Unfortunately, the full consequences of today's chemical-dependent and waste-producing economies may not become apparent for another generation. In December 1999, Dr. John Peterson of the W. Alton Jones Foundation in the United States told a conference of scientists in Japan that "a hundred or more novel chemicals are swilling around in our bloodstream, chemicals which, before this century, were not found in human beings. It makes all of us, as well as our children and grandchildren, a walking experiment—one with completely unknown results."[6]

Some of these chemicals disrupt the endocrine system and therefore affect all aspects of human development from the embryo onward. Because the chemical and pharmaceutical industries are so central to modern economies and so powerful, governments have been slow to investigate, regulate, or ban these harmful substances.

Scientists and environmental NGOs (non-government organizations) are worried about the long-term consequence of these

---

[5] "How Much Water Is Needed to Produce Food and How Much Do We Waste?" *Guardian,* January 10, 2013.

[6] Quoted in Sean McDonagh, "Water: Source of Life or Death," *The Word* (May 2002).

chemicals and have demanded that substances that are suspected of acting as endocrine blockers and that accumulate in human tissue should be banned. The Women's Environmental Network in Britain claims that between 1 percent and 8 percent of babies in Britain have suffered slight nervous-system damage and memory loss as a result of being exposed to dioxins and PCBs.[7] These is a group of persistent toxic chemicals that can cause serious health problems, such as cancer and immune system disorders.

Water and Poverty

Laudato Si' proclaims that "access to safe, drinkable water is a basic and universal human right, since it is essential to human survival and, as such, is a condition for the exercise of other human rights" (no. 30). Still, the poor pay much more for their water. A person who lives in Canada receives twenty-six times more water than a person who lives in Mexico. Sixty percent of the world's population lives in Asia yet Asia only receives 36 percent of the world's fresh water. Pope Francis is aware that "the quality of water available to the poor" is often poor quality (no. 29). The rich have much more access to water than the poor. In many rich countries water is readily available from taps, and some people have swimming pools in or attached to their houses. The cost of water varies a lot. People in Tanzania pay 5.7 percent of their daily wages on water. In Pakistan it costs 1.1 percent of the daily wage. In Britain the average yearly cost to a household for water and sewage services amounts to only 0.013 percent of the average industrial wage. In the United States people pay as little as 0.006 percent of their wages on water.[8]

But even in the wealthy nations, water costs have been surging. A *USA Today* article notes that its study of "residential water rates over the past 12 years for large and small water agencies

---

[7] Michael S. Serrill, "Well Running Dry," Special Issue of *Time (Our Precious Planet),* November 1997.

[8] "Earth," *Guardian,* August 7, 2002.

nationwide found that monthly costs doubled or more in 29 localities. . . . A resource long taken for granted will continue to become more costly for millions of Americans."[9]

Yet while the wealthier nations worry about the increasing scarcity and resultant rise in the cost of water, most people have no regular access to drinking water at all. According to the World Health Organization, 84 percent live in rural areas or places where the supply of drinking water is limited.[10] Pope Francis draws attention to the fact that "water poverty especially affects Africa, where large sectors of the population have no access to safe drinking water or experience droughts which impede agricultural production" (no. 28).

Water and Health

Polluted water is one of the main causes of illness in poor countries. Pope Francis recognizes this when he says that, "dysentery and cholera are linked to inadequate hygiene and water supplies" (no. 29). As a result, two million people, mainly in Africa, die needlessly each year from illnesses like diarrhea, malaria, and other water-borne diseases.[11] This is the equivalent of ten jumbo jets crashing each day. One of the most appalling statistics of all is that about six thousand children die each day from water-borne diseases like gastro-enteritis. This figure is almost twice the number of people killed in the September 11, 2001, attacks on the World Trade Center and the Pentagon, which led to massive retaliation in Afghanistan and huge resources being poured into the "war on terrorism." Unfortunately, there is no crusade to provide clean water for everyone on the planet despite the high death toll across much of the Third World.

---

[9] Kevin McCoy, "USA Today Analysis: Water Costs Gush Higher," *USA Today,* September 29, 2012.

[10] Pontifical Council for Justice and Peace, *Water*, 93.

[11] Paul Brown, "Failure to Manage Water Kills Two Million a Year—UN," *Guardian,* April 11, 2002.

Water and World Peace

Today the water situation in the Middle East and North Africa is precarious. Northeastern China, western and southern India, Pakistan, much of South America, and countries in Central America, as well as large parts of Mexico, face water scarcity in the future. Around the world 260 rivers flow through two or more countries. Only a handful of these countries have signed treaties regulating their respective access to this water.[12] As a result, competition between adjacent countries for access to water resources is causing friction that could lead to hostilities in the future.

The conflict between Israel and Palestine is one of the running sores of our time. We know it has the potential to destabilize both the Middle East and the world. But the potential for water wars is not confined to Israel and Palestine. The Tigris-Euphrates river valley is another potential hot spot. Turkey has spent thirty billion dollars on dams and irrigation systems. This has forced countries situated downstream, like Syria and Iraq, to curtail their water requirements. In 1989, Turkey threatened to cut water flow in the Euphrates because of Syria's support for Kurdish guerrillas in Turkey.[13]

Until very recently, Egypt, Ethiopia, and other countries that share the Nile's waters seemed to be on a collision course over access to a fair share of the water. Almost sixty million people in Egypt depend on the Nile for their water, but the river rises elsewhere. About 85 percent of the waters of the Nile come from rainfall in Ethiopia, flowing as the Blue Nile into Sudan. The rest comes from the White Nile, with its headwaters at Lake Victoria in Tanzania. The Nile is the longest river in the world and supplies water to nine countries. Under the auspices of the United Nations, in 1999 these countries reached agreement on equitable access to the Nile's waters.[14] In 2015, a five billion dollar dam on the

---

[12] Dr. William Reville, "Water, Water Everywhere, But Not for Everyone," *Irish Times,* May 15, 2000.

[13] Sandra Postel, "The Politics of Water," *WorldWatch Magazine* (July/August 1993), 14.

[14] Brown, "Failure to Manage Water Kills Two Million a Year—UN."

Blue Nile threatened to lead to war between Egypt and Ethiopia. Fortunately, scientists seem to have solved this potential conflict with a win-win situation, giving more water and electricity to both countries.[15]

There is the potential for tension between Pakistan and India over sharing the waters of the Indus. The Indus and its tributaries rise in the Indian Himalayas. On its journey to the sea it flows through Kashmir and into Pakistan. Pakistan relies on the Indus and its tributaries for crop irrigation and hydroelectric power. After years of bickering following independence and partition in 1947, India and Pakistan signed the Indus Water Treaty in 1960. This treaty ceded all the water in the western tributaries to India. The water in the eastern tributaries is assigned to Pakistan. The ongoing guerrilla war in Kashmir has come close to driving both countries to war in recent years and has put enormous strain on the treaty. In May 2002, prominent Indian politicians called on their government to scrap the treaty unless the government of Pakistan prevented terrorists from crossing over into Kashmir.[16]

All of these tensions are now exacerbated by the fact that the volume of water in the Indus has fallen in recent years, probably because global warming has decreased the amount of snow that falls annually in the mountains. Less water will in turn lead to a food shortage as irrigation projects dry up. This will add enormously to the problems facing seventeen million people in Pakistan who already live in poverty.

Conflict on the Indian subcontinent also looms between India and Bangladesh. In December 2002, Indian Prime Minister Atai Behari Vajpayee announced plans to pump water from the rivers in the north of the country through a series of canals to replenish the rivers in the south of India. The plan would "redraw the hydrological map of India, the waters from 14 Himalayan tributaries of the Ganges and the Brahmaputra rivers in Northern India and Nepal, and transfer them south via a series of canals and pumping

---

[15] Fred Pearce, "Avoiding War over Ethiopia's Nile Dam," *New Scientist* 226, no. 3023 (May 30–June 5, 2015): 16.

[16] Fred Pearce, "Water War," *New Scientist* (May 18, 2002): 18.

stations across the Vindhya mountains to replenish 17 southern rivers including the Godavari, Krishna and Cauvery."[17] If India implements this plan, there is no doubt that Bangladesh will resist it. According to the Ganges Treaty signed by both countries in 1996, India agreed not to reduce water flow over the boundaries in the future. But the plan would breach this agreement. Even a 10 percent reduction in water could have a huge impact on Bangladeshi farmers and leave their farms dry for much of the year.

Elsewhere in Asia the Salween River is a source of tension among Thailand, Myanmar, and China. Each of these countries has stated that it plans to dam the river in order to benefit more from the water. The Mekong is potentially a source of conflict among Cambodia, Laos, Vietnam, and Thailand. In 2008, the Mekong River Commission with the various governments prepared a navigation strategy and program. The long-term goal of the strategy is to develop sustainable, effective, and safe navigation on the Mekong and to increase the international trade opportunities for the mutual support of the member countries of the Mekong River Commission.

It is no wonder that Ismail Serageldin, the World Bank's vice president for environmentally sustainable development, is on record as stating that while many of the wars of the twentieth century were about oil, the wars of twenty-first century will be about water. The prestigious business magazine *Fortune* concurs. It states that water promises to be to the twenty-first century what oil was to the twentieth century.[18]

Access to Water

Dams have been built on almost every major river in the world in the twentieth century. The purpose of these dams is to generate electricity and store water for irrigation. The pressure to build

---

[17] Fred Pearce, "Conflict Looms over India," *New Scientist* (March 1, 2003): 4.

[18] Shawn Tully, "H2O Will Be to the 21st Century What Oil Was to the 20th," *Fortune* (May 15, 2000).

more dams is evident, particularly in Asia. India, Nepal, Bhutan, and Pakistan are planning to build more than four hundred hydroelectric dams. China is planning to build one hundred dams on major rivers that rise in Tibet. A further sixty or more dams are being planned for the Mekong River, which also rises in Tibet. There is a danger that in the next twenty years more dams could be built in the Himalayas than anywhere else on earth. Very few studies have been done on the geological, human, and environmental impact of all these dams in such a sensitive area. The effects could be disastrous and cause prolonged droughts and even earthquakes. They could also lead to major conflict between India and China.[19]

In the United States there are disagreements among the various states about access to water. Throughout the twentieth century there was conflict between Arizona and California about the allocation of the waters of the Colorado River. The Colorado River Compact in 1922 was supposed to settle the matter. It did not, and to this day it continues to be an irritant between these states. On New Year's Day 2003, by order of the Federal Government, "three of the eight pumps that tap into the glistening reservoir of Colorado River water . . . are sitting idle."[20] The scarcity of water in this arid region could have major implications for agriculture in the United States. Six other states draw water from the Colorado River.

In many of these conflict areas the church has not entered into the discussion as an ecclesial entity. A number of exceptions are worth mentioning.

On World Ocean Day, June 8, 2004, the seven Catholic bishops of the state of Queensland in Australia issued a pastoral letter on the threatened and damaged Great Barrier Reef. They celebrated the reef with its coral trout, huge groupers, sea snakes, large green turtles, humpback whales, sea

---

[19] John Vidal and Kumkum Dasgupta, "China and India 'Water Grab' Dams Put Ecology of Himalayas in Danger," *Observer* (September 11, 2013), 19.

[20] Dean E. Murphy, "In a First, US Officials Put Limits on California's Thirst," *New York Times,* January 5, 2003.

grasses, sea fern, sponges, and anemones as beautiful gifts of God that arouse wonder, gratitude, and praise. They assessed the serious dangers facing the reef and called on their people to take responsibility for its survival and its health.[21]

On the feast of St. Francis of Assisi, October 4, 2004, eleven bishops of the Murray-Darling Basin (the longest river in Australia) endorsed a statement of Catholic Earthcare Australia that supports political action on reducing the salinity and increasing river flow. The statement also called for a commitment to conserve and reuse water. Denis Edwards points out

> that (1) the response is local, involving local church leaders taking a position on an ecological issue that arises in their own bioregion, and (2) in adopting political options, such as increased environmental river flow, the bishops are not only defending the good of human beings but also explicitly extending their moral commitment and advocacy to include the animals, plants and fish of the Murray-Darling and the Great Barrier Reef.[22]

Climate Change and Water

Some of the main global consequences of climate change are severe weather patterns and a warming of the earth. Severe weather is evident in more frequent, heavy precipitation followed by drought. Recent satellite data indicate that, while countries in the northern latitudes and in the tropics are becoming wetter, countries in the mid-latitudes are facing water shortages and even droughts. This includes areas such as California, North Africa, the Middle East, Brazil, and South Asia. Since 2003, "parts of Turkey, Syria,

---

[21] Denis Edwards, *Ecology at the Heart of Faith: The Change of Heart that Leads to a New Way of Living on Earth* (Maryknoll, NY: Orbis Books, 2006), 114.

[22] Ibid., 115.

Iraq and Iran along the Tigris and Euphrates rivers lost 144 cubic kilometres of stored water."[23]

One of the most evident results of current global warming is the melting of glaciers around the world. The melting of glaciers in the Himalayas and in the Andes could be catastrophic for hundreds of millions of people. By 2006, snow and ice on the eastern Himalayas had decreased by 30 percent since the 1970s.[24] In 2002, it was predicted that as many as forty lakes could be formed by melting ice in the Himalayas, especially in Nepal. In 2002, Paul Brown wrote that "there are thought to be hundreds more liquid time bombs in India, Pakistan, Afghanistan, Tibet, and China."[25] The impact of melting glaciers on agriculture and human settlement patterns could be catastrophic. If large sections of the glaciers on the Himalayas melt in the next few decades, this will affect the melt waters of the Ganges, Bramaputra, Irrawaddy, Mekong, Salween, Yangtze, and Yellow rivers. One-quarter of the world's population depends on these rivers.[26]

Privatizing Water

In the 1980s transnational water corporations began to view the provision of water as a highly profitable business in both the developing and the developed world. From Ghana, Bolivia, and the Philippines to the United Kingdom, the United States, and Canada private companies have been attempting to capture the "water market" and in the process make huge profits. In May 2000 *Fortune* magazine predicted that water is about to become one of the world's greatest business opportunities.

---

[23] Suzanne Goldenbery, "Why Global Shortages Pose Threat of Terror and War," *The Observer* (February 9, 2014).

[24] David Adam, "UN Urged to Save Glaciers and Reefs," *Guardian,* March 16, 2006.

[25] Paul Brown, "Global Warming Meets Glaciers and Produces Unstable Lakes," *Guardian,* April 17, 2002.

[26] Quoted in Dinyar Godrei, "On the Challenge Posed by the World's Freshwater Crisis," *New Internationalist* (March 2003), 12.

In many countries the provision of water is no longer seen as a public service. At the Third World Water Forum in Kyoto, Japan, in March 2003, Archbishop Renato Martino presented a document entitled *Water: An Essential Element for Life.* Even the title of the document reflects the concern of the Holy See for the many complex water-related challenges. The document argues that water is a good that must serve the development of the whole person and of every person. The cardinal stated

> The water concerns of the poor must become the concern of all in a perspective of solidarity. This solidarity is a firm and persevering determination to commit oneself to the common good, to the good of all and of each individual. It presupposes the effort for a more just social order and requires a preferential attention to the situation of the poor. The same duty of solidarity that rests on individuals exists also for nations; advanced nations have a very heavy obligation to help developing nations.[27]

In *Laudato Si'* Pope Francis warns that "it is also conceivable that the control of water by large multinational businesses may become a major source of conflict in this century" (no. 31).

The 2004 *Compendium of the Social Doctrine of the Church* states unambiguously

> By its very nature water cannot be treated as just another commodity among many, and it must be used rationally and in solidarity with others. The distribution of water is traditionally among the responsibilities that fall to public agencies, since water is considered a public good. If water distribution is entrusted to the private sector it should still be considered a public good. *The right to water,* as all human rights, finds its basis in human dignity and not in any kind

---

[27] Pontifical Council for Justice and Peace, "A Contribution of the Delegation of the Holy See on the Occasion of the Third World Water Forum," Kyoto, March 16–23, 2003.

of merely quantitative assessment that considers water as a merely economic good. Without water, life is threatened. Therefore, the right to safe drinking water is a universal and inalienable right. (no. 485)

Consequently, water policies must give priority to those living in poverty and to those living in areas endowed with fewer resources. A few individuals or corporations cannot be allowed to control or exhaust a resource such as water, which is meant for everyone. Catholic social thought has always stressed that the defense and preservation of certain common goods cannot be safeguarded simply by market forces, since they touch on fundamental human needs which escape market logic.

In an era when privatization of essential services is being promoted by many countries, the Pontifical Council for Justice and Peace in 2003 warns that

it has however proved to be extremely difficult to establish the right balance of public-private partnerships and serious errors have been committed. At times individual enterprises attained almost monopoly powers over public goods. A prerequisite for effective privatization is that it be set within a clear legislative framework which allows government to ensure that private interventions do in actual fact protect the public interest.[28]

In the "Message of His Holiness Pope John Paul II for the Celebration of the World Day of Peace" in 2003 the pope drew attention to the fact that the right to drinkable water is far from being guaranteed, especially for the poor (no. 5).

Water and Christianity

The Bible has much to teach Christians today about how to deal with the many complex development and ethical issues concerning

---

[28] Ibid., p. 29.

water. In fact, water plays a central role in the Bible. At the beginning of the book of Genesis we find God's spirit hovering over the water. The author believes that Yahweh has the power to tame the area of most unpredictability—the oceans. We find this theme once again in Yahweh's challenge to Job:

> Or who shut in the sea with doors
>   when it burst out from the womb?—
> when I made the clouds its garment,
>   and thick darkness its swaddling band,
> and prescribed bounds for it,
>   and set bars and doors,
> and said, "Thus far shall you come, and no
>   farther,
>   and here shall your proud waves be stopped"?
> (Job 38:8–11)

In the book of Exodus water is seen as a source of Israel's liberation from slavery in Egypt. Yahweh drives back the sea to make an escape route for the Israelites and uses the returning waves as a way of punishing the Egyptians (Exod 14:21b–31).

Water is seen as a source of health and abundance. One of the most powerful presentations of this teaching is to be found in Ezekiel where the prophet extols the healing and life-giving qualities of clean water. It brings fruitfulness and abundance (47:1–12).

Living water is so important in the New Testament that Jesus applies the term to himself. In response to the Samaritan woman who was taken aback by Jesus' request for a drink, he says: "If you knew the gift of God, and who it is that is saying to you, 'Give me a drink,' you would have asked him, and he would have given you living water" (John 4:10).

In reply, the Samaritan woman expresses surprise at how Jesus, who has no bucket, could give her water. She also wonders whether Jesus is on a par with Jacob, the patriarch who gave them the well and used it himself. Jesus replies: "Everyone who drinks of this water will be thirsty again, but those who drink of the water that I will give them will never be thirsty. The water that I will give will become in them a spring of water gushing up to eternal life" (John 4:13–14).

In the New Testament, Christ's own baptism in the Jordan is linked to his mission to bring about justice and peace for all. Benedictine Kilian McDonnell describes the cosmic dimension of the baptism of Jesus. He recalls the writings of Gregory of Nazianzus who had Jesus "carrying the cosmos with him as he ascended out of the water at the Jordan." He continues: "The cosmic dimensions of the baptism of Jesus are part of antiquity's broader conviction, rooted in the incarnation and resurrection, that the material world, as the home of a redeemed humanity, is destined for transfiguration through the power of the Spirit manifested in the risen body of Christ."[29]

Water as a symbol of cleansing and life is very much to the fore in the rite of baptism, whereby believers (catechumens) are incorporated into the Christian community. In baptism the symbol of water operates at a number of different levels. For St. Paul it represents both death and new life through the resurrection of Christ. "Do you not know that all of us who have been baptized into Christ Jesus were baptized into his death? Therefore we have been buried with him by baptism into death, so that, just as Christ was raised from the dead by the glory of the Father, so we too might walk in newness of life" (Rom 6:3–4).

In the rite of baptism in the early church this death or cleansing from sin together with bestowal of new life was clearly symbolized by the catechumen having to walk down into the baptismal water to emerge transformed.

During the baptismal ceremony the priest or deacon blesses the waters that will be used to baptize the catechumens using the following words:

> Father, you give us grace through sacramental signs, which tell us of the wonders of your unseen power. In baptism we use your gift of water, which you have made a rich symbol

---

[29] Kilian McDonnell, *Baptism of Jesus in the Jordan: The Trinitarian and Cosmic Order of Salvation* (Collegeville MN: Liturgical Press, 1996), 23.

of the grace you give us in this sacrament. At the very dawn of creation your Spirit breathed on the waters, making them the wellspring of all holiness. The waters of the great flood you made a sign of the waters of baptism, that make an end of sin and a new beginning of goodness.

Through the waters of the Red Sea you led Israel out of slavery, to be an image of God's holy people, set free from sin by baptism. In the waters of the Jordan your Son was baptized by John and anointed with the Spirit. Your Son willed that water and blood should flow from his side as he hung upon the cross.

After his resurrection he told his disciples: "Go out and teach all nations, baptizing them in the name of the Father, and of the Son, and of the Holy Spirit." Father, look now with love upon your Church, and unseal for her the fountain of baptism. By the power of the Spirit give to the water of this font the grace of your Son. You created man in your own likeness: cleanse him from sin in a new birth to innocence by water and the Spirit.

It is clear from these prayers that water is seen as the source of life and of cleansing from sin. This, of course, presumes that the water that is being used in baptism is both life-giving and has the power to cleanse. This is where the difficulty arises in our modern world, when in many instances water has been so polluted in many countries around the world.

In baptism we incorporate the newly baptized person into the body of Christ and into the community that is the church. However, we need to widen the parameters of the community into which the newly baptized is being incorporated. It includes not only Christians or the wider human community, but the community of all creation, not only that which exists now, but all that has existed during the long, wonderful, emergent journey of our universe, from the initial flaring forth 13.8 billion years ago to the world in which we live. This is not a metaphorical claim. The carbon in each cell of our bodies was forged in the cauldron of the great supernova explosions twelve billion years ago. The same is true for the iron in our blood and the oxygen in our lungs. Every emergent phase of that story is both instructive and awe inspiring.

The *Compendium of the Social Teaching of the Church* confirms that

> as a gift from God, water is a vital element essential to survival; thus everyone has a right to it. Satisfying the needs of all, especially those who live in poverty, must be fundamental to the use of water and the services connected with it. Inadequate access to safe drinking water affects the well-being of a huge number of people and is often the cause of disease, suffering, conflict, poverty and even death. For a suitable solution to this problem, it must be set in context in order to establish moral criteria based precisely on the value of life and the respect for the rights and dignity of all human beings. (no. 484)

Unfortunately, this teaching has not received the attention it should have at international, national, or local levels. It is particularly relevant when governments are no longer willing to provide water for all as a public service and are allowing private or semi-public bodies to become the main providers of water for the community.

The Catholic bishops of California, which is experiencing its worst drought since 1895, have recognized the moral issues at stake in water preservation. In their Lenten message for 2014, they linked water conservation with stewardship for the common good, writing, "May we receive the grace to better conserve our natural resources and expend our energies in works of charity so that justice and mutual respect may flow like a river through the cities, towns and fields of our State."[30]

---

[30] Monica Clarke, "California Bishops Urge Water Conservation as Lenten Practice," *National Catholic Reporter*, March 10, 2014.

Bibliography

Ball, Philip, *H2O: A Biography of Water* (London: Phoenix Paperback, 1999).

Lohan, Tara, ed., *Water Consciousness: How We All Have to Change to Protect Our Most Critical Resource* (San Francisco: AlterNet books, 2008).

McDonagh, Sean, *Dying for Water* (Dublin: Veritas, 2003).

Pearce, Fred, *When the Rivers Run Dry: What Happens When Our Water Runs Out?* (London: Transworld Publisher, 2007).

Peppard, Christiana Z., *Just Water: Theology, Ethics, and the Global Water Crisis* (Maryknoll, NY: Orbis Books, 2014).

Pontifical Council for Justice and Peace, *Water: An Essential Element for Life,* (Vatican City: 2013).

Powledge, Fred, *Water: The Nature, Uses, and Future of Our Most Precious and Abused Resource* (Toronto: McGraw-Hill Ryerson, 1983).

Woodford, Chris, *Water Pollution: An Introduction,* Explainthat Stuff! 2015, http://www.explainthatstuff.com/waterpolution.html.

5

The Oceans

We call our planet earth (meaning *ground*) because our culture views the planet from a land-based perspective. If an astronaut had been asked to name the planet he or she would probably have called it water. From space it is abundantly clear that 70 percent of the planet's surface is covered by water. Most of this water is found in the oceans.

For many it might come as a surprise to learn that we know more about the surface of the moon and about Mars than we do about what happens in the deepest parts of the oceans. There are only a few robots or submersibles capable of transporting people to depths beyond even half of the ocean's deepest regions. In 2010, the United States Center for Coastal and Ocean Mapping found that the Mariana Trench reaches a maximum depth of 6.8 miles.

In *Laudato Si'* Pope Francis calls our attention to the fact that our "oceans not only contain the bulk of our planet's water supply, but also most of the immense variety of living creatures, many of them still unknown to us and threatened for various reasons" (no. 40). The oceans are home to 80 percent of all life on Earth. About 300,000 marine species have been identified, but it is commonly held by marine scientists that there are at least double that number. Some scientists believe that the ocean floor alone may contain up to ten million species.

Without the oceans our planet would be as barren and inhospitable as Mars. There would be no meadows, no forests, no birds, no animals, and no people. Life on earth began in the oceans over

3.8 billion years ago and was nurtured there for over three billion years before it began to colonize the land. When life did come ashore four hundred million years ago, it brought the oceans with it. Water makes up approximately 70 percent of most living beings, including human beings.

Oceans Threatened by Human Activity

At this point in the history of our planet the oceans of the earth are under threat from human activity. The most tragic aspect of the present moment is that much of its marine life may be destroyed long before it is even identified. The pressure on the oceans comes from many sources, including industrial pollution, mounting population pressures along coastal zones, and fishing methods that are akin to strip mining. There are about thirty-five major seas in the world, some coastal and some enclosed by land. Seven of these seas—the Baltic, Mediterranean, Black, Caspian, Bering, Yellow, and South China seas—have been seriously damaged in recent decades. As a result of human activity the Yellow River can in a single year dump 751 tons of heavy metals such as cadmium, mercury, lead, zinc, arsenic, and chromium into the South China Sea, along with twenty-one thousand tons of oil. The pulp and paper mills of Sweden and Finland, which now supply 10 percent of the world market for paper, also unload 400,000 tons of toxic chloride compounds into the Baltic Sea each year.

All marine life in both the Black Sea and the Sea of Marmara is under serious threat. Tezcan Yaramanci, president of the Turkish Marine Environment Protection Association, has warned that unless the necessary steps are taken soon the status of the sea will move down from "too dirty" to "dead sea" category. According to Yaramanci, the oxygen content of the water has plummeted, and the seabed fauna is also seriously damaged.[1]

Ninety percent of the pollution of the Black Sea is caused by domestic and industrial pollution. The Danube is responsible

---

[1] Quoted in Aydin Albayrak, "Black Sea in Danger of Becoming 'Dead Sea,'" *Today's Zaman*, May 6, 2012.

for 48 percent of the pollution; it carries domestic and industrial pollution from many European countries into the Black Sea. It is responsible for 53 percent of decomposed nitrogen and 66 percent of the total phosphorus flowing into the Black Sea.[2] Some people think that Turkey should take the pollution issue of the Black Sea to the European Union, because much of the pollution comes from Europe.

While the Turks might point the finger at Europeans polluting the Black Sea, local pollution is not negligible. Turkish Statistics Institute data reveal that in 2010, 715 of the 2,950 municipalities in Turkey did not have a sewage treatment plant. It is estimated that one billion cubic meters of waste water is discharged each year into the environment without undergoing any kind of treatment whatever. The situation is better in Istanbul, according to Kadir Topbas, mayor of the Istanbul Metropolitan Municipality. He claims that it is safe to swim in 421 kilometers (261.6 miles) out of a total 623 kilometers (387 miles) of the waters around Istanbul.[3]

Overfishing and the effects of the polluted waters of the River Volga have led to the near collapse of sturgeon fishing along the southern shores of the Caspian Sea. Yields fell from sixty-seven hundred tons in 1960 to half a ton in the early 1990s.

A report by Crude Accountability describes ongoing pollution that has been captured on satellite images and analyzed by the American Association for the Advances of the Sciences (AAAS). It indicates a serious threat to the environment of the Turkmen section of the Caspian Sea. The research shows that since the year 2000 there have been hundreds of oil discharges in the Caspian Sea by local and international oil companies. Even the Khazar Nature Reserve, which is identified by the Ramsar Convention as a protected area because of its importance to migratory birds, has been affected.[4]

---

[2] Ibid.

[3] Ibid.

[4] Crude Accountability, "Hidden in Plain Sight: Environmental and Human Rights Violations in the Turkmen Section of the Caspian Sea" (April 2013); Crude Accountability, "Satellite Images of the Caspian Sea Indicate that Oil Spills and Oil Wealth Rob Citizens of Their Environmental and Human Rights in Western Turkmenistan" (May 6, 2013).

Acidification of the Oceans

Laudato Si' recognizes that "carbon dioxide pollution increases the acidification of the oceans and compromises the marine food chain" (no. 24). It is only in the past two decades that scientists have become aware of the fact that fossil fuel emissions which drive climate change also have a very negative impact on the oceans. As carbon dioxide is absorbed by the oceans, this changes their chemistry, making them about 25 percent more acidic.[5] As a result, there is a negative impact on many species of plankton, which make up an important component in the marine food chain. Some marine scientists fear that within ten years this will have an impact too on ocean phytoplankton, which provides 50 percent of the oxygen humans and other creatures breathe. In the final paragraph of the *Scientific Synthesis of the Impact of Ocean Acidification on Marine Biodiversity*, the authors claim that "ocean acidification is irreversible on short-term timeframes, and substantial damage to ocean ecosystems can only be avoided through urgent and rapid reduction in global emissions of CO_2 by at least 50% by 2050 and much more thereafter."[6]

Dr. Carol Turley, a scientist at Plymouth University's Marine Laboratory, believes that global warming is also leading to a marked increase in jellyfish numbers. Jellyfish devour huge quantities of plankton, thus depriving smaller fish of the food they need. "This restricts the transfer of energy up the food chain because jellyfish are not readily consumed by other predators."[7]

Ocean Deoxygenation

Ocean deoxygenation happens when there is a reduction of dissolved oxygen (O_2) in seawater. Climate change is a contributory

---

[5] Tracy McVeigh, "Explosion in Jellyfish Numbers May Lead to Ecological Disaster, Warn Scientists," *Observer,* June 2, 2012.

[6] Secretariat of the Convention on Biological Diversity, *Scientific Synthesis of the Impacts of Ocean Acidification on Marine Biodiversity,* CBD Technical Series no. 46 (Montreal: Secretariat on the Convention on Biological Diversity, 2009), 61.

[7] McVeigh, "Explosion in Jellyfish Numbers May Lead to Ecological Disaster, Warn Scientists."

factor, particularly because, as with the warming effect, the higher temperature reduces oxygen solubility. Furthermore, an increase in temperature in the surface water is likely to create a more strati-fied ocean, decreasing the downward oxygen from the surface. Ocean acidification and nutrient runoff from rivers can also lead to deoxygenation. Deoxygenation will have a negative impact on fish and other marine organisms. Extended zones of low oxygen often result in the exclusion of fish and other organisms in the area. There are beneficiaries however. Organisms such as microbes thrive in a low-oxygen environment. This, in turn, leads to a change in the balance of living organisms in waters. Recent ocean models project that there will be a decline of between 1 percent and 7 percent in the global ocean oxygen in this century.

Stripping the Oceans Bare

"Uncontrolled fishing [is] leading to a drastic depletion of certain species" (no. 40). It is like killing the goose that lays the golden egg. In the past people might have felt that the oceans were so vast and that the variety of fish was so abundant that there would always be vast quantities of fish in the sea. We are now learning how false those assumptions were. According to a 1995 report by the UN Food and Agriculture Organization (FAO), over 70 percent of the world's marine fish stocks were either "fully-to-heavily exploited, overexploited, depleted, or slowly recovering."[8] The depletion is most notable in many of the world's most productive fishing grounds. These include the Grand Banks of Canada and New England. Cod fishing has also collapsed in the North Sea. A study by IUCN in 2012 found that 12 percent of all the marine species in the tropical eastern Pacific Ocean are threatened with extinction.[9]

As fisheries collapse in shallow waters through overfishing, the fishing industry has focused its attention on the deep ocean. As a

---

[8] Don Hinrichsen, "The Ocean Planet," *People and the Planet* 7, no. 2 (1998): 6–7.

[9] Mark Conlin, "More Than One in 10 Marine Species in Tropical Eastern Pacific Face Extinction," *Guardian,* February 23, 2012.

result, deep-sea-bottom trawls have done enormous damage to the ocean beds. Some of the trawls reach depths of 1.25 miles. Les Watling and Gilles Boeuf point out that the deep ocean is "home to countless species, including some of the oldest known living animal and life forms found on earth."[10] It is often forgotten that many of the creatures that live in the deep sea metabolize and reproduce very slowly. When their habitat is invaded by deep-sea trawling they are often forced into extinction.

Most of the damage to the oceans has taken place during the twentieth century. Fish catches have increased from three metric tons at the beginning of the century to almost ninety million metric tons in 1989. Most of the increase happened after World War II, when sonar and radar tracking technologies that had been developed for military purposes were used to locate and catch fish. Furthermore, super-trawlers—the size of a football field—were built to accommodate nets thousands of feet long. In a single netting, these boats can take up to four hundred tons of marine creatures. Modern trawlers can remain at sea for months at a time and are equipped to process and freeze the catch. Their fishing methods are so indiscriminate and destructive that a huge percentage of the catch, deemed unsuitable for commercial purposes, is simply dumped back into the oceans. It is estimated that 27 million tons, or more than 25 percent of the total annual catch worldwide, is thrown away. These throwaways (known as bycatch) are a main cause of the disastrous drop in the North Sea herring population. *Laudato Si'* criticizes this practice (no. 40).

Ninety percent of the population of the largest fish species have disappeared over the past fifty years.[11] The fact that a sizable portion of the annual catch consists of immature fish means that the breeding stock is being decimated. This will inevitably mean smaller catches in the future. It is now clear that since World War II, what can only be described as a war on the fish species of the world has been pursued relentlessly. The net result is that

---

[10] Les Watling and Gilles Boeuf, "Deep-Sea Plunder and Ruin," *New York Times,* October 2, 2013.

[11] "Big-Fish Stocks Fall 90 Percent Since 1950, Study Says," *National Geographic News,* May 15, 2003.

global fish catches peaked in 1989. They have been falling ever since, despite improved gear and tracking and snaring technology, and despite the fact that more species at different depths in the ocean are being targeted. Given present trends, it is inevitable that there will be a further decline if not an outright collapse of fishing worldwide. Daniel Pauly, the author of a study on global fishing trends, predicts that "if things go unchecked, we might end up with a marine junkyard dominated by plankton."[12]

It is essential that human beings begin to recognize that the destruction of the oceans impoverishes the planet for all future generations. The main losers in the human community are the two hundred million small-scale fishermen in third-world countries and in coastal regions in first-world countries. These have lived for generations from fish catches they have made around their native shores without causing ecological damage.

Giant Trawlers Plunder the Seas

At the moment many of the huge trawlers that are responsible for the slaughter of creatures of the oceans are heavily subsidized by governments. The subsidies take different forms, from providing fuel-tax exemptions to low-interest loans or outright grants for boat building and equipment. These kinds of subsidies have skewed the economics of global fishing to a remarkable degree. At present it costs approximately $124 billion annually to catch $70 billion worth of fish. The huge shortfall is bridged by governments. It is because of these subsidies that fishing can be a lucrative business for the large-scale operator. On the other hand, the present policies are driving the small-scale operators out of business. Once the coastal waters are fished bare, small-scale fishermen are forced out of business. Unlike the wealthy owners of multinational fishing fleets, they cannot operate too far from shore and, furthermore, they do not have the money to invest in another profitable business when fish stocks collapse. If the

---

[12] Originally published in *Science* (February 1998); quoted in Peter Montague, "Oceans without Fish," *Third World Resurgence* (April 1998), 5.

livelihood of small-scale fishermen, who provide much more employment than their large-scale competitors, is to be protected, it is essential that the subsidies paid to factory-fish-ship operators be discontinued. This will not be easy to achieve. It will take a lot of courageous political action at local, national, and international levels. Churches should also lobby for quotas and robust enforcement structures.

One of the best ways to protect fish and the wider marine environment is to establish more marine reserves around the world. Unfortunately, less than 2 percent of the world's oceans is fully protected in "no take" marine reserves, compared to 15 percent of land.[13] Where it happens the results can be spectacular. In Tonga Island Marine Reserve some fish stocks, such as blue cod, have improved by a factor of forty. Crawfish stocks have improved by a factor of seven.[14] Further protected areas are planned in the near future. Local churches should support such initiatives.

Industrial and Agricultural Waste

As if all the above were not enough, humans are also polluting the oceans with industrial waste that includes heavy metals, organochlorines (such as DDT), polychlorinated biphenyl (PCBs), nuclear waste, and agricultural effluent. Eighty percent of urban sewage discharged into the Mediterranean is untreated.[15] The destruction wrought by industrial, chemical, and radioactive pollution is not confined to the coastal areas in which it is dumped. It can be carried around the world by ocean currents. DDT and PCBs, for example, have turned up in the fatty tissue of seals in the Arctic and penguins in the Antarctic. In the past fifty years or so, over seventy thousand chemical compounds, pesticides,

---

[13] PEW Charitable Trusts, "Global Ocean Legacy," http://www.pewtrusts.org/en/global-ocean-legacy/about.

[14] Isaac Davison, "Smith Wants More Sea Sanctuaries," *New Zealand Herald,* January 9, 2014.

[15] WWF, "Marine Problems: Pollution: Over 80% of Marine Pollution Comes from Land-Based Activities," online.

cleaning agents, dioxins, and pharmaceuticals have entered the global environment.

There is increasing evidence that chemical pollution poses a very serious threat to the survival of whales and dolphins. Even low-level contamination can increase their susceptibility to disease and affect their fertility with disastrous long-term effects. Sian Pullen, head of the marine unit of the World Wide Fund for Nature in the run up to the Convention for the Protection of Marine Environment of the North East Atlantic OSPAR Conference, stated that "some of the most exotic sea creatures around Irish and British coasts, and some hundreds of species in total, are threatened by large-scale dumping of industrial chemicals, heavy metals and oil pollution."[16]

Plastic and Marine Life

The ubiquitous plastic bag also causes damage and great suffering to many marine creatures. A plastic bag bobbing up in the ocean looks like a jellyfish to a turtle. Once consumed, the plastic blocks the turtle's intestines and causes a slow, painful death. Huge amounts of plastic are also found in the Great Pacific Garbage Patch, which is located in the waters between North America and Japan. Oceanographers and ecologists have discovered that about 75 percent of the marine rubbish actually sinks to the bottom of the ocean. Both on the surface of the ocean and on its floor, plastic does enormous damage to marine creatures.

Eutrophication

Agricultural effluent is also a problem. Runoff of chemicals such as nitrates and phosphates from the land increases nitrification and oxygen deficiency in waterways (eutrophication). The North Sea, the Baltic Sea, and the Black Sea have all been particularly

---

[16] Quoted in Kevin O'Sullivan, "Action on Sea Pollution Sought to Ensure Survival of Marine Species," *Irish Times,* July 21, 1988.

affected. Eutrophication causes die-back in sea-grass meadows, an increase in algal blooms, and a consequent decline in fisheries.

Mining the Oceans

Many people are now afraid that mining for copper, manganese, nickel, cobalt, and rare earth metals on the floor of the Pacific Ocean, 2.5 miles beneath the surface, will do irreparable damage to parts of the earth which we are only beginning to explore. According to Greg Stone, vice-president for Conservation International, "it is tampering with ecosystems we hardly understand that are really at the frontier of our knowledge base. We are starting mining operations in a place where we don't fully understand how it works yet. So that is our concern—disturbing the deep sea habitat."[17] Suzanne Goldenberg, the author of the article, points out that "the ore content of the nodules of copper, manganese, cobalt and rare earths strewn across the ocean floor promises to be 10 times greater than the richest seam on land, making the cost of their retrieval from the extreme depths more attractive to companies."[18] The stakes are so high that some people fear a Klondike-like gold rush on the floor of the oceans, with terrible and irreversible consequences.

Coral Reefs and Mangrove Forests

Because the bulk of marine life everywhere is found close to coasts, even localized pollution can cause enormous damage. Two marine ecosystems are particularly vital to ensure a vibrant and healthy marine environment: the coral reefs and the mangrove forests. Both these ecosystems have been under attack for decades and now are in a precarious state globally. *Laudato Si'* points out that "in tropical and subtropical seas, we find coral reefs comparable to the great forest on dry land, for they shelter approximately

---

[17] Quoted in Suzanne Goldenberg, "Marine Mining: Underwater Gold Rush Sparks Fears of Ocean Catastrophe," *Guardian*, March 2, 2014.

[18] Ibid.

a million species, including fish, crabs, mollusks, sponges and algae. Many of the world's coral reefs are already barren or in a state of constant decline" (no. 41). Coral reefs provide shelter and livelihood security for almost 500 million people across the globe. The destruction of coral reefs also reduces the capacity of the coastlines to buffer the impact of sea level rise and increased storm surge.[19]

> According to a report co-authored by British and Australian scientists . . . researchers examined more than 800 reefs in 64 locations around the world and found that 83% had lost more than half of their fish, most of these losses having occurred since the 1970s. . . . Coral reefs occupy less than 0.1 percent of the world's ocean surface, but provide homes for more than a quarter of all marine species.[20]

Laudato Si' asserts that much of the damage "is due largely to pollution which reaches the sea as the result of deforestation, agricultural monocultures, industrial waste and destructive fishing methods, especially those using cyanide and dynamite" (no. 41).

Even in Australia, the Great Barrier Reef, which runs for 1,284 miles along the east coast, is under threat because of rising ocean temperatures caused by global warming and pollution. The reef has more than four hundred species of coral and fifteen hundred species of fish; it is worth £2.6 billion to the Australian tourism economy.[21]

In the past thirty years the reef has lost half of its corals due to rising sea temperatures, ocean acidification, increased number of cyclones, and fertilizer runoff from farms and sewage. In June 2015, UNESCO ruled that, though the Great Barrier Reef was deteriorating, it would not list it as "in danger." It nevertheless

---

[19] UNEP Emerging Issues, "Environmental Consequences of Ocean Acidification: A Threat to Food Security" (UNEP, 2010), 6.

[20] "The Observer View on the Destruction of the World's Great Coral Reefs," *Guardian,* April 11, 2015.

[21] Ibid.

called upon the Australian government to halt the deterioration of the natural icon as a matter of urgency.[22]

The fact that corals are dying in such large numbers ought to act as a wakeup call to humans to recognize that the oceans are sick and that if no remedial action is taken in the near future, dying and polluted oceans could have dire, irreversible consequences for the future of the planet. Pope Francis decries what is happening to the oceans with a sentence taken from "What Is Happening to Our Beautiful Land?" the Philippine bishops' pastoral letter on the environment: "Who turned the wonder-world of the seas into underwater cemeteries bereft of color and life?" (no. 41).

Mangrove forests are another marine ecosystem in the shallow oceans that are under threat (no. 39). The trees are salt tolerant *(halophytes)* and have adapted to thrive in harsh coastal conditions. Trees in mangrove forests have complex salt filtration systems and root systems to cope with salt water immersion and wave action. They are also adapted to the low oxygen (anoxic) conditions of waterlogged mud.

Like coral reefs, mangrove forests are an extraordinary productive life system, because they provide food and shelter for fish. Over the past forty years millions of acres of mangrove areas have been destroyed. Thailand has lost 27 percent of its mangrove forests, Malaysia 20 percent, the Philippines 45 percent, and Indonesia 40 percent. The expansion of fish farming and tourist resorts has contributed to the destruction of mangrove forests. Many forget that they protect coastlines in many tropical countries. The communities where mangrove forests were intact fared better during the 2004 tsunami in Asia because they acted as a buffer and therefore lessened the impact of the tsunami.

Caring for the Oceans

The Ocean Health Index was launched by Conservation International in 2012 in order to assess the health of the oceans based on measures such as biodiversity, food provisioning, coastal liveli-

---

[22] Joshua Robertson, "UNESCO Spares Great Barrier Reef 'In-Danger' Listing But Issues Warning," *Guardian,* July 1, 2015.

hoods, artisanal fishing opportunities, tourism and recreation, and carbon storage. In the 2013 update to the index the ability of the oceans to provide food only scored 33 out of 100. The 2013 Ocean Health Index ranked the current overall health of the oceans as 65 out of 100.

For thousands of years the sea has taken care of human beings. We now know that we are intimately connected with the oceans. If they become toxic, our food and our bodies will also become toxic. The time has come for humans to start taking care of the sea. We need to act quickly and comprehensively. Only 20 of the 177 countries that have coastlines have implemented effective coastal-management plans. To combat overfishing it is essential to limit the kind of technology that is allowed in fishing and to create areas where fishing is simply not allowed.

To combat pollution it is essential to enforce the Oslo Convention on dumping waste and toxic substances at sea, which was ratified as far back as 1972. This was followed two years later by the Paris Convention on dumping from land sources. This includes radioactive waste. Both these conventions were superseded by the OSPAR Convention in 1992. The OSPAR Convention requires the contracting parties to take all possible steps to prevent and eliminate pollution. The OSPAR ministerial statement, which emanated from the first ministerial meeting of the OSPAR Commission at Sintra, Portugal, in July 1998, adopted strong measures to protect the marine environment. It included a commitment to reduce radioactive waste to as close to zero as is technically feasible by the year 2020.

The Sintra statement prohibits the dumping of oil rigs at sea unless it can be proven that this will not cause environmental problems. This was a significant ruling in light of the controversy that surrounded the decision by Shell Oil to dump the oil rig *Brent Spar* at sea a few years ago.

Political and economic pressure needs to be brought to bear on corporations to persuade them to stop producing polluting chemicals and to move instead toward clean production techniques that would end the dumping of toxic substances into the ocean. But as Bruce McKay, a researcher for Sea Web, writes,

"Change will not come easily. Much of humanity has developed a profound dependency on nitrogen-based fertilizers, fossil fuels pesticides, and a host of other environmentally damaging goods and services."[23]

On a global level the provisions of the UN Convention on the Law of the Sea, which was negotiated in the early 1980s and came into force in 1994, need to be enforced more rigorously, and its enabling bodies, like the Tribunal for the Law of the Sea, require adequate funding and staff. Given the pressure on the oceans globally from fishing, oil and gas exploration, and dumping, the traditional notion of "freedom of the sea" will have to be abandoned.

Laudato Si' acknowledges that international and regional conventions do exist to promote the governance of the oceans. However, "they are fragmented" and the "lack of strict mechanisms of regulation, control and penalization end up undermining these efforts" (no. 174).

If remedial policies are vigorously implemented, nature will respond positively. Places such as the Great Lakes in North America, or the Hudson River and the Thames, rivers that were formerly very polluted, are now healthy and productive fishing areas.

The Ocean in the Bible

Because the Israelites were not seafaring people like the Phoenicians or the Vikings, the oceans get very little mention in the Bible. This is in stark contrast to the wealth of material on land. Norman Habel argues that there are at least six biblical perspectives on land.[24] Animals, both domestic and wild, and birds also figure prominently in the scriptures.[25]

The oceans, on the other hand, seem to be on the periphery of the Israelites' cultural and religious consciousness. Pious Jews

---

[23] Bruce McKay, "Cleaning Up the Seas," *People and the Planet* (1998): 16.

[24] Norman Habel, *The Land Is Mine* (Minneapolis: Fortress Press, 1995), 190.

[25] John Eaton, *The Circle of Creation* (London: SCM Press, 1995), 1–116.

would automatically expect to experience Yahweh's power on land, whether in the desert, on the mountain, or in the vineyard, the farm, the city, or especially, in the Temple. But in Psalm 107 the author argues that this power is also encountered in unexpected places, namely, the oceans:

> Some went down to the sea in ships
>   doing business on the mighty waters;
> they saw the deeds of the Lord ,
>   his wondrous works in the deep. (Ps 107:23–24)

In Psalm 107 the ocean is not seen as a benign, human-friendly place.[26] Rather, the fearsome nature of the ocean and the fragility of the seafarers riding in small fragile boats are emphasized:

> For he commanded and raised the stormy wind,
>   which lifted up the waves of the sea
> They mounted up to heaven, they went down to
>   the depths;
>   their courage melted away in their calamity;
> they reeled and staggered like drunkards,
>   and were at their wits' end. (Ps 107:25–27)

Jonah's trip from Joppa to Tarshish, the lone sea journey of the Old Testament, reinforces this negative image of the sea as a dangerous place, possibly not far from the gates of Sheol (Jonah 2:7). In Job, the sea is seen as the home of the sea monster (Job 7:12). Even in the New Testament the sea is a dangerous and even demonic place. The demons that terrorized the Gerasene demoniac beseeched Jesus to allow them to enter the swine, who then "charged over the cliff into the lake, and there they were drowned" (Mark 5:13). Mark portrays Jesus as having power over the sea. At the height of the storm, his "Be quiet! Be calm" caused the wind to stop and quiet to reign (Mark 4:39).

---

[26] See also Genesis 7:11–12; 9:11; 15.

The sea as a dangerous and threatening place can function as a metaphor for any kind of personal danger. In Psalm 69 the Psalmist, recognizing he is in difficulty and facing grave danger, says,

> I have come into deep waters,
>> and the flood sweeps over me. (Ps 69:2b)

In the Old Testament there appeared to be a pervasive fear that the waters might invade the land (Prov 8:29). In response to this fear, Yahweh displayed both his power over all the elements, even rebellious ones like the oceans, and his concern for the people by imposing limits to the seas at the dawn of creation (Gen 1:9ff.). Even Psalm 104, which is one of the most insightful and observant pieces of natural-history writing in the Bible, still shares an ambivalent attitude toward the oceans. Only Yahweh's word can keep the waters in check:

> You set a boundary that they may not pass,
>> so that they might not again cover the earth.
> (Ps 104:9; cf. Job 38:8–11)

The underlying fear evoked by the ocean is even present at the end of the New Testament in the vision of the future portrayed in the book of Revelation. "Then I saw a new heaven and a new earth; for the first heaven and the first earth had passed away, and the sea was no more" (Rev 21:1).

There is, of course, a more positive approach to the oceans in the Bible. The Bible teaches that the oceans are created by God (Gen 1:9–10). As God's creature it invites the "oceans and all that move in them" to praise God (Ps 69:34). We find the same theme in the three young men in the furnace in the book of Daniel: "Seas and rivers, bless the Lord" (Dan 3:78).

As Christians, living in a world where the oceans are under threat from human activity, we need to develop this positive strand in the biblical teaching in order to shape a positive theology of the oceans that will help give us energy and support in our efforts to protect the seas in today's world. Because the biblical view of the oceans is both scant and ambivalent, we will need to augment this with the positive understanding of the place of the oceans in our world that has become available to us through the research of modern science. This story of the earth, or more correctly, the story of the waters of the planet, ought to become the basis for a new understanding and regard for the oceans. The stories and myths of various maritime and indigenous peoples, like the following Inuit song that expresses their delight and love for the oceans, can be woven into the new caring attitude toward the oceans.

> The Great sea has set me in motion,
> Set me adrift,
> And I move as a weed in the river.
> The arch of the sky
> and the mightiness of storms
> Encompasses me,
> And I am left
> Trembling with joy.[27]

Bibliography

Dawson, James, *Superspill: The Future of Ocean Pollution* (London: Jane's Publishing Company, 1980).

Field, Michael, *The Catch: How Fishing Companies Reinvented Slavery and Plunder the Oceans* (London: Awe Press, 2014).

Hilborn, Ray, with Ulrike Hilborn, *Overfishing: What Everyone Needs to Know* (Oxford: Oxford University Press, 2012).

---

[27] "The Great Sea Has Set Me in Motion," in *A Book of Uncommon Prayer*, ed. Theo Dorgan (New York: Penguin Books, 2007).

6

Sustainable Food

In 2015, the human population of planet earth reached 7.3 billion people. This is expected to jump to nearly 10 billion by 2050, which poses a very real question: How will we adequately feed all these people? At the moment, even though we have the resources and the capacity to produce enough food for all, the number of people suffering from chronic hunger increased from under eight hundred million in 1996 to over one billion in 2009.[1] Undernourishment is still responsible for 15 percent of global diseases, and even when there is sufficient caloric intake, the diet is often deficient in micronutrients or of poor quality and diversity. In 2005, 2.2 million children under five years of age died from malnutrition; approximately forty million children are blinded each year by vitamin A deficiency.[2] On the other side of the scale, one and a half billion overconsume to a degree that increases their risk from chronic health-related diseases.[3]

Farmers grow enough to provide everyone on the planet with thirty-five hundred calories a day. Pope Francis recognizes that the majority of people are fed by small-scale food production systems (no. 129). However, world hunger persists, largely because of

---

[1] United Nations' Food and Agriculture Organization (FAO), *How to Feed the World in 2050* (Rome: FAO, 2009).

[2] World Health Organization (WHO), Nutrition, "Micronutrient Deficiencies: Vitamin A Deficiency," online.

[3] Foresight, "Tackling Obesities: Future Choices," project report (London: Government Office for Science, 2007).

unequal access to food; the problems are food distribution and poverty rather than inadequate agricultural capacity.

Laudato Si' notes that industrialized agriculture has forced "smallholders to sell their land or to abandon their traditional crops. Their attempts to move to other, more diversified, means of production prove fruitless because of the difficulty of linkage with regional and global markets, or because the infrastructure for sales and transport is geared to larger businesses" (no. 129). Without access to land to grow their own food, the urban poor do not have money to buy food even if it is available.

The agricultural output of industrialized countries roughly doubled in the second half of the twentieth century. Much of this newfound productivity came from increasing reliance on chemicals and fertilizers. The ready availability of cheap nitrogen led farmers to abandon traditional crop rotation and periodic fallowing in favor of continuous cultivation of row crops. From the early 1960s to 2000, there is an almost perfect correlation among global fertilizer use, global grain production, and the rise in population levels. However, researchers are becoming concerned that food demands for the growing global population could lead to food crises, especially in countries where land and water resources are scarce.[4]

New Agricultural Paradigm

A new agricultural paradigm has become dominant in industrialized countries. The maintenance of soil fertility almost exclusively depends now on artificial fertilizers, pesticides, and herbicides, all of which are manufactured from petroleum. A wide variety of different machines, all powered by oil, are the central feature of industrialized agriculture. It comes as no surprise, though it is seldom commented on, that agriculture today consumes 30 percent of oil used worldwide. Ninety-five percent of all food production depends on oil; one-third of this goes to make artificial fertilizers;

---

[4] FAO, IFAD and WFP, *The State of Food Insecurity in the World 2014: Strengthening the Enabling Environment for Food Security and Nutrition* (Rome: FAO, 2014).

a further one-third drives tractors, harvesters, and other equipment; and the remaining one-third is used in irrigation and in the manufacture of pesticides and herbicides.[5]

Between 1961 and 1984, fertilizer use increased tenfold in developing countries, especially in Asia. This did not end hunger, because population growth increased in line with the increased productivity. Throughout the 1990s, the world regularly stored more than one hundred days of grain supplies. Since the year 2000, grain stocks have been below seventy-five days on six occasions. In 2013, global supplies of rice, corn, soybeans, wheat, and other grain stocks dipped to seventy-one days because of droughts in Australia, Eastern Europe, and the United States. In the autumn of 2014, world supplies of corn, rice, soybeans, wheat, and other staple grains were forecast to reach their highest levels in fifteen years. However, food experts say the increase will do little to reverse an upward trend in food prices.[6] More and more, our global food reserves are being reduced.

It must be said that this new model of agriculture is highly productive and efficient, particularly in terms of the volume of food produced. But if the energy costs and the associated social and environmental costs are acknowledged, it is very inefficient. When these are factored in, the opposite is the case. On older, traditional farms ten kilocalories of food energy could be produced for every one kilocalorie expended on the cultivation. On the modern farm the equation is reversed: for every ten kilocalories put in (most of it from fossil fuel), we get one kilocalorie in food.[7]

Although industrial agriculture resolved the nutrient bottleneck easily and cheaply, it did so by failing to maintain fertility sustainably. It did away with the drudgery of working on the land, but it

---

[5] Colin Tudge, *So Shall We Reap (How everyone who is liable to be born in the next ten thousand years could eat very well indeed; and why, in practice, our immediate descendants are likely to be in serious trouble)* (London: Penguin, 2003).

[6] Codi Kozacek, "World Food Supplies Recover from Drought and Reach 15-Year High," Circle of Blue, November 27, 2014.

[7] Richard Manning, "The Oil We Eat: Following the Food Chain Back to Iraq," *Harpers* (May 24, 2004), 43.

released most people from direct dependent contact with the land and the security of local food. Hundreds of millions of people were forced off the land, often into slums in megacities in Asia and Latin America.

Greenhouse Gases and Global Warming

Another very important cost that needs to be factored in to climate change is industrial agriculture. Industrialized farming contributes between one quarter and one third of greenhouse gas emissions. Eighteen percent of global emissions is due to land use change, mainly deforestation, and a further 12–14 percent is associated with direct agricultural greenhouse emissions, including petroleum-based fertilizers and methane from livestock.[8] Methane is twenty-five times more potent as a greenhouse gas than carbon dioxide. For example, when farmers spread nitrogen on their crops, much of it is wasted because it is carried elsewhere by rain and fertilizes other areas. Some of the nitrogen reacts chemically with its surroundings to produce nitrous oxide. This greenhouse gas also contributes to climate change. Normally, cultivating plants offsets climate change because it removes carbon dioxide from the air. However, when nitrogen is applied liberally, it has the opposite effect.

In a time of increasing human population and climate change worldwide, agriculture will have to produce more food while it faces floods, droughts, and warmer and rising sea levels, all of which are part of climate change.

The negative effects of climate change are likely to be disproportionate in areas that already suffer from food insecurity, particularly for subsistence farmers in Africa and parts of Southeast Asia who rely on rain-fed agriculture.[9] For example, the anticipated rise in sea level due to climate change will inundate and flood coastal

---

[8] Royal Society, *Reaping the Benefits: Science and the Sustainable Intensification of Global Agriculture* (London: The Royal Society, 2009).

[9] William R. Sutton, Jitendra P. Srivastava, and James E. Neumann, *Looking beyond the Horizon: How Climate Change Impacts and Adaptation Responses Will Reshape Agriculture in Eastern Europe and Central China* (Washington DC: World Bank, 2013).

lands where half of all humans live and where much of the world's best farmland is situated.

Petroleum production is expected to peak before the middle of this century. As supplies dwindle, oil and gas will become too valuable to use for fertilizer production. And we know that we must leave 70 percent of the oil in the ground if the average increase in global temperature is to remain less than a 2-degree Celsius rise above preindustrial levels. As a result, the price of fertilizers will continue to increase in the years and decades ahead, putting it beyond the reach of the majority of farmers in those parts of the world in greatest need of sustainable agriculture.

Another major cause for concern in terms of producing enough food to feed a growing global population is that the development of biofuels will compromise food security. As Richard Manning points out, "We spend more calories of fossil-fuel energy making ethanol than we gain from it. The Department of Agriculture says that the ratio is closer to a gallon and a quart of ethanol for every gallon of fossil fuel we invest."[10] The question whether to expand biofuel production was debated at length by the Committee on World Food Security at a meeting in Rome in October 2013. The meeting was attended by nearly 750 people, including more than 130 government delegations. The committee stressed that biofuel development "should not compromise food security, and should especially consider women and children."[11]

Food Consumption

Apart from the challenges that relate to the actual production of food, there are significant issues that relate to the way food is consumed in the modern world. Wheat, rice, and maize provide one-half of the calories of all humanity and two-thirds of its protein. As living standards increase worldwide, people want to emulate Western lifestyles—and in diet this means more food that is high

---

[10] Manning, "The Oil We Eat," 44.

[11] FAO, "Biofuel Development Should Not Compromise Food Security, Says CFS," October 11, 2013.

in meat, dairy, fat, salt, and sugar. Most people would agree that a certain amount of meat and animal products is desirable for a range of reasons. Still, it would be incorrect to think that our daily protein requirement can come only from eating meat. Cereals combined with pulses also provide complete protein.

Meat Consumption

Because of the increased focus on climate change in recent years, most of us are aware that generating our electricity and fueling our transportation activities release greenhouse gases into the atmosphere; this, in turn, causes climate change. We are not so aware, however, that our diet, especially if it is based on meat, can have a similar impact. According to an FAO study in 2006, meat consumption is expected to increase significantly from its current level of 15 percent of the total global human diet. The study found that the production of meat in our world today contributes thirty-six billion tons of CO_2 or between 14 and 22 percent of all greenhouse gas emissions.[12]

The shift toward higher consumption of calories from fats and animal products will put much greater pressure on land resources because animals require much more land, water, and energy and make a greater contribution to anthropogenic greenhouse gas emissions.

The yield of protein and energy per hectare (approximately two and one-half acres) is about ten times higher from land under cultivation than from grazing land. Half of the world's wheat and barley is fed to livestock, as is 80 percent of the maize and nearly all of the soya. It takes a little over fifteen pounds of grain to make approximately two pounds of beef, or a ratio of over 7:1. For pigs, the ratio is around 4:1, and it is less again for chickens. In addition, water consumption for beef production is huge, approximately two thousand gallons for one pound of beef (this includes the "water cost" of growing feed).[13]

---

[12] Nathan Fiala, "How Meat Contributes to Global Warming," *Scientific American* (February 2009).

[13] Alex Proud," We All Need to Stop Eating Meat, and This Is Why," *The Telegraph,* July 28, 2015.

By 2050, there will be nine to ten billion people on the planet. Our livestock will be consuming enough grain and pulses to feed another four billion people.[14] Ten tons of wheat would solve the nutritional problems of fifty people for a year. But if it is fed to pigs and poultry and cattle it will feed only five people. This means that more will have to be grown and sold to satisfy the ever-growing market. We also discard most of the animal because we believe that the most expensive animal cuts are the only parts worth eating.[15] David Pimentel, who at the time was working on food and energy at Cornell University, states: "If all the world ate the way the United States eats, humanity would exhaust all known fossil-fuel reserves in just over seven years." Richard Manning quotes Pimentel and adds that "Pimentel has his detractors. Some have accused him of being off on other calculations by as much as 10 percent. Fine. Make it ten years."[16]

Other cultures are beginning to consume much more meat and to feed their grain to livestock. In 2004, Mexico was feeding 45 percent of its grain to livestock, while in 1960 it was only 5 percent. Egypt went from 3 percent to 31 percent in the same period, and China from 8 percent to 26 percent.[17] Religious people need to assess whether a meat-rich diet is a moral option in the twenty-first century.

Loss of Genetic Diversity

Another facet of the dominance of industrial agriculture is the loss of genetic diversity in farm animals and food crops all over the world. Genetic diversity is essential in the face of climatic uncertainty. We have lost an enormous amount already. Seventy-five percent of the world's agricultural diversity was lost over the

---

[14] Helena Norberg-Hodge, Todd Merrifield, and Steven Gorelick, *Bringing the Food Economy Home: Local Alternatives to Global Agribusiness* (Westport, CT: Kumarian Press, 2002).

[15] Michael Pollan, *The Omnivore's Dilemma: The Search for a Perfect Meal in a Fast-Food World* (New York: Bloomsbury, 2011).

[16] Manning, "The Oil We Eat," 11–12.

[17] Ibid., 18.

course of the twentieth century. For example, in 1949, ten thousand varieties of wheat were being grown in China; by the 1970s only one thousand remained.[18] The loss of such locally adapted varieties, or landraces, as they are called, is a biological disaster. When a crop with a uniform genetic structure succumbs to a disease, as happened in the United States in the 1970s, researchers had to go back to the landraces to find varieties with genes that might protect the crop against the diseases.[19]

Consumption and Waste

Pope Francis tells us that "approximately a third of all food produced is discarded" (no. 50). At the production end of the food chain, post-harvest losses can be reduced through investment to support the development of the necessary infrastructure for storage and cooling facilities, correct packaging, and improved transportation and marketing of food. At the retail end, quality standards often require that fruit, vegetables, or other perishable commodities that are cosmetically imperfect must be withdrawn. Direct marketing of farm produce, such as farmers' markets, can help to reduce the amount of rejected crops, because the often unnecessarily strict quality standards of supermarkets do not apply.

Need for a New Model in Agriculture

We urgently need a new model of food production if we are to improve the lives of those who do not have enough to eat while, at the same time, not exhausting the fertility of the land and leaving it barren. This will involve farming with intelligence and compassion rather than by habit or convenience. It will involve merging traditional agricultural knowledge and experience with a modern

---

[18] FAO, *World Agriculture: Toward 2030/2050: Prospects for Good Nutrition: Agriculture and Major Commodity Groups*, Interim Report (Rome: Global Perspective Studies Unit, FAO, 2006).

[19] A. J. Ullstrup, "The Impacts of the Southern Corn Leaf Blight Epidemics of 1970–1971," *Annual Review of Phytopathology* 10 (September 1972): 37–50.

understanding of ecology in order to sustain agriculture in a way that can feed the population of the twenty-first century.

Cultivating more land is no longer an option for us, because most of the land capable of cultivation is already farmed. The extent of farm land globally has grown from 17.4 million square miles in 1966 to 19.3 million square miles in 2014. According to the Global Environment Facility, land degradation affects 33 percent of the earth's land surface and affects the lives of more than 2.6 billion people in more than one hundred countries. Land degradation is caused by soil erosion, salinization, and nutrient depletion.

Since there is limited scope for land expansion, sustainable intensification will be a key strategy in increased food production. It will not be an extension of the highly intensive and mechanized agriculture that has emerged since World War II. At the heart of modern sustainable agriculture is the realization that retaining the soil's organic matter is the key to sustainable productivity. Soil carbon sequestration is among the most important techniques for the mitigation of greenhouse gas emissions in agriculture. One-third of the total carbon dioxide buildup in the atmosphere since the Industrial Revolution has come not from fossil fuels, but from the degradation of organic matter in soil. Traditional rotations replaced the organic matter and nutrients in the soil. Sustainable, low-input methods of agriculture rely on enhancing and building up soil fertility by growing diversified crops, adding animal manure and green compost, and using natural pest control and crop rotation rather than having synthetic nutrients provided by chemical manufacturing.

Enlightened Agriculture

In other words, we will require enlightened agriculture to feed the world. The future will need good farmers and lots of them. Farming requires skill and the experience of generations, as well as vibrant and supportive agrarian communities. It cannot be practiced by one farmer on a thousand acres, which is the goal today. Good farming needs to be labor intensive, but the modern economic system is making it impossible to be labor intensive. There will be many more opportunities to work on the land as envisaged by Pope Francis (nos. 124, 128). More people are needed on the land, practicing intensive, enlightened agriculture on smaller farms, using appropriate technology. In the words of *Laudato Si'*, "This way of experiencing work makes us more protective and respectful of the environment; it imbues our relationship to the world with a healthy sobriety" (no. 126).

Enlightened agriculture is mixed and small-scale farming. It combines the accumulated agronomic wisdom of millennia with the best scientific understanding. It provides the best and freshest possible food and leads to national self-reliance worldwide. If even the poorest countries had new agrarian economies geared to their own local variety of enlightened agriculture, they could be self-reliant in producing food. Trade in commodities would apply only to excess goods for which there are guaranteed markets.

Urban Farming as Part of the Answer

Urban agriculture will be part of the solution. "Fifty percent of the global population now lives in cities and this is expected to rise to 70 percent by 2050." At least a dozen cities will have populations in excess of fifty million people. "Seventy percent of urban households in developing countries participate in agricultural activities."[20] Where conditions are favorable, it can provide up to 60 percent of the family's food requirements. According to *Worldwatch* magazine, urban agriculture in Asia and some parts of Africa already provides some eight hundred million people with most of their food.[21]

International Assessment of Agricultural Science and Technology (IAASTD)

Small-scale, mixed agriculture is also the approach recommended in a 2008 report by the IAASTD in one of the most comprehensive

---

[20] Leslie Lipper, Wendy Mann, Alexandre Meybeck, and Reuben Sessa, "'Climate-Smart' Agriculture: Policies, Practices, and Financing for Food Security, Adaptation, and Mitigation" (Rome: FAO, 2010).

[21] Worldwatch Institute, *State of the World: Innovations that Nourish the Planet* (New York: W. W. Norton and Company, 2011).

studies ever conducted on the effectiveness of agricultural knowledge, science, and technology. The report, initiated by the World Bank, was the result of a collaborative process involving nine hundred participants and 110 countries. The results and conclusions of the study were reviewed and ratified during the Intergovernmental Plenary Meeting held in Johannesburg, South Africa, April 7–12, 2008. The report did not endorse the claims of the biotech industry that genetically modified crops will feed the world. It argues that small-scale farmers and ecologically sensitive methods of farming are the way forward.

Laudato Si', while endorsing this approach, adds a vital moral and legal element to the argument when it calls for the necessity to cultivate a public conscience that considers food and access to water as universal rights of all human beings, without distinction or discrimination. I would argue that this right makes patents on food crops morally questionable. This is particularly true in light of the principle of gratuitousness that runs like a thread throughout the encyclical.

The Contribution of Genetic Engineering

The promise of greatly increased crop yields from genetic engineering, which was promoted in the 1990s by Robert Shapiro, the CEO of Monsanto, has so far proved elusive. Proponents of GMOs (genetically modified organisms) have not been able to alleviate worries that transgenic foods have the potential for creating unexpected reactions in humans unless these foods are rigorously tested in accordance with universally recognized precautionary principles. Neither have they been able to allay worries that nontarget species might be negatively affected by genetic modifications aimed at specific pests; for example, some have argued that Bt-corn has had a negative impact on the monarch butterfly. Nor have they dispelled the very real threat of loss of biodiversity posed by GMOs.

In *Laudato Si'* Pope Francis makes the claim that "no conclusive proof exists that GM cereals may be harmful for humans" (no. 134). While his purpose is not to advocate the use of GMOs, many people, myself included, would disagree with this assertion.

In 2015, "the European Network of Scientists for Social and Environmental Responsibility collected more than 300 signatures from independent researchers endorsing a statement rejecting the claim that there is a consensus on the safety of genetically modified organisms (GMOs)."[22]

French scientist Gilles-Éric Séralini, a professor of molecular biology at the University of Caen, has published research concluding that genetically modified food is unsafe for consumption. Recent studies by Professor Séralini and his colleagues report high levels of toxic contaminants in the standard feeds used in animal testing across five continents, undermining any consensus that GM foods are safe.[23]

In 1996, a team of scientists led by Dr. Árpád Pusztai carried out research at the prestigious Rowett Institute in Scotland on rats that had been fed with GM potatoes. The researchers found that the GM potatoes adversely affected virtually every organ of the young rats and that the damage was done by the "genetic modification process itself." Dr. Pusztai spoke about the research on television with the permission of the director of the institute. For two days he was the hero of the institute. Then, it is alleged, two phone calls from Downing Street were forwarded by the receptionist to the director. The next day Dr. Pusztai, who had worked at the institute for thirty-five years, was sacked. He was also silenced with threats of lawsuits. His team of twenty scientists was disbanded. This research is still the most extensive GMO feeding study ever published.[24]

While Pope Francis is neutral on the science of recombinant DNA technology, he is very critical of the social impact of GM crops. He writes:

---

[22] Erik Millstone, Andy Stirling, and Dominic Glober, "Regulating Genetic Engineering: The Limits of Politics of Knowledge," *Perspectives* (Summer 2015), 25.

[23] R. Mesnage, Gilles-Éric Séralini, et al., "Laboratory Rodent Diets Contain Toxic Levels of Environmental Contaminants: Implications for Regulatory Tests," *PLOS ONE* 10, no. 7 (2015): 7.

[24] Jeffrey M. Smith, *Genetic Roulette: The Documented Health Risks of Genetically Engineered Foods* (Fairfield, IA: Yes! Books, 2007), 23.

In many places, following the introduction of these crops, productive land is concentrated in the hands of a few owners "due to the progressive disappearance of small producers, who, as a consequence of the loss of the exploited lands, are obliged to withdraw from direct production." The most vulnerable of these become temporary laborers, and many rural workers end up moving to poverty-stricken urban areas. (no. 134)

The pope is also aware of the power of transnational agribusiness corporations. "In various countries, we see an expansion of oligopolies for the production of cereals and other products needed for their cultivation" (no. 139). In 2002, Jorge Eduardo Fuli stated that "our brief history of submission to the world biotechnology giants has been so disastrous that we fervently hope other Latin American nations will take it as an example of what not to do."[25]

But agribusiness companies such as Monsanto are also loathed and feared in the United States. In 2008, *Vanity Fair* carried an article entitled "Monsanto's Harvest of Fear." The article describes "Monsanto's fierce reputation for enforcing its patents and suing anyone who allegedly violated them." The article alleges that "Monsanto relies on a shadowy army of private investigators and agents in the American heartland to strike fear into farm country. . . . Lawyers who have represented farmers sued by Monsanto say that intimidating actions like these are commonplace."[26] Monsanto is a major player in global mechanized and chemical agriculture.

The Christian Response

The enormity of the challenges we face to feed the world calls to mind the challenge confronting Jesus following his discourse

---

[25] Sue Branford, "Why Argentina Can't Feed Itself: How GM Soya Is Destroying Livelihoods and the Environment in Argentina," *The Ecologist* (October 2002), 23.

[26] Donald L. Barlett and James R. Steele, "Monsanto's Harvest of Fear," *Vanity Fair* (May 2008), 112–23.

in a remote place on the fringes of cultivation when he fed five thousand men, "not counting women and children," with seven loaves and with two fishes, twelve basketfuls of broken pieces being gathered when all had eaten (Matt 14:13–21; Mark 6:31–44; Luke 9:10–17; John 6:5–15).

We can feed all the people living on this planet. We have the knowledge and the resources, if we can apply them, guided by wisdom and virtue instead of primarily in pursuit of excessive profit and misguided self-interest.

The significance of all of this for Christians is highlighted by the story of the feeding of the multitudes, but it is elevated onto an altogether different plane through the central Christian mystery of the Eucharist. Through the sharing of bread and wine we receive the body and blood of Christ. The bread and wine are not incidental to the sacrament. They are real bread and real alcoholic wine, standing in for all the fruit of human endeavor in the fields. This becoming the body and blood of Christ is not some added thing that makes the material, substantial ordinary bread irrelevant, something that falls away as soon as Christ becomes present. The reality of bread and wine is of the essence of the sacrament.

Food and the Eucharist

We celebrate the Eucharist within our Christian communities so that, fortified through the grace we receive, we may attempt to realize in our lives the central commandment to love our neighbor who, in Christ's own uncompromising words, is all of humankind. According to Pope Francis, the "Eucharist is also the source of light and motivation for our concerns for the environment, directing us to be stewards of all creation" (no. 236).

When we bring bread and wine to the altar for the Eucharist, we bring with them the whole of creation. These "fruits of the earth" and "work of human hands" represent crops and vineyards, sunshine and rain, the God-given bounty of the earth. The gifts of bread and wine represent all God's creatures. It is in these signs of the whole creation that the risen Christ bestows himself on us.

In the Eucharist we not only bring creation to the altar, but we praise God with all creatures and give thanks to God for all creatures. This idea is at the heart of the Eucharist. In the "Third Eucharistic Prayer," immediately after the "Sanctus," the priest prays on behalf of the community in these words: "You are indeed Holy, O Lord, and all you have created rightly gives you praise."

Every creature on earth and in some way the whole universe is involved with us when we pray the Eucharist. Each Eucharist is an event of communion. Sharing in the Eucharist, we participate in the divine life of the blessed Trinity. In this divine communion we are brought into communion with one another, with the church throughout the world, with the Communion of Saints, and with all God's creatures. The communion in which we share embraces all of earth's peoples and all its living creatures. Our communion with God is also a communion with God's beloved creation.

The Eucharist, as a memorial of the cross, calls us into solidarity with the human victims of injustice, wars, and ecological disasters. We remember those who have lost their families and their homes in tragic climate events, and the threat to millions of others living in low-lying areas. And we remember the rest of God's creation, "groaning in labor pains until now" (Rom 8:22), with so much threatened, damaged, or destroyed by human action. In the Eucharist we participate in God's feeling for our planetary community and commit ourselves again to ecological action as people of Easter hope.

Laudato Si' has a wonderful section on the Eucharist (nos. 236–237). The pope says that "it is in the Eucharist that all that has been created finds it greatest exaltation." He continues that "he comes not from above, but from within, he comes that we might find him in this world of ours." He quotes Pope John Paul II, who taught that the "Eucharist was an act of cosmic love. . . . The Eucharist joins heaven and earth; it embraces and penetrates all creation." Yes, cosmic! Because even when it is celebrated on the humble altar of a country church, the "Eucharist is always in some way celebrated on the altar of the world. The Eucharist joins heaven and earth and penetrates all creation" (no. 236). When we participate in it, we commit ourselves to a way of acting that respects the integrity of other creatures before God.

Finally, the Eucharist is the sacrament of ecology. The goal of ecological thinking and action is to create a mutually enhancing relationship between humankind and the rest of creation. This is what happens in the Eucharist. We do not use wheat or grape juice, but rather bread and wine, which combines the fertility of God's creation, "fruit of the earth," with human creativity in farming, baking, cultivation of vines, and wine making, "and work of human hands." The hope is that the faithful who celebrate the Eucharist on Sundays will try to live their daily lives in a way that protects and enhances all God's creation.

Bibliography

Berry, Thomas, *The Dream of the Earth* (Berkeley, CA: Counterpoint Press, 2015; < Sierra Club Books, 1988>).

———, with Thomas Clark, *Befriending the Earth: A Theology of Reconciliation between Humans and the Earth* (Mystic, CT: Twenty-Third Publications, 1991).

———, with Brian Swimme, *The Universe Story* (San Francisco: HarperSanFrancisco, 1994).

———, *The Great Work: Our Way into the Future* (New York: Harmony/Bell Tower, 2000).

———, *Evening Thoughts: Reflecting on Earth as Sacred Community,* ed. Mary Evelyn Tucker (Berkeley, CA: Counterpoint Press, 2015 < Sierra Club, 2006>).

———, *The Sacred Universe: Earth, Spirituality, and Religion in the Twenty-first Century,* ed. and foreword Mary Evelyn Tucker (New York: Columbia University Press, 2009).

———, *The Christian Future and the Fate of Earth,* ed. Mary Evelyn Tucker and John Grim (Maryknoll, NY: Orbis Books, 2009).

McDonagh, Sean, *Patenting Life? Stop! Is Corporate Greed Forcing Us to Eat Genetically Engineered Food?* (Dublin: Dominican Publications, 2003).

Pollan, Michael, *The Omnivore's Dilemma: The Search for a Perfect Meal in a Fast-food World* (New York: Bloomsbury, 2001).

Smith, Jeffrey M., *Genetic Roulette: The Documented Health Risks of Genetically Engineered Foods* (Fairfield, IA: Yes! Books, 2007).

Tucker, Mary Evelyn, and John Grim, eds., *Thomas Berry: Selected Writings on the Earth Community* (Maryknoll, NY: Orbis Books, 2014).

United Nations Food and Agriculture Organization (FAO), *How to Feed the World in 2050* (Rome: FAO, 2009).

Worldwatch Institute, *State of the World: Innovations that Nourish the Planet* (New York: W.W. Norton and Company, 2001).

7

Responsibility for Protecting
the Environment

In *Laudato Si'* Pope Francis states that his message about environmental deterioration is addressed to "all men and women of good will" (no. 3). He notes that every effort to protect and improve our world entails profound changes in "lifestyles, models of production and consumption" (no. 5). Pope Francis is not overwhelmed by the sheer magnitude of the ecological crisis because he believes that "things can change" (no. 13). He is adamant that "young people demand change. . . . They wonder how anyone can claim to be building a better future without thinking of the environmental crisis and the sufferings of the excluded" (no. 13). Of course, Pope Francis realizes that "change is impossible without motivation and a process of education" (no. 15). He notes that some progress is being made. "Investments have also been made in means of production and transportation which consume less energy and require fewer raw materials, as well as in methods of construction and renovating buildings which improve their energy efficiency. But these good practices are still far from widespread" (no. 26).

In lamenting the incalculable loss that extinction represents for our fertile planet, Pope Francis states that "we cannot be silent witnesses to terrible injustices if we think that we can obtain significant benefits by making the rest of humanity, present and future, pay the extremely high cost of environmental destruction" (no. 36).

He insists that "a legal framework which can set clear boundaries and ensure the protection of ecosystems has become indispensable; otherwise the new power structures based on the techno-economic paradigm may overwhelm not only our politics but also freedom and justice" (no. 53).

While commending the achievements in some countries to address environmental problems, the pope writes that "these achievements do not solve global problems, but they do show that men and women are still capable of intervening positively" (no. 58).

Need for Ecological Education

Pope Francis is very clear that "many things have to change, but it is we human beings above all who need to change" (no. 202). He is convinced that "we lack an awareness of our common origin, of our mutual belonging, and of a future to be shared with everyone. He continues, "No system can completely suppress our openness to what is good, true and beautiful, or our God-given ability to respond to his grace at work deep in our hearts" (no. 205). It is also true that a change in lifestyle could put pressure on those who wield political, economic, and social power (no. 208).

The pope talks about the wider responsibility of environmental education. Initially it centered on gathering scientific data and raising people's awareness. Today it needs to broaden this to include a "critique of the 'myths' of a modernity grounded in a utilitarian mindset (individualism, unlimited progress, competition, consumerism, the unregulated market)." We need to live in "harmony with ourselves, with others, with nature and other living creatures, and with God." The key ideas for genuine ecological education need to revolve around "solidarity, responsibility and compassionate care" (no. 210). The goal is to create "an ecological citizenship" (no. 211).

This, of course, will lead to practical action such as "avoiding the use of plastic and paper, reducing water consumption, separating refuse, cooking only what can reasonably be consumed, showing care for other living beings, using public transport or car-pooling, planting trees, turning off unnecessary lights, or any number of other practices" (no. 211). "Ecological education can take place in a variety of settings: at school, in families, in the media, in catechesis and elsewhere" (no. 213). The family must be at the heart of all of this because it is there that we "first learn how to show love and respect for life; we are taught the proper use of things, order and cleanliness, respect for the local ecosystem and care for all creatures" (no. 213). The church has an important role to play also in this process. "It is my hope that our seminaries and houses of formation will provide an education in responsible simplicity of life, in grateful contemplation of God's world, and in concern for the poor and the protection of the environment" (no. 214). Good education in promoting what is beautiful and aesthetic will also help in the maintenance of a healthy and beautiful environment (no. 215). Above all, what we need is a profound ecological conversion. The pope reminds Catholics that "the Sacraments are a privileged way in which nature is taken up by God to become a means of mediating supernatural life. . . . Water, oil, fire and colours are taken up in all their symbolic power and incorporated in our act of praise" (no. 235). The Eucharist is an "act of cosmic love!" which "embraces and penetrates all creation" (no. 326).

As I read this section of *Laudato Si',* I asked myself whether this transformative education will happen. Will humans turn from being "masters, consumers, [and] ruthless exploiters" to feeling "intimately united to all that exists" (no. 11)? As someone who has been involved in environmental theology in the Philippines and Ireland for almost forty years, I am convinced that without serious education at both individual and community levels *Laudato Si'* will be ineffective. What is called for here will involve massive changes.

I am reminded that on World Peace Day, January 1, 1990, Pope John Paul II published a document on ecology entitled "Peace with God the Creator: Peace with All of Creation." In its first paragraph that document states: "In our day, there is a growing awareness that world peace is threatened not only by the arms race, regional conflicts and continued injustices among peoples and nations, but also by a lack of *due respect for nature*, by the plundering of natural resources and by a progressive decline in the quality of life." Pope John Paul II ends that first paragraph with the words "moreover, a new *ecological awareness* is beginning to emerge which, rather than being downplayed, ought to be encouraged to develop into concrete programmes and initiatives." Later in the document Pope John Paul II states that "*an education in ecological responsibility* is urgent: responsibility for oneself, for others, and for the earth" ("Peace," no. 13). He goes on to claim that "Christians, in particular, realize that their responsibility within creation and their duty towards nature and the Creator are an essential part of their faith. As a result, they are conscious of a vast field of ecumenical and interreligious cooperation opening up before them" ("Peace," no. 15). Unfortunately, this vision of Pope John Paul II failed miserably. Very few Catholic communities embraced the task of working to protect the poor and the embattled earth. The document called for a "*more internationally coordinated approach to the management of the earth's goods*" ("Peace," no. 9). This also has not happened, because resources were not committed to making it happen.

To bring the message of *Laudato Si'* to the Catholic Church and beyond, the church will have to establish and properly resource justice, peace, and ecology committees in every diocese and parish around the world. Such initiatives will require money, energy, and organizational ability. And many clergy and committed Catholics might see little need for such committees unless there are specific problems in their community related to these issues such as struggles over water rights. Ecological concerns are often seen as purely secular concerns. This is the kind of barrier that Pope Francis is hoping to breach with the encyclical *Laudato Si'*.

These committees will first of all have to educate themselves about justice and ecology issues on the local, national, and global levels. They will also have to study *Laudato Si'* closely as the teaching of this document on crucial ecological issues such as climate change or the extinction of species is much more radical than the position shared by most Catholics, especially in the United States.

Catholic colleges and universities will have to set up programs in justice, peace, and ecology so that those involved in this ministry will be competent and credible. Once again, theology departments in Catholic universities have devoted very little time or research to creation theology. This will have to change drastically if *Laudato Si'* is going to be implemented in a coherent and competent way.

But the focus of *Laudato Si'* is not about empowering experts or the elite within the church. It is aimed at bringing about a major cultural change through an ecological conversion across the church and the wider society. Therefore, church leaders will have to find new ways to communicate this message to everyone in the church. Younger Catholics could play a vital role in disseminating this new call for the care of God's creation, and church leaders should be open to harnessing their enthusiasm and talents in this new ministry.

For example, in the section on climate change *Laudato Si'* states: "If present trends continue, the century may well witness extraordinary climate change and an unprecedented destruction of ecosystems, with serious consequences for all of us" (no. 24). One can ask, is there going to be an education program on climate change? The same question is true for biodiversity, fresh water, the oceans, and sustainable food. Who will do it? And how will it be managed? Communities will have to grapple with all of these issues at both local, national, and international levels. According to the pope, "The problem is that we still lack the culture needed to confront this crisis. We lack leadership capable of striking out on new paths and meeting the needs of the present with concern for all and without prejudice towards coming generations" (no. 53). How will we combat the special-interest groups and economic systems that "end up trumping the common good and manipulating information so that their own plans will not be affected" (no. 54)? There is also an "evasiveness [that] serves as a licence to carry on with our present lifestyles and models of production and consumption" (no. 59). Part of the problem, as Pope Francis sees it, is that "our immense technological development has not been accompanied by a development in human responsibility, values and conscience" (no. 105). We will have to confront the "lie that there is an infinite supply of the earth's goods" (no. 106).

Pope Francis believes that we must develop "an educational programme, a lifestyle and a spirituality which together generate resistance to the technological paradigm" (no. 111). We also need to extricate ourselves from "today's self-centred culture of instant gratification" (no. 162).

A Synod on Ecology at Local, National, and International Levels

One way the church could begin educating itself about these issues would be through a synodal process. A synod is a council of the church that is usually convened to make decisions on doctrine or issues that are considered important by the church at a particular time. So, given the importance of working for the poor and protecting the environment, as highlighted in *Laudato Si'* it would make a lot of sense to hold a synod on these topics. The synod should run for at least three years. The first year might be spent coming to know the local environment in each parish and diocese. What are the ecosystems in the area? How have they been affected in recent times? Obviously, people with knowledge and skills in this area could be called to share their expertise with the members of the synod, most of whom would be laypeople. It would be important that there be a good age mix at the synod.

The synod could begin by asking the questions that Pope Francis has raised in *Laudato Si'*. In terms of climate change, for example, the synod would discuss the level of greenhouse gas emissions in that area from either transportation or agriculture. It could help suggest various ways to reduce these emissions quickly. In some synods this might raise the question of the morality of a heavy meat diet, not just on the local environment but on the planet as well. If our diet is going to have to be changed significantly because it contributes to global warming, this will happen only in the context of robust debate and dialogue. Naturally, if these changes are to take root, other profitable farming alternatives would have to be suggested and supported so that the members of the farming community could pursue their livelihood.

Similar issues will emerge in terms of our use of energy, water, and waste. The synod would also attempt to develop a spirituality to make it easier for local Catholic groups to honor their relationship with God, their fellow humans, other creatures, and the natural world. Appropriate liturgies could also be developed as the synod members try to tease out what this new, more harmonious way of living might entail.

For the second year of the synod a similar process should take place at the national level. In the third year an international synod could be held. This would be a huge boost to ecological thinking and action around the world, and the Catholic Church could play a vital role as a catalyst facilitating the whole process.

Sources of Hope

Pope Francis is not pessimistic. He tells us that "all is not lost. Human beings, while capable of the worst, are also capable of rising above themselves, choosing again what is good, and making new starts, despite their mental and social conditioning" (no. 204).

Even though grave damage is being done to our home, Pope Francis says that "hope would have us recognize that there is always a way out, that we can always redirect our steps, that we can always do something to solve our problems" (no. 61). Our Christian faith is always a source of great hope: "The Spirit of God has filled the universe with possibilities and therefore, from the very heart of things, something new can always emerge" (no. 80). And, as he notes in a classic statement: "All it takes is one good person to restore hope!" (no. 71). He points to one such individual later in the encyclical, St. Thérèse of Lisieux, who practiced the "little way of love" by her smiles, kind words, and gestures of friendship (no. 230). To this I would add the example of four people who each showed what "one good person" can achieve. They have much to teach those who are involved in an ecological ministry.

Rachel Carson: A Visionary

On September 29, 1962, Rachel Carson published the book *Silent Spring.* Many people believe that the modern environmental movement owes its origins to this book, so great was its impact, particularly in raising consciousness about the harmful effects of DDT and other pesticides. DDT was first synthesized in 1874, but its value as an insecticide was only discovered by the Swiss chemist Paul Hermann in 1939. DDT was used throughout World War II to control malaria; as a result, Hermann won a Nobel Prize in Medicine in 1947. After World War II, commercial and agricultural use of DDT was widespread in the United States. "During the 30 years prior to its cancellation, a total of approximately 1,350,000,000 pounds [approximately 675,000 tons] of DDT was used domestically." The high point for use of DDT was in 1959, when forty thousand tons were used. By the early 1970s the figure had dropped dramatically, to six thousand tons, most of which was used in agriculture, especially in cotton-growing areas. "The decline in DDT usage was the result of (1) increased insect resistance; (2) the development of more effective alternative pesticides; (3) growing public concern over the adverse environmental side effects; and (4) increasing government restrictions on DDT use."[1] Rachel Carson's book had made an impact.

Silent Spring begins with a story about the lack of birdsong in the countryside in the spring. The dawn chorus of birds had been silenced because DDT had made it difficult for birds' eggs to be viable. Major concentrates of chlorinated hydrocarbons do not necessarily kill birds, but they do affect the bird's calcium metabolism, making their eggshells much thinner. These thin eggshells break easily.

From this, Carson went on to describe and question the logic of releasing large amounts of synthetic chemicals, especially organochlorines such as DDT, into the natural world. As she argued, the chemicals not only kill insects that humans call pests, but as they make their way up the food chain they threaten bird and

---

[1] Environmental Protection Agency, "DDT Regulatory History: A Brief Survey (to 1975)" (July 1975), an excerpt from "DDT, A Review of Scientific and Economic Aspects of the Decision to Ban Its Use as a Pesticide," prepared for the Committee on Appropriations of the US House of Representatives by EPA, July 1975, EPA-540/1–75/022.

fish populations, and ultimately human beings. The book claimed that DDT and other pesticides had been shown to cause cancer. She pointed out that once these pesticides enter the biosphere, they are carried by the food chain right around the world and affect bird and fish populations in places such as the Arctic, where such pesticides were never used.

Much of the data and case studies used by Carson in *Silent Spring* were already known to the scientific community. What Carson did was to make the scientific data understandable to ordinary citizens and to use it to draw stark and far-reaching conclusions. By doing this, she spawned a revolution and encouraged others to attempt similar feats in other scientific disciplines, such as nuclear power. She popularized modern ecology and opened up the discourse of environmental issues to non-scientists who were passionate about protecting the natural world. Though not an overtly religious person, Carson did add a moral argument to the arsenal of scientific reasons to be very careful with this chemical. She argued that humans did not have the right to poison other creatures by the belief that nature's purpose is simply to serve human beings.

There were many challenges to *Silent Spring.* Velsicol, a manufacturer of DDT, threatened to sue the publisher, Houghton Mifflin, as well as the *New Yorker,* which serialized the book in the summer of 1962. Other attacks were more vitriolic. Carson was accused of being a sympathizer with communism because she was attempting to torpedo American agriculture. Some claimed that she wanted to reduce the capability of the non-communist world to feed itself. Carson was well aware that in writing what she herself called the "poison" book, she would be challenging some of the largest and most politically powerful corporations, particularly in the chemical industry. Yet, while her detractors created a storm, Carson did have powerful allies, among them President John F. Kennedy, who established a presidential committee to investigate pesticides.

Silent Spring was a great success. The book sold more than two million copies. It made a powerful case for the idea that, if we poison nature, nature will, in turn, poison us. Studies have shown that breast cancer and other cancers, male infertility, and diseases of the nervous system have been associated with DDT. Carson emphasized this point when she testified on June 4, 1964, before a US Senate subcommittee on pesticides. She told the senators, "Our heedless and destructive acts enter into the vast cycles of the earth and in time return to bring hazard to ourselves."[2] None of the senators was aware at the time that although she was only fifty-six years old, Carson was dying of cancer. She had already had a radical mastectomy. The cancer had spread to her pelvis, which was fractured in so many places that she could barely sit down. She wore a wig to hide the baldness caused by chemotherapy.

During the 1970s and 1980s, DDT was banned in most developed countries. In the United States the ban came into effect in 1972. The United Kingdom, however, continued to use DDT as an insecticide until 1984. The Stockholm Convention banned DDT worldwide in 2001, though it is still used in places. Many believe that the worldwide ban has contributed to the comeback in the numbers of eagles and peregrine falcons in recent years.

Even though the environmental movement has grown in the past sixty years, no other work has had the impact of *Silent Spring*. This has not been for lack of effort. In the United States, in 1989, Bill McKibben made a compelling case for addressing climate change in *The End of Nature*. In 2006 Elizabeth Kolbert wrote *Field Notes from a Catastrophe* about the impact of climate change on communities around the world. She also spoke with many scientists about their research and challenged transnational corporations such as Exxon Mobil and General Motors about attempting to influence politicians and discredit scientists. Former Vice President Al Gore sounded an alarm in 2006 with a documentary film on climate change entitled *An Inconvenient Truth*. Despite all of this widely disseminated information, huge numbers of people in the United States do not "believe" in climate change, and the issue barely surfaced in the 2012 presidential election.

Rachel Carson would agree with many of Pope Francis's comments in *Laudato Si'*, as when he writes that "nuclear energy, biotechnology, information technology, knowledge of our DNA,

---

[2] Quoted in Eliza Griswold, "How 'Silent Spring' Ignited the Environmental Movement," *New York Times*, September 21, 2012.

and many other abilities which we have acquired, have given . . .
those with the knowledge, and especially the economic resources
to use them, an impressive dominance over the whole of humanity and the entire world" (no. 104). The chemical companies of
Carson's era had that power, but they did not have the wisdom to
know when not to use it because "contemporary man has not been
trained to use power well" (no. 105, quoting Romano Guardini).
She would have subscribed to the belief that every advance in
technology is not necessarily, as Romano Guardini writes, "an
increase in progress itself" (no. 105). Carson viewed the world as
flexible and dynamic and knew that "merely technical solutions
run the risk of addressing symptoms and not the more serious
underlying problems" (no. 144).

Joe Farman: An Ominous Discovery

Though I never met Joe Farman, who died in May 2013, he is
one of my heroes. In 1956, after completing studies at Corpus
Christi College, Cambridge, he joined the Falkland Island Dependency Survey, later renamed the British Antarctic Survey, as
a geophysicist.

For decades humans had been releasing tons of dangerous
chemical compounds into the atmosphere. Unknown to most
people, some of these chemicals were causing drastic changes
to the earth's atmosphere, especially the ozone layer. In the up-
per atmosphere the ozone layer plays a vital role in blocking the
ultraviolet rays of the sun, which can cause skin cancer and other
health problems in humans and other creatures.

In the 1970s two American scientists, Mario Molina and F. Sherwood Rowlands, discovered that chlorofluorocarbons (CFCs) found
in propellants in everyday products such as hairsprays, household
refrigerators, and solvents were contributing to the destruction of
the ozone layer. The chemical companies that manufactured CFCs
were very powerful politically and were unwilling to concede that
their products might be doing such enormous damage. In response
to the research of the above scientists, the NASA Space Center in
the United States began to collect data on the ozone layer.

With the arrival of Margaret Thatcher as prime minister in England in 1979, there were major cuts across the public services. Yet Mrs. Thatcher, a chemist herself, supported Farman's work and protected the Antarctic Survey budget. Nevertheless, as the data had hardly changed during the twenty-five years Farman had been collecting it, even some of his superiors urged him to give it up. They also felt that the NASA data from satellites would be much more accurate than land-based data. All the same, Farman continued taking his ground-level readings.

In the beginning of the 1980s things began to change dramatically. The data that Farman and his colleagues collected with his twenty-five-year-old Dobson spectrophotometer[3] was so unusual that he thought the machine was faulty. Farman ordered new machines. He repeated his study over a number of years with the new equipment and found that the results were even more startling. In May 1984, Farman and two colleagues, Jonathan Shanklin and Brian Gardiner, published their results in the prestigious journal *Nature.* Based on the data they had collected, they claimed that ozone levels over the Antarctic had fallen by 40 percent from 1975 to 1984.

The article came as a shock to the scientific community. After all, the much better resourced and technologically superior NASA program had not picked up the data or sounded the alarm. What transpired was bizarre. NASA was forced to admit that while its satellites had picked up the data, its computers did not highlight the depletion of the ozone layer because they were programmed to disregard data that seemed infeasible. When the data was rechecked, the satellites picked up a hole in the ozone layer over the Antarctic as large as the United States. The importance of Farman's findings was underscored by a study undertaken by the United States Environmental Protection Agency (EPA) in 1986. "A draft assessment by the Environmental Protection Agency projects Americans could suffer 40 million cases of skin cancer and

---

[3] A spectrophotometer measures the amount of light absorbed by a sample material. Farman was using the instrument to measure the amount of ultraviolet radiation penetrating the atmosphere.

800,000 cancer deaths in the next 88 years because of depletion of atmospheric ozone." Those rates would be double the ones at the time of the study in 1986.[4]

Sharon Roan, author of the 1989 book *Ozone Crises: The Fifteen Year Evolution of a Sudden Global Emergency,* writes that Farman's willingness to do basic research even when others were not convinced of its value "made him a model scientist. He wasn't looking for anything astonishing—just doing a little job, and persevering at it. And he came up with the most astonishing discovery."[5] As a direct result of Farman's work, a treaty called the Montreal Protocol, designed to phase out ozone-depleting compounds, was signed by twenty-four countries in 1987. It has now been ratified by two hundred countries.

In 2003, Kofi Annan, then Secretary-General at the United Nations, called the Montreal Protocol "perhaps the single most successful international agreement to date."[6] The depletion of ozone leveled off in the early 2000s. Nevertheless, it could take between eighty and one hundred years to repair the damage already done.

All humans and other creatures living now and all future creatures owe Joe Farman a huge debt of gratitude. When people ask what one person can do in terms of preventing environmental damage, I point to the achievements of Joe Farman.

Dorothy Stang: A Martyr for the Earth

Sister Dorothy Stang was born on July 7, 1931, in Dayton, Ohio. She decided early in life to become a Sister of Notre Dame de Namur so that she could live and work with the poor. After teaching assignments in Chicago and Phoenix she was assigned in 1966 to mission work in Brazil, where she lived until her murder in 2005. Sister Dorothy's work with poor farmers in the Amazon

---

[4] "EPA Cites Skin Cancer Increase from Depletion of Earth's Ozone," *New York Times*, November 6, 1986.

[5] Quoted in Paul Vitello, "Joseph Farman, 82, Is Dead; Discovered the Ozone Hole," *New York Times,* May 18, 2013.

[6] United Nations, "International Day for the Preservation of the Ozone Layer, 16 September," no date, online.

region became joined with her passion for protecting the Amazon from the depredations of big loggers and ranchers. She was often seen wearing a tee-shirt with the slogan,"The death of the forest is the end of our life." Her work was appreciated by many people. She received the Woman of the Year award from the state of Para for her work in the Amazon region. The Brazilian Bar Association recognized her as the Humanitarian of the Year for her work with local rural workers.

But many people, especially those involved in illegal logging and ranching, did not approve of Sister Dorothy's work and tried to intimidate and threaten her at various times. Some police who had been bought off by ranchers also made her life difficult. "On one occasion the police arrested her for passing out 'subversive' material. It was the United Nations' Universal Declaration of Human Rights."[7]

On the morning of February 12, 2005, Sister Dorothy was on her way to address a meeting on human rights for those working in the Amazon region. A farmer who was also on his way to that meeting saw what happened. Sister Dorothy was stopped by two men, Clodoaldo Carlos Tatista and Raifran das Neves Sales. They asked her whether she was carrying any weapons. She replied that her only weapon was the Bible. She opened it and began to read from the Beatitudes, "Blessed are the poor in spirit . . . " until Raifran fired a round into her abdomen. As she fell to the ground, Raifran continued to shoot her both in the back and in the head.

In June 2005 the two gunmen were charged with conspiracy to murder Sister Dorothy. They were convicted on December 10, 2005. A series of further trials followed, resulting in 2010 in the conviction of a rancher, Vitalmiro Bastos de Moura, who was sentenced to thirty years for hiring the gunmen to kill Sister Dorothy. He was released after three years.

Since her death, books and documentaries have helped circulate the story of Sister Dorothy. Along with rubber-tapper Chico Mendes, who was killed in 1988, she represents a new kind of

---

[7] John Dear, SJ, "Sister Dorothy Stang: Martyr of the Amazon," *National Catholic Reporter*, October 2, 2007.

martyr for our times: a witness for ecological sustainability willing to die for the poor and for the well-being of our planet.

The publication of *Laudato Si'* in June 2015 presented another opportunity to celebrate her life and work. Sister Dorothy's ministry is a clear reminder of what the mission of the church ought to be. In line with the gospel and ministry of Jesus, his followers are called to stand with those who are on the margins of society and to support the poor, oppressed, and endangered earth even when such a course of action might have dire consequences. Like Jesus, Dorothy gave her life for "the life of the world."

Thomas Berry: The New Story

The writings of Thomas Berry, CP, from the 1970s onward, provide a comprehensive intellectual framework both for understanding our relationship to the universe and for critiquing human activity as it affects the wider earth community. On the positive side he helped us appreciate that we and everything else on planet earth are made of stardust. At the same time he was aware that "the encompassing technocratic, manipulative world that we have established" has taken a horrendous toll on other species, driving many of them to extinction.[8]

Thomas Berry was born in Greensboro, North Carolina, in 1914. He was called William after his father, William Nathan Berry. It was when he joined the Passionist Order in 1933 that he took the religious name Thomas, after Aquinas, which he retained throughout his life.

After ordination in 1942 Berry studied at the Catholic University of America, where he was awarded a doctorate in history. In 1948 he was sent as a missionary to China. There he immersed himself in the study of the Chinese language and culture and took a particular interest in the insights of Confucian thinkers. His stay in China was cut short by the Communist victory under Mao Zedong in 1949.

---

[8] Thomas Berry, *The Dream of the Earth* (San Francisco; Sierra Club Books, 1988), 8–9.

He expanded his knowledge of Asia by learning Sanskrit, which opened up for him the religious world of India. Later he developed an interest in the religion of the First Nations people, especially their teachings on shamanism. He also studied the writings of Jesuit paleontologist Pierre Teilhard de Chardin (and served as president of the American Teilhard Association from 1975 to 1987). In the 1960s Berry established the History of Religions program at Fordham, the Jesuit University in New York. He also created the Riverdale Center for Religious Research.

After the publication of Rachel Carson's *Silent Spring,* Berry turned his attention to the massive ecological destruction that was occurring in many parts of the world. Until very recently this went unnoticed amid the human fascination with ever-more sophisticated and powerful technologies.

Berry believed that religion might play an important role in helping us move away from technologies that were destroying the earth and instead lead us to embrace an ecological age in which humans might live in a mutually enhancing relationship with the rest of creation. He often called himself a *geologian*, meaning that our appreciation of the earth must be comprehensive and develop from the rocks upward to life forms.

In both *The Dream of the Earth* and *The Universe Story* he describes what he calls the "New Story." This sets out to capture the proper place of humans within the larger evolutionary story of the emergence of our universe, our planet, and all life on earth. Berry argued that this story, drawing on a variety of sciences and our best religious reflections, must now become the touchstone of reality and value for a new ecological age—the era humanity must enter if we are to live in a mutually enhancing way with the rest of creation.

Thomas Berry would applaud Pope Francis's understanding of the damage powerful technologies have wreaked on planet earth. Like Pope Francis and Patriarch Bartholomew he would consider these sins (no. 8). He would share Pope Francis's concern about the "pollution that affects everyone, caused by transport, industrial fumes, substances which contribute to the acidification of soil and water, fertilisers, insecticides, fungicides, herbicides and agrotoxins in general" (no. 20). In the next paragraph Pope Francis points out that "each year hundreds of millions of tons of waste are generated, most of it non-biodegradable, highly toxic and radioactive, from homes and business, from construction and demolition sites, from clinical, electronic and industrial sources" (no. 21). Unlike any of his predecessors, Pope Francis has grasped the magnitude of the ecological damage that is now taking place; he states that "the earth, our home is beginning to look more and more like an immense pile of filth" (no. 21).

Thomas Berry would have been thrilled to hear a pope declare that other species have intrinsic value independent of their usefulness to humans (no. 140). The pope writes that "in our time, the Church does not simply state that other creatures are completely subordinated to the good of human beings, as if they have no worth in themselves and can be treated as we wish. The German bishops have taught that, where other creatures are concerned, we can speak of the priority of being over that of *being useful.* The Catechism clearly and forcefully criticises a distorted anthropocentrism: 'Each creature in its own particular goodness and perfection. . . . Each of the various creatures, willed in its own being, reflects in its own way a ray of God's infinite wisdom and goodness. Man must therefore respect the particular goodness of every creature, to avoid the disordered use of things.'" (no. 69). And Pope Francis writes that "every creature is thus the object of the Father's tenderness who gives it its place in the world. Even the fleeting life of the least of beings is the object of his love, and in its few seconds of existence, God enfolds it with his affections" (no. 77). An oft-repeated statement of Thomas Berry, that "the world is not a collection of objects but a communion of subjects," is celebrated and honored in these texts.

Thomas Berry would welcome Pope Francis's critique of modern intrusive and destructive technology in chapter 3 of *Laudato Si'.* This section is called "The Human Roots of the Ecological Crisis." The pope believes that "we have the freedom to limit and direct technology; we can put it at the service of another type of progress, one which is healthier, more human, more social and more integral" (no. 112). Berry would see this chapter as an attempt by the pope to shake us out of the "technological trance" into which we have fallen during the past century. The pope writes that "contemporary man has not been trained to use power well" (no. 105).

The pope calls us to respect the "structures of nature" in reframing our understanding of how humans should live in relation to other creatures (no. 116). Here we are back again to the search for our true place in the universe. Throughout the encyclical Pope Francis emphasizes the connectedness of all reality:

> Time and space are not independent of one another, and not even atoms or subatomic particles can be considered in isolation. Just as the different aspects of the planet – physical, chemical, and biological – are interrelated, so too living species are part of a network which we will never fully explore and understand. A good part of our genetic code is shared by many living beings. It follows that the fragmentation of knowledge and the isolation of bits of information can actually become a form of ignorance, unless they are integrated into a boarder vision of reality. (no. 138)

This is where Berry sees the value and power of this New Story, which began with the mysterious fireball 13.8 billion years ago. It tells us how the elements were forged in the galactic cauldron of the first generation of stars as they collapsed in supernova explosions. These new elements seeded our solar system and gave rise to the sun, the planets, and our own planet earth. The story goes on to tell how, over hundreds of millions of years, our earth was formed in its physical dimensions. Finally, it tells how life arrived on earth in the oceans, first as a tentative flicker, and later in great profusion and diversity, culminating in the emergence of a creature with reflective self-consciousness. It tells us that everything in the universe is linked, and that we are literally cousins with every creature on the planet. The earth is here primarily to give glory to God and not to be a quarry for humans to exploit. Tracing that journey to where we are now is an exciting and extraordinary voyage that both connects us with all reality and gives us the possibility of designing a way of living which will be less predatory and destructive.

The New Story also helps human beings to grasp and understand the significance of cosmic and geological time and the fact that our universe is an emergent one. In 1654 James Ussher, the Church of Ireland archbishop of Armagh, used his extensive knowledge of Semitic texts and mathematics to calculate that the earth was created on October 23, 4004 BCE.

Modern science, however, tells us that our universe is 13.8 billion years old. If we were to condense that time into a single year, the fireball would have happened on January 1. The supernovas, which created the heavy elements, took place on May 1. The earth was formed on August 1, and single-celled life began on September 15. Multi-celled life emerged on December 13.Vertebrates left the sea and came ashore on December 20.The dinosaurs flourished on December 29 and 30. On December 31 mammals arrived at 4 pm. At 11 pm primates evolved. Homo sapiens burst forth at 11:58 pm. Human cultures flourished at 11:59:40, and the technological age developed at 11:59:59.6. This is an extraordinary chronicle.

In Pope Francis's world Thomas Berry did make a difference, and his thought still guides and inspires people in the United States and elsewhere who are trying to make this move to a more ecologically sensitive age.

In 1980 I had the great privilege of spending four months living and studying with Thomas Berry at the Riverdale Center for Religious Research in New York. The clarity of his insights, especially in critiquing the "technological trance" that has gripped the Western and now the global culture helped me make sense of the ecological disaster I was witnessing in the Philippines, particularly with the destruction of so much of the tropical forests. Berry is very clear that the task of humankind is to design a way of living in a sustainable way with the rest of the natural world.

In the early 1980s I brought Thomas Berry to the Philippines on two occasions. At that time there was often a rift between religious people who were involved in working for a more just and peaceful society during the dictatorship of Ferdinand Marcos and those who were concerned with the massive destruction of the environment that was occurring at the time. Those who focused on liberation theology often felt that environmental issues were being championed by people from the North (the First World) who did not understand the pain, suffering, and grinding poverty of many people in the South (the Third World). Thomas Berry understood this tension and in his talks and seminars in various cities throughout the Philippines he helped to bridge this gap, just as Pope Francis's *Laudato Si'* has done more recently. Finally, Thomas Berry was a man of enormous erudition, which he wore very lightly—always willing to share his time, knowledge, and books with people he met. I, and many others, owe him a huge debt of gratitude.

The lives of these four people, Carson, Farman, Stang, and Berry, challenge us to do what we can to eradicate poverty and to protect our planet.

I began these reflections by stating that *Laudato Si'* was one of the most important documents to come from Rome since the beginning of modern Catholic social teaching at the end of the nineteenth century.

Pope Francis's mission in writing the encyclical was to ensure that every human being can live in dignity and peace, with his or her basic needs met while, at the same time, protecting planet earth. If Pope Francis's encyclical encourages and helps sustain this process, the outcome will be a great victory for humans, for other creatures, and for the planet itself. If, however, the invitation to be part of this new world fails and humans continue with the exploitative behavior that they have shown in recent years, it will be tragic for humans, for other creatures, and for the planet. The stakes are very high. In fact, they could not be higher!

PART II

LAUDATO SI'

POPE FRANCIS

ENCYCLICAL LETTER
LAUDATO SI'
OF THE HOLY FATHER
FRANCIS
ON CARE FOR OUR COMMON HOME

1. *"LAUDATO SI', mi' Signore"—"Praise be to you, my Lord"*. In the words of this beautiful canticle, Saint Francis of Assisi reminds us that our common home is like a sister with whom we share our life and a beautiful mother who opens her arms to embrace us. "Praise be to you, my Lord, through our Sister, Mother Earth, who sustains and governs us, and who produces various fruit with coloured flowers and herbs".[1]

2. This sister now cries out to us because of the harm we have inflicted on her by our irresponsible use and abuse of the goods with which God has endowed her. We have come to see ourselves as her lords and masters, entitled to plunder her at will. The violence present in our hearts, wounded by sin, is also reflected in the symptoms of sickness evident in the soil, in the water, in the air and in all forms of life. This is why the earth herself, burdened and laid waste, is among the most abandoned and maltreated of our poor; she "groans in travail" (*Rom* 8:22). We have forgotten that

---

[1] Canticle of the Creatures, in *Francis of Assisi: Early Documents*, vol. 1, New York-London-Manila, 1999, 113-114.

we ourselves are dust of the earth (cf. *Gen* 2:7); our very bodies are made up of her elements, we breathe her air and we receive life and refreshment from her waters.

Nothing in this world is indifferent to us

3. More than fifty years ago, with the world teetering on the brink of nuclear crisis, Pope Saint John XXIII wrote an Encyclical which not only rejected war but offered a proposal for peace. He addressed his message *Pacem in Terris* to the entire "Catholic world" and indeed "to all men and women of good will". Now, faced as we are with global environmental deterioration, I wish to address every person living on this planet. In my Apostolic Exhortation *Evangelii Gaudium*, I wrote to all the members of the Church with the aim of encouraging ongoing missionary renewal. In this Encyclical, I would like to enter into dialogue with all people about our common home.

4. In 1971, eight years after *Pacem in Terris*, Blessed Pope Paul VI referred to the ecological concern as "a tragic consequence" of unchecked human activity: "Due to an ill-considered exploitation of nature, humanity runs the risk of destroying it and becoming in turn a victim of this degradation."[2] He spoke in similar terms to the Food and Agriculture Organization of the United Nations about the potential for an "ecological catastrophe under the effective explosion of industrial civilization", and stressed "the urgent need for a radical change in the conduct of humanity", inasmuch as "the most extraordinary scientific advances, the most amazing technical abilities, the most astonishing economic growth, unless they are accompanied by authentic social and moral progress, will definitively turn against man".[3]

---

[2] Apostolic Letter *Octogesima Adveniens* (14 May 1971), 21: AAS 63 (1971), 416-417.

[3] Address to FAO on the 25th Anniversary of its Institution (16 November 1970), 4: AAS 62 (1970), 833.

5. Saint John Paul II became increasingly concerned about this issue. In his first Encyclical he warned that human beings frequently seem "to see no other meaning in their natural environment than what serves for immediate use and consumption".[4] Subsequently, he would call for a global ecological *conversion*.[5] At the same time, he noted that little effort had been made to "safeguard the moral conditions for an authentic *human ecology*".[6] The destruction of the human environment is extremely serious, not only because God has entrusted the world to us men and women, but because human life is itself a gift which must be defended from various forms of debasement. Every effort to protect and improve our world entails profound changes in "lifestyles, models of production and consumption, and the established structures of power which today govern societies".[7] Authentic human development has a moral character. It presumes full respect for the human person, but it must also be concerned for the world around us and "take into account the nature of each being and of its mutual connection in an ordered system".[8] Accordingly, our human ability to transform reality must proceed in line with God's original gift of all that is.[9]

6. My predecessor Benedict XVI likewise proposed "eliminating the structural causes of the dysfunctions of the world economy and correcting models of growth which have proved incapable of ensuring respect for the environment".[10] He observed that the

---

[4] Encyclical Letter *Redemptor Hominis* (4 March 1979), 15: AAS 71 (1979), 287.

[5] Cf. *Catechesis* (17 January 2001), 4: *Insegnamenti* 41/1 (2001), 179.

[6] Encyclical Letter *Centesimus Annus* (1 May 1991), 38: AAS 83 (1991), 841.

[7] Ibid., 58: AAS 83 (1991), p. 863.

[8] JOHN PAUL II, Encyclical Letter *Sollicitudo Rei Socialis* (30 December 1987), 34: AAS 80 (1988), 559.

[9] Cf. ID., Encyclical Letter *Centesimus Annus* (1 May 1991), 37: AAS 83 (1991), 840.

[10] *Address to the Diplomatic Corps Accredited to the Holy See* (8 January 2007): AAS 99 (2007), 73.

world cannot be analyzed by isolating only one of its aspects, since "the book of nature is one and indivisible", and includes the environment, life, sexuality, the family, social relations, and so forth. It follows that "the deterioration of nature is closely connected to the culture which shapes human coexistence".[11] Pope Benedict asked us to recognize that the natural environment has been gravely damaged by our irresponsible behaviour. The social environment has also suffered damage. Both are ultimately due to the same evil: the notion that there are no indisputable truths to guide our lives, and hence human freedom is limitless. We have forgotten that "man is not only a freedom which he creates for himself. Man does not create himself. He is spirit and will, but also nature".[12] With paternal concern, Benedict urged us to realize that creation is harmed "where we ourselves have the final word, where everything is simply our property and we use it for ourselves alone. The misuse of creation begins when we no longer recognize any higher instance than ourselves, when we see nothing else but ourselves".[13]

United by the same concern

7. These statements of the Popes echo the reflections of numerous scientists, philosophers, theologians and civic groups, all of which have enriched the Church's thinking on these questions. Outside the Catholic Church, other Churches and Christian communities—and other religions as well—have expressed deep concern and offered valuable reflections on issues which all of us find disturbing. To give just one striking example, I would mention the statements made by the beloved Ecumenical Patriarch Bartholomew, with whom we share the hope of full ecclesial communion.

---

[11] Encyclical Letter *Caritas in Veritate* (29 June 2009), 51: AAS 101 (2009), 687.

[12] *Address to the Bundestag*, Berlin (22 September 2011): AAS 103 (2011), 664.

[13] Address to the Clergy of the Diocese of Bolzano-Bressanone (6 August 2008): AAS 100 (2008), 634.

8. Patriarch Bartholomew has spoken in particular of the need for each of us to repent of the ways we have harmed the planet, for "inasmuch as we all generate small ecological damage", we are called to acknowledge "our contribution, smaller or greater, to the disfigurement and destruction of creation".[14] He has repeatedly stated this firmly and persuasively, challenging us to acknowledge our sins against creation: "For human beings . . . to destroy the biological diversity of God's creation; for human beings to degrade the integrity of the earth by causing changes in its climate, by stripping the earth of its natural forests or destroying its wetlands; for human beings to contaminate the earth's waters, its land, its air, and its life—these are sins".[15] For "to commit a crime against the natural world is a sin against ourselves and a sin against God".[16]

9. At the same time, Bartholomew has drawn attention to the ethical and spiritual roots of environmental problems, which require that we look for solutions not only in technology but in a change of humanity; otherwise we would be dealing merely with symptoms. He asks us to replace consumption with sacrifice, greed with generosity, wastefulness with a spirit of sharing, an asceticism which "entails learning to give, and not simply to give up. It is a way of loving, of moving gradually away from what I want to what God's world needs. It is liberation from fear, greed and compulsion".[17] As Christians, we are also called "to accept the world as a sacrament of communion, as a way of sharing with God and our neighbours on a global scale. It is our humble conviction that the divine and

---

[14] *Message for the Day of Prayer for the Protection of Creation* (1 September 2012).

[15] *Address in Santa Barbara, California* (8 November 1997); cf. JOHN CHRYSSAVGIS, *On Earth as in Heaven: Ecological Vision and Initiatives of Ecumenical Patriarch Bartholomew*, Bronx, New York, 2012.

[16] Ibid.

[17] *Lecture at the Monastery of Utstein, Norway* (23 June 2003).

the human meet in the slightest detail in the seamless garment of God's creation, in the last speck of dust of our planet".[18]

Saint Francis of Assisi

10. I do not want to write this Encyclical without turning to that attractive and compelling figure, whose name I took as my guide and inspiration when I was elected Bishop of Rome. I believe that Saint Francis is the example par excellence of care for the vulnerable and of an integral ecology lived out joyfully and authentically. He is the patron saint of all who study and work in the area of ecology, and he is also much loved by non-Christians. He was particularly concerned for God's creation and for the poor and outcast. He loved, and was deeply loved for his joy, his generous self-giving, his openheartedness. He was a mystic and a pilgrim who lived in simplicity and in wonderful harmony with God, with others, with nature and with himself. He shows us just how inseparable the bond is between concern for nature, justice for the poor, commitment to society, and interior peace.

11. Francis helps us to see that an integral ecology calls for openness to categories which transcend the language of mathematics and biology, and take us to the heart of what it is to be human. Just as happens when we fall in love with someone, whenever he would gaze at the sun, the moon or the smallest of animals, he burst into song, drawing all other creatures into his praise. He communed with all creation, even preaching to the flowers, inviting them "to praise the Lord, just as if they were endowed with reason".[19] His response to the world around him was so much more than intellectual appreciation or economic calculus, for to him each and every creature was a sister united to him by bonds

---

[18] "Global Responsibility and Ecological Sustainability", Closing Remarks, Halki Summit I, Istanbul (20 June 2012).

[19] THOMAS OF CELANO, *The Life of Saint Francis*, I, 29, 81: in *Francis of Assisi: Early Documents*, vol. 1, New York-London-Manila, 1999, 251.

of affection. That is why he felt called to care for all that exists. His disciple Saint Bonaventure tells us that, "from a reflection on the primary source of all things, filled with even more abundant piety, he would call creatures, no matter how small, by the name of 'brother' or 'sister'".[20] Such a conviction cannot be written off as naive romanticism, for it affects the choices which determine our behaviour. If we approach nature and the environment without this openness to awe and wonder, if we no longer speak the language of fraternity and beauty in our relationship with the world, our attitude will be that of masters, consumers, ruthless exploiters, unable to set limits on their immediate needs. By contrast, if we feel intimately united with all that exists, then sobriety and care will well up spontaneously. The poverty and austerity of Saint Francis were no mere veneer of asceticism, but something much more radical: a refusal to turn reality into an object simply to be used and controlled.

12. What is more, Saint Francis, faithful to Scripture, invites us to see nature as a magnificent book in which God speaks to us and grants us a glimpse of his infinite beauty and goodness. "Through the greatness and the beauty of creatures one comes to know by analogy their maker" (*Wis* 13:5); indeed, "his eternal power and divinity have been made known through his works since the creation of the world" (*Rom* 1:20). For this reason, Francis asked that part of the friary garden always be left untouched, so that wild flowers and herbs could grow there, and those who saw them could raise their minds to God, the Creator of such beauty.[21] Rather than a problem to be solved, the world is a joyful mystery to be contemplated with gladness and praise.

---

[20] *The Major Legend of Saint Francis*, VIII, 6, in *Francis of Assisi: Early Documents*, vol. 2, New York-London-Manila, 2000, 590.

[21] Cf. THOMAS OF CELANO, *The Remembrance of the Desire of a Soul*, II, 124, 165, in *Francis of Assisi: Early Documents*, vol. 2, New York-London-Manila, 2000, 354.

My appeal

13. The urgent challenge to protect our common home includes a concern to bring the whole human family together to seek a sustainable and integral development, for we know that things can change. The Creator does not abandon us; he never forsakes his loving plan or repents of having created us. Humanity still has the ability to work together in building our common home. Here I want to recognize, encourage and thank all those striving in countless ways to guarantee the protection of the home which we share. Particular appreciation is owed to those who tirelessly seek to resolve the tragic effects of environmental degradation on the lives of the world's poorest. Young people demand change. They wonder how anyone can claim to be building a better future without thinking of the environmental crisis and the sufferings of the excluded.

14. I urgently appeal, then, for a new dialogue about how we are shaping the future of our planet. We need a conversation which includes everyone, since the environmental challenge we are undergoing, and its human roots, concern and affect us all. The worldwide ecological movement has already made considerable progress and led to the establishment of numerous organizations committed to raising awareness of these challenges. Regrettably, many efforts to seek concrete solutions to the environmental crisis have proved ineffective, not only because of powerful opposition but also because of a more general lack of interest. Obstructionist attitudes, even on the part of believers, can range from denial of the problem to indifference, nonchalant resignation or blind confidence in technical solutions. We require a new and universal solidarity. As the bishops of Southern Africa have stated: "Everyone's talents and involvement are needed to redress the damage caused by human abuse of God's creation".[22] All of us can cooperate as

---

[22] SOUTHERN AFRICAN CATHOLIC BISHOPS' CONFERENCE, *Pastoral Statement on the Environmental Crisis* (5 September 1999).

instruments of God for the care of creation, each according to his or her own culture, experience, involvements and talents.

15. It is my hope that this Encyclical Letter, which is now added to the body of the Church's social teaching, can help us to acknowledge the appeal, immensity and urgency of the challenge we face. I will begin by briefly reviewing several aspects of the present ecological crisis, with the aim of drawing on the results of the best scientific research available today, letting them touch us deeply and provide a concrete foundation for the ethical and spiritual itinerary that follows. I will then consider some principles drawn from the Judaeo-Christian tradition which can render our commitment to the environment more coherent. I will then attempt to get to the roots of the present situation, so as to consider not only its symptoms but also its deepest causes. This will help to provide an approach to ecology which respects our unique place as human beings in this world and our relationship to our surroundings. In light of this reflection, I will advance some broader proposals for dialogue and action which would involve each of us as individuals, and also affect international policy. Finally, convinced as I am that change is impossible without motivation and a process of education, I will offer some inspired guidelines for human development to be found in the treasure of Christian spiritual experience.

16. Although each chapter will have its own subject and specific approach, it will also take up and re-examine important questions previously dealt with. This is particularly the case with a number of themes which will reappear as the Encyclical unfolds. As examples, I will point to the intimate relationship between the poor and the fragility of the planet, the conviction that everything in the world is connected, the critique of new paradigms and forms of power derived from technology, the call to seek other ways of understanding the economy and progress, the value proper to each creature, the human meaning of ecology, the need for forthright and honest debate, the serious responsibility of international and

local policy, the throwaway culture and the proposal of a new lifestyle. These questions will not be dealt with once and for all, but reframed and enriched again and again.

CHAPTER ONE

WHAT IS HAPPENING TO OUR COMMON HOME

17. Theological and philosophical reflections on the situation of humanity and the world can sound tiresome and abstract, unless they are grounded in a fresh analysis of our present situation, which is in many ways unprecedented in the history of humanity. So, before considering how faith brings new incentives and requirements with regard to the world of which we are a part, I will briefly turn to what is happening to our common home.

18. The continued acceleration of changes affecting humanity and the planet is coupled today with a more intensified pace of life and work which might be called "rapidification". Although change is part of the working of complex systems, the speed with which human activity has developed contrasts with the naturally slow pace of biological evolution. Moreover, the goals of this rapid and constant change are not necessarily geared to the common good or to integral and sustainable human development. Change is something desirable, yet it becomes a source of anxiety when it causes harm to the world and to the quality of life of much of humanity.

19. Following a period of irrational confidence in progress and human abilities, some sectors of society are now adopting a more critical approach. We see increasing sensitivity to the environment and the need to protect nature, along with a growing concern, both genuine and distressing, for what is happening to our planet. Let us review, however cursorily, those questions which are troubling us today and which we can no longer sweep under the carpet. Our goal is not to amass information or to satisfy curiosity, but rather to become painfully aware, to dare to turn what is happening to the

world into our own personal suffering and thus to discover what each of us can do about it.

I. POLLUTION AND CLIMATE CHANGE

Pollution, waste and the throwaway culture

20. Some forms of pollution are part of people's daily experience. Exposure to atmospheric pollutants produces a broad spectrum of health hazards, especially for the poor, and causes millions of premature deaths. People take sick, for example, from breathing high levels of smoke from fuels used in cooking or heating. There is also pollution that affects everyone, caused by transport, industrial fumes, substances which contribute to the acidification of soil and water, fertilizers, insecticides, fungicides, herbicides and agrotoxins in general. Technology, which, linked to business interests, is presented as the only way of solving these problems, in fact proves incapable of seeing the mysterious network of relations between things and so sometimes solves one problem only to create others.

21. Account must also be taken of the pollution produced by residue, including dangerous waste present in different areas. Each year hundreds of millions of tons of waste are generated, much of it non-biodegradable, highly toxic and radioactive, from homes and businesses, from construction and demolition sites, from clinical, electronic and industrial sources. The earth, our home, is beginning to look more and more like an immense pile of filth. In many parts of the planet, the elderly lament that once beautiful landscapes are now covered with rubbish. Industrial waste and chemical products utilized in cities and agricultural areas can lead to bioaccumulation in the organisms of the local population, even when levels of toxins in those places are low. Frequently no measures are taken until after people's health has been irreversibly affected.

22. These problems are closely linked to a throwaway culture which affects the excluded just as it quickly reduces things to rubbish. To

cite one example, most of the paper we produce is thrown away and not recycled. It is hard for us to accept that the way natural ecosystems work is exemplary: plants synthesize nutrients which feed herbivores; these in turn become food for carnivores, which produce significant quantities of organic waste which give rise to new generations of plants. But our industrial system, at the end of its cycle of production and consumption, has not developed the capacity to absorb and reuse waste and by-products. We have not yet managed to adopt a circular model of production capable of preserving resources for present and future generations, while limiting as much as possible the use of non-renewable resources, moderating their consumption, maximizing their efficient use, reusing and recycling them. A serious consideration of this issue would be one way of counteracting the throwaway culture which affects the entire planet, but it must be said that only limited progress has been made in this regard.

Climate as a common good

23. The climate is a common good, belonging to all and meant for all. At the global level, it is a complex system linked to many of the essential conditions for human life. A very solid scientific consensus indicates that we are presently witnessing a disturbing warming of the climatic system. In recent decades this warming has been accompanied by a constant rise in the sea level and, it would appear, by an increase of extreme weather events, even if a scientifically determinable cause cannot be assigned to each particular phenomenon. Humanity is called to recognize the need for changes of lifestyle, production and consumption, in order to combat this warming or at least the human causes which produce or aggravate it. It is true that there are other factors (such as volcanic activity, variations in the earth's orbit and axis, the solar cycle), yet a number of scientific studies indicate that most global warming in recent decades is due to the great concentration of greenhouse gases (carbon dioxide, methane, nitrogen oxides and others) released mainly as a result of human activity. Concentrated

in the atmosphere, these gases do not allow the warmth of the sun's rays reflected by the earth to be dispersed in space. The problem is aggravated by a model of development based on the intensive use of fossil fuels, which is at the heart of the world-wide energy system. Another determining factor has been an increase in changed uses of the soil, principally deforestation for agricultural purposes.

24. Warming has effects on the carbon cycle. It creates a vicious circle which aggravates the situation even more, affecting the availability of essential resources like drinking water, energy and agricultural production in warmer regions, and leading to the extinction of part of the planet's biodiversity. The melting in the polar ice caps and in high altitude plains can lead to the dangerous release of methane gas, while the decomposition of frozen organic material can further increase the emission of carbon dioxide. Things are made worse by the loss of tropical forests which would otherwise help to mitigate climate change. Carbon dioxide pollution increases the acidification of the oceans and compromises the marine food chain. If present trends continue, this century may well witness extraordinary climate change and an unprecedented destruction of ecosystems, with serious consequences for all of us. A rise in the sea level, for example, can create extremely serious situations, if we consider that a quarter of the world's population lives on the coast or nearby, and that the majority of our megacities are situated in coastal areas.

25. Climate change is a global problem with grave implications: environmental, social, economic, political and for the distribution of goods. It represents one of the principal challenges facing humanity in our day. Its worst impact will probably be felt by developing countries in coming decades. Many of the poor live in areas particularly affected by phenomena related to warming, and their means of subsistence are largely dependent on natural reserves and ecosystemic services such as agriculture, fishing and forestry. They have no other financial activities or resources which

can enable them to adapt to climate change or to face natural disasters, and their access to social services and protection is very limited. For example, changes in climate, to which animals and plants cannot adapt, lead them to migrate; this in turn affects the livelihood of the poor, who are then forced to leave their homes, with great uncertainty for their future and that of their children. There has been a tragic rise in the number of migrants seeking to flee from the growing poverty caused by environmental degradation. They are not recognized by international conventions as refugees; they bear the loss of the lives they have left behind, without enjoying any legal protection whatsoever. Sadly, there is widespread indifference to such suffering, which is even now taking place throughout our world. Our lack of response to these tragedies involving our brothers and sisters points to the loss of that sense of responsibility for our fellow men and women upon which all civil society is founded.

26. Many of those who possess more resources and economic or political power seem mostly to be concerned with masking the problems or concealing their symptoms, simply making efforts to reduce some of the negative impacts of climate change. However, many of these symptoms indicate that such effects will continue to worsen if we continue with current models of production and consumption. There is an urgent need to develop policies so that, in the next few years, the emission of carbon dioxide and other highly polluting gases can be drastically reduced, for example, substituting for fossil fuels and developing sources of renewable energy. Worldwide there is minimal access to clean and renewable energy. There is still a need to develop adequate storage technologies. Some countries have made considerable progress, although it is far from constituting a significant proportion. Investments have also been made in means of production and transportation which consume less energy and require fewer raw materials, as well as in methods of construction and renovating buildings which improve their energy efficiency. But these good practices are still far from widespread.

II. THE ISSUE OF WATER

27. Other indicators of the present situation have to do with the depletion of natural resources. We all know that it is not possible to sustain the present level of consumption in developed countries and wealthier sectors of society, where the habit of wasting and discarding has reached unprecedented levels. The exploitation of the planet has already exceeded acceptable limits and we still have not solved the problem of poverty.

28. Fresh drinking water is an issue of primary importance, since it is indispensable for human life and for supporting terrestrial and aquatic ecosystems. Sources of fresh water are necessary for health care, agriculture and industry. Water supplies used to be relatively constant, but now in many places demand exceeds the sustainable supply, with dramatic consequences in the short and long term. Large cities dependent on significant supplies of water have experienced periods of shortage, and at critical moments these have not always been administered with sufficient oversight and impartiality. Water poverty especially affects Africa where large sectors of the population have no access to safe drinking water or experience droughts which impede agricultural production. Some countries have areas rich in water while others endure drastic scarcity.

29. One particularly serious problem is the quality of water available to the poor. Every day, unsafe water results in many deaths and the spread of water-related diseases, including those caused by microorganisms and chemical substances. Dysentery and cholera, linked to inadequate hygiene and water supplies, are a significant cause of suffering and of infant mortality. Underground water sources in many places are threatened by the pollution produced in certain mining, farming and industrial activities, especially in countries lacking adequate regulation or controls. It is not only a question of industrial waste. Detergents and chemical products, commonly used in many places of the world, continue to pour into our rivers, lakes and seas.

30. Even as the quality of available water is constantly diminishing, in some places there is a growing tendency, despite its scarcity, to privatize this resource, turning it into a commodity subject to the laws of the market. Yet *access to safe drinkable water is a basic and universal human right, since it is essential to human survival and, as such, is a condition for the exercise of other human rights.* Our world has a grave social debt towards the poor who lack access to drinking water, because *they are denied the right to a life consistent with their inalienable dignity.* This debt can be paid partly by an increase in funding to provide clean water and sanitary services among the poor. But water continues to be wasted, not only in the developed world but also in developing countries which possess it in abundance. This shows that the problem of water is partly an educational and cultural issue, since there is little awareness of the seriousness of such behaviour within a context of great inequality.

31. Greater scarcity of water will lead to an increase in the cost of food and the various products which depend on its use. Some studies warn that an acute water shortage may occur within a few decades unless urgent action is taken. The environmental repercussions could affect billions of people; it is also conceivable that the control of water by large multinational businesses may become a major source of conflict in this century.[23]

III. LOSS OF BIODIVERSITY

32. The earth's resources are also being plundered because of short-sighted approaches to the economy, commerce and production. The loss of forests and woodlands entails the loss of species which may constitute extremely important resources in the future, not only for food but also for curing disease and other uses. Different species contain genes which could be key resources in years

---

[23] Cf. *Greeting to the Staff of FAO* (20 November 2014): AAS 106 (2014), 985.

ahead for meeting human needs and regulating environmental problems.

33. It is not enough, however, to think of different species merely as potential "resources" to be exploited, while overlooking the fact that they have value in themselves. Each year sees the disappearance of thousands of plant and animal species which we will never know, which our children will never see, because they have been lost for ever. The great majority become extinct for reasons related to human activity. Because of us, thousands of species will no longer give glory to God by their very existence, nor convey their message to us. We have no such right.

34. It may well disturb us to learn of the extinction of mammals or birds, since they are more visible. But the good functioning of ecosystems also requires fungi, algae, worms, insects, reptiles and an innumerable variety of microorganisms. Some less numerous species, although generally unseen, nonetheless play a critical role in maintaining the equilibrium of a particular place. Human beings must intervene when a geosystem reaches a critical state. But nowadays, such intervention in nature has become more and more frequent. As a consequence, serious problems arise, leading to further interventions; human activity becomes ubiquitous, with all the risks which this entails. Often a vicious circle results, as human intervention to resolve a problem further aggravates the situation. For example, many birds and insects which disappear due to synthetic agrotoxins are helpful for agriculture: their disappearance will have to be compensated for by yet other techniques which may well prove harmful. We must be grateful for the praiseworthy efforts being made by scientists and engineers dedicated to finding solutions to man-made problems. But a sober look at our world shows that the degree of human intervention, often in the service of business interests and consumerism, is actually making our earth less rich and beautiful, ever more limited and grey, even as technological advances and consumer goods continue to abound limitlessly. We seem to think that we can substitute an

irreplaceable and irretrievable beauty with something which we have created ourselves.

35. In assessing the environmental impact of any project, concern is usually shown for its effects on soil, water and air, yet few careful studies are made of its impact on biodiversity, as if the loss of species or animals and plant groups were of little importance. Highways, new plantations, the fencing-off of certain areas, the damming of water sources, and similar developments, crowd out natural habitats and, at times, break them up in such a way that animal populations can no longer migrate or roam freely. As a result, some species face extinction. Alternatives exist which at least lessen the impact of these projects, like the creation of biological corridors, but few countries demonstrate such concern and foresight. Frequently, when certain species are exploited commercially, little attention is paid to studying their reproductive patterns in order to prevent their depletion and the consequent imbalance of the ecosystem.

36. Caring for ecosystems demands far-sightedness, since no one looking for quick and easy profit is truly interested in their preservation. But the cost of the damage caused by such selfish lack of concern is much greater than the economic benefits to be obtained. Where certain species are destroyed or seriously harmed, the values involved are incalculable. We can be silent witnesses to terrible injustices if we think that we can obtain significant benefits by making the rest of humanity, present and future, pay the extremely high costs of environmental deterioration.

37. Some countries have made significant progress in establishing sanctuaries on land and in the oceans where any human intervention is prohibited which might modify their features or alter their original structures. In the protection of biodiversity, specialists insist on the need for particular attention to be shown to areas richer both in the number of species and in endemic, rare or less protected species. Certain places need greater protection because of their immense importance for the global ecosystem, or because

they represent important water reserves and thus safeguard other forms of life.

38. Let us mention, for example, those richly biodiverse lungs of our planet which are the Amazon and the Congo basins, or the great aquifers and glaciers. We know how important these are for the entire earth and for the future of humanity. The ecosystems of tropical forests possess an enormously complex biodiversity which is almost impossible to appreciate fully, yet when these forests are burned down or levelled for purposes of cultivation, within the space of a few years countless species are lost and the areas frequently become arid wastelands. A delicate balance has to be maintained when speaking about these places, for we cannot overlook the huge global economic interests which, under the guise of protecting them, can undermine the sovereignty of individual nations. In fact, there are "proposals to internationalize the Amazon, which only serve the economic interests of transnational corporations".[24] We cannot fail to praise the commitment of international agencies and civil society organizations which draw public attention to these issues and offer critical cooperation, employing legitimate means of pressure, to ensure that each government carries out its proper and inalienable responsibility to preserve its country's environment and natural resources, without capitulating to spurious local or international interests.

39. The replacement of virgin forest with plantations of trees, usually monocultures, is rarely adequately analyzed. Yet this can seriously compromise a biodiversity which the new species being introduced does not accommodate. Similarly, wetlands converted into cultivated land lose the enormous biodiversity which they formerly hosted. In some coastal areas the disappearance of ecosystems sustained by mangrove swamps is a source of serious concern.

---

[24] FIFTH GENERAL CONFERENCE OF THE LATIN AMERICAN AND CARIBBEAN BISHOPS, *Aparecida Document* (29 June 2007), 86.

40. Oceans not only contain the bulk of our planet's water supply, but also most of the immense variety of living creatures, many of them still unknown to us and threatened for various reasons. What is more, marine life in rivers, lakes, seas and oceans, which feeds a great part of the world's population, is affected by uncontrolled fishing, leading to a drastic depletion of certain species. Selective forms of fishing which discard much of what they collect continue unabated. Particularly threatened are marine organisms which we tend to overlook, like some forms of plankton; they represent a significant element in the ocean food chain, and species used for our food ultimately depend on them.

41. In tropical and subtropical seas, we find coral reefs comparable to the great forests on dry land, for they shelter approximately a million species, including fish, crabs, molluscs, sponges and algae. Many of the world's coral reefs are already barren or in a state of constant decline. "Who turned the wonderworld of the seas into underwater cemeteries bereft of colour and life?"[25] This phenomenon is due largely to pollution which reaches the sea as the result of deforestation, agricultural monocultures, industrial waste and destructive fishing methods, especially those using cyanide and dynamite. It is aggravated by the rise in temperature of the oceans. All of this helps us to see that every intervention in nature can have consequences which are not immediately evident, and that certain ways of exploiting resources prove costly in terms of degradation which ultimately reaches the ocean bed itself.

42. Greater investment needs to be made in research aimed at understanding more fully the functioning of ecosystems and adequately analyzing the different variables associated with any significant modification of the environment. Because all creatures are connected, each must be cherished with love and respect, for all of us as living creatures are dependent on one another. Each area is responsible for the care of this family. This will require undertak-

---

[25] CATHOLIC BISHOPS' CONFERENCE OF THE PHILIPPINES, Pastoral Letter *What is Happening to our Beautiful Land?* (29 January 1988).

ing a careful inventory of the species which it hosts, with a view to developing programmes and strategies of protection with particular care for safeguarding species heading towards extinction.

IV. DECLINE IN THE QUALITY OF HUMAN LIFE AND THE BREAKDOWN OF SOCIETY

43. Human beings too are creatures of this world, enjoying a right to life and happiness, and endowed with unique dignity. So we cannot fail to consider the effects on people's lives of environmental deterioration, current models of development and the throwaway culture.

44. Nowadays, for example, we are conscious of the disproportionate and unruly growth of many cities, which have become unhealthy to live in, not only because of pollution caused by toxic emissions but also as a result of urban chaos, poor transportation, and visual pollution and noise. Many cities are huge, inefficient structures, excessively wasteful of energy and water. Neighbourhoods, even those recently built, are congested, chaotic and lacking in sufficient green space. We were not meant to be inundated by cement, asphalt, glass and metal, and deprived of physical contact with nature.

45. In some places, rural and urban alike, the privatization of certain spaces has restricted people's access to places of particular beauty. In others, "ecological" neighbourhoods have been created which are closed to outsiders in order to ensure an artificial tranquillity. Frequently, we find beautiful and carefully manicured green spaces in so-called "safer" areas of cities, but not in the more hidden areas where the disposable of society live.

46. The social dimensions of global change include the effects of technological innovations on employment, social exclusion, an inequitable distribution and consumption of energy and other services, social breakdown, increased violence and a rise in new forms of social aggression, drug trafficking, growing drug use by

young people, and the loss of identity. These are signs that the growth of the past two centuries has not always led to an integral development and an improvement in the quality of life. Some of these signs are also symptomatic of real social decline, the silent rupture of the bonds of integration and social cohesion.

47. Furthermore, when media and the digital world become omnipresent, their influence can stop people from learning how to live wisely, to think deeply and to love generously. In this context, the great sages of the past run the risk of going unheard amid the noise and distractions of an information overload. Efforts need to be made to help these media become sources of new cultural progress for humanity and not a threat to our deepest riches. True wisdom, as the fruit of self-examination, dialogue and generous encounter between persons, is not acquired by a mere accumulation of data which eventually leads to overload and confusion, a sort of mental pollution. Real relationships with others, with all the challenges they entail, now tend to be replaced by a type of internet communication which enables us to choose or eliminate relationships at whim, thus giving rise to a new type of contrived emotion which has more to do with devices and displays than with other people and with nature. Today's media do enable us to communicate and to share our knowledge and affections. Yet at times they also shield us from direct contact with the pain, the fears and the joys of others and the complexity of their personal experiences. For this reason, we should be concerned that, alongside the exciting possibilities offered by these media, a deep and melancholic dissatisfaction with interpersonal relations, or a harmful sense of isolation, can also arise.

V. GLOBAL INEQUALITY

48. The human environment and the natural environment deteriorate together; we cannot adequately combat environmental degradation unless we attend to causes related to human and social degradation. In fact, the deterioration of the environment and of society affects the most vulnerable people on the planet:

"Both everyday experience and scientific research show that the gravest effects of all attacks on the environment are suffered by the poorest".[26] For example, the depletion of fishing reserves especially hurts small fishing communities without the means to replace those resources; water pollution particularly affects the poor who cannot buy bottled water; and rises in the sea level mainly affect impoverished coastal populations who have nowhere else to go. The impact of present imbalances is also seen in the premature death of many of the poor, in conflicts sparked by the shortage of resources, and in any number of other problems which are insufficiently represented on global agendas.[27]

49. It needs to be said that, generally speaking, there is little in the way of clear awareness of problems which especially affect the excluded. Yet they are the majority of the planet's population, billions of people. These days, they are mentioned in international political and economic discussions, but one often has the impression that their problems are brought up as an afterthought, a question which gets added almost out of duty or in a tangential way, if not treated merely as collateral damage. Indeed, when all is said and done, they frequently remain at the bottom of the pile. This is due partly to the fact that many professionals, opinion makers, communications media and centres of power, being located in affluent urban areas, are far removed from the poor, with little direct contact with their problems. They live and reason from the comfortable position of a high level of development and a quality of life well beyond the reach of the majority of the world's population. This lack of physical contact and encounter, encouraged at times by the disintegration of our cities, can lead to a numbing of conscience and to tendentious analyses which neglect parts of reality. At times this attitude exists side by side with a "green"

---

[26] BOLIVIAN BISHOPS' CONFERENCE, Pastoral Letter on the Environment and Human Development in Bolivia *El universo, don de Dios para la vida* (23 March 2012), 17.

[27] Cf. GERMAN BISHOPS' CONFERENCE, Commission for Social Issues, *Der Klimawandel: Brennpunkt globaler, intergenerationeller und ökologischer Gerechtigkeit* (September 2006), 28-30.

rhetoric. Today, however, we have to realize that a true ecological approach *always* becomes a social approach; it must integrate questions of justice in debates on the environment, so as to hear *both the cry of the earth and the cry of the poor.*

50. Instead of resolving the problems of the poor and thinking of how the world can be different, some can only propose a reduction in the birth rate. At times, developing countries face forms of international pressure which make economic assistance contingent on certain policies of "reproductive health". Yet "while it is true that an unequal distribution of the population and of available resources creates obstacles to development and a sustainable use of the environment, it must nonetheless be recognized that demographic growth is fully compatible with an integral and shared development".[28] To blame population growth instead of extreme and selective consumerism on the part of some, is one way of refusing to face the issues. It is an attempt to legitimize the present model of distribution, where a minority believes that it has the right to consume in a way which can never be universalized, since the planet could not even contain the waste products of such consumption. Besides, we know that approximately a third of all food produced is discarded, and "whenever food is thrown out it is as if it were stolen from the table of the poor".[29] Still, attention needs to be paid to imbalances in population density, on both national and global levels, since a rise in consumption would lead to complex regional situations, as a result of the interplay between problems linked to environmental pollution, transport, waste treatment, loss of resources and quality of life.

51. Inequity affects not only individuals but entire countries; it compels us to consider an ethics of international relations. A true "ecological debt" exists, particularly between the global north and south, connected to commercial imbalances with effects on

---

[28] PONTIFICAL COUNCIL FOR JUSTICE AND PEACE, *Compendium of the Social Doctrine of the Church*, 483.

[29] *Catechesis* (5 June 2013): *Insegnamenti* 1/1 (2013), 280.

the environment, and the disproportionate use of natural resources by certain countries over long periods of time. The export of raw materials to satisfy markets in the industrialized north has caused harm locally, as for example in mercury pollution in gold mining or sulphur dioxide pollution in copper mining. There is a pressing need to calculate the use of environmental space throughout the world for depositing gas residues which have been accumulating for two centuries and have created a situation which currently affects all the countries of the world. The warming caused by huge consumption on the part of some rich countries has repercussions on the poorest areas of the world, especially Africa, where a rise in temperature, together with drought, has proved devastating for farming. There is also the damage caused by the export of solid waste and toxic liquids to developing countries, and by the pollution produced by companies which operate in less developed countries in ways they could never do at home, in the countries in which they raise their capital: "We note that often the businesses which operate this way are multinationals. They do here what they would never do in developed countries or the so-called first world. Generally, after ceasing their activity and withdrawing, they leave behind great human and environmental liabilities such as unemployment, abandoned towns, the depletion of natural reserves, deforestation, the impoverishment of agriculture and local stock breeding, open pits, riven hills, polluted rivers and a handful of social works which are no longer sustainable".[30]

52. The foreign debt of poor countries has become a way of controlling them, yet this is not the case where ecological debt is concerned. In different ways, developing countries, where the most important reserves of the biosphere are found, continue to fuel the development of richer countries at the cost of their own present and future. The land of the southern poor is rich and mostly unpolluted, yet access to ownership of goods and resources for meeting vital needs is inhibited by a system of commercial relations and

---

[30] BISHOPS OF THE PATAGONIA-COMAHUE REGION (ARGENTINA), *Christmas Message* (December 2009), 2.

ownership which is structurally perverse. The developed countries ought to help pay this debt by significantly limiting their consumption of non-renewable energy and by assisting poorer countries to support policies and programmes of sustainable development. The poorest areas and countries are less capable of adopting new models for reducing environmental impact because they lack the wherewithal to develop the necessary processes and to cover their costs. We must continue to be aware that, regarding climate change, there are *differentiated responsibilities*. As the United States bishops have said, greater attention must be given to "the needs of the poor, the weak and the vulnerable, in a debate often dominated by more powerful interests".[31] We need to strengthen the conviction that we are one single human family. There are no frontiers or barriers, political or social, behind which we can hide, still less is there room for the globalization of indifference.

VI. WEAK RESPONSES

53. These situations have caused sister earth, along with all the abandoned of our world, to cry out, pleading that we take another course. Never have we so hurt and mistreated our common home as we have in the last two hundred years. Yet we are called to be instruments of God our Father, so that our planet might be what he desired when he created it and correspond with his plan for peace, beauty and fullness. The problem is that we still lack the culture needed to confront this crisis. We lack leadership capable of striking out on new paths and meeting the needs of the present with concern for all and without prejudice towards coming generations. The establishment of a legal framework which can set clear boundaries and ensure the protection of ecosystems has become indispensable; otherwise, the new power structures based on the

---

[31] UNITED STATES CONFERENCE OF CATHOLIC BISHOPS, *Global Climate Change: A Plea for Dialogue, Prudence and the Common Good* (15 June 2001).

techno-economic paradigm may overwhelm not only our politics but also freedom and justice.

54. It is remarkable how weak international political responses have been. The failure of global summits on the environment make it plain that our politics are subject to technology and finance. There are too many special interests, and economic interests easily end up trumping the common good and manipulating information so that their own plans will not be affected. The *Aparecida Document* urges that "the interests of economic groups which irrationally demolish sources of life should not prevail in dealing with natural resources".[32] The alliance between the economy and technology ends up sidelining anything unrelated to its immediate interests. Consequently the most one can expect is superficial rhetoric, sporadic acts of philanthropy and perfunctory expressions of concern for the environment, whereas any genuine attempt by groups within society to introduce change is viewed as a nuisance based on romantic illusions or an obstacle to be circumvented.

55. Some countries are gradually making significant progress, developing more effective controls and working to combat corruption. People may well have a growing ecological sensitivity but it has not succeeded in changing their harmful habits of consumption which, rather than decreasing, appear to be growing all the more. A simple example is the increasing use and power of air-conditioning. The markets, which immediately benefit from sales, stimulate ever greater demand. An outsider looking at our world would be amazed at such behaviour, which at times appears self-destructive.

56. In the meantime, economic powers continue to justify the current global system where priority tends to be given to speculation and the pursuit of financial gain, which fail to take the context into

---

[32] FIFTH GENERAL CONFERENCE OF THE LATIN AMERICAN AND CARIBBEAN BISHOPS, *Aparecida Document* (29 June 2007), 471.

account, let alone the effects on human dignity and the natural environment. Here we see how environmental deterioration and human and ethical degradation are closely linked. Many people will deny doing anything wrong because distractions constantly dull our consciousness of just how limited and finite our world really is. As a result, "whatever is fragile, like the environment, is defenceless before the interests of a deified market, which become the only rule".[33]

57. It is foreseeable that, once certain resources have been depleted, the scene will be set for new wars, albeit under the guise of noble claims. War always does grave harm to the environment and to the cultural riches of peoples, risks which are magnified when one considers nuclear arms and biological weapons. "Despite the international agreements which prohibit chemical, bacteriological and biological warfare, the fact is that laboratory research continues to develop new offensive weapons capable of altering the balance of nature".[34] Politics must pay greater attention to foreseeing new conflicts and addressing the causes which can lead to them. But powerful financial interests prove most resistant to this effort, and political planning tends to lack breadth of vision. What would induce anyone, at this stage, to hold on to power only to be remembered for their inability to take action when it was urgent and necessary to do so?

58. In some countries, there are positive examples of environmental improvement: rivers, polluted for decades, have been cleaned up; native woodlands have been restored; landscapes have been beautified thanks to environmental renewal projects; beautiful buildings have been erected; advances have been made in the production of non-polluting energy and in the improvement of public transportation. These achievements do not solve global problems, but they do

---

[33] Apostolic Exhortation *Evangelii Gaudium* (24 November 2013), 56: AAS 105 (2013), 1043.

[34] JOHN PAUL II, *Message for the 1990 World Day of Peace*, 12: AAS 82 (1990), 154.

show that men and women are still capable of intervening positively. For all our limitations, gestures of generosity, solidarity and care cannot but well up within us, since we were made for love.

59. At the same time we can note the rise of a false or superficial ecology which bolsters complacency and a cheerful recklessness. As often occurs in periods of deep crisis which require bold decisions, we are tempted to think that what is happening is not entirely clear. Superficially, apart from a few obvious signs of pollution and deterioration, things do not look that serious, and the planet could continue as it is for some time. Such evasiveness serves as a licence to carrying on with our present lifestyles and models of production and consumption. This is the way human beings contrive to feed their self-destructive vices: trying not to see them, trying not to acknowledge them, delaying the important decisions and pretending that nothing will happen.

VII. A VARIETY OF OPINIONS

60. Finally, we need to acknowledge that different approaches and lines of thought have emerged regarding this situation and its possible solutions. At one extreme, we find those who doggedly uphold the myth of progress and tell us that ecological problems will solve themselves simply with the application of new technology and without any need for ethical considerations or deep change. At the other extreme are those who view men and women and all their interventions as no more than a threat, jeopardizing the global ecosystem, and consequently the presence of human beings on the planet should be reduced and all forms of intervention prohibited. Viable future scenarios will have to be generated between these extremes, since there is no one path to a solution. This makes a variety of proposals possible, all capable of entering into dialogue with a view to developing comprehensive solutions.

61. On many concrete questions, the Church has no reason to offer a definitive opinion; she knows that honest debate must be encouraged among experts, while respecting divergent views. But

we need only take a frank look at the facts to see that our common home is falling into serious disrepair. Hope would have us recognize that there is always a way out, that we can always redirect our steps, that we can always do something to solve our problems. Still, we can see signs that things are now reaching a breaking point, due to the rapid pace of change and degradation; these are evident in large-scale natural disasters as well as social and even financial crises, for the world's problems cannot be analyzed or explained in isolation. There are regions now at high risk and, aside from all doomsday predictions, the present world system is certainly unsustainable from a number of points of view, for we have stopped thinking about the goals of human activity. "If we scan the regions of our planet, we immediately see that humanity has disappointed God's expectations".[35]

CHAPTER TWO

THE GOSPEL OF CREATION

62. Why should this document, addressed to all people of good will, include a chapter dealing with the convictions of believers? I am well aware that in the areas of politics and philosophy there are those who firmly reject the idea of a Creator, or consider it irrelevant, and consequently dismiss as irrational the rich contribution which religions can make towards an integral ecology and the full development of humanity. Others view religions simply as a subculture to be tolerated. Nonetheless, science and religion, with their distinctive approaches to understanding reality, can enter into an intense dialogue fruitful for both.

I. THE LIGHT OFFERED BY FAITH

63. Given the complexity of the ecological crisis and its multiple causes, we need to realize that the solutions will not emerge from just one way of interpreting and transforming reality. Respect

---

[35] ID., *Catechesis* (17 January 2001), 3: *Insegnamenti* 24/1 (2001), 178.

must also be shown for the various cultural riches of different peoples, their art and poetry, their interior life and spirituality. If we are truly concerned to develop an ecology capable of remedying the damage we have done, no branch of the sciences and no form of wisdom can be left out, and that includes religion and the language particular to it. The Catholic Church is open to dialogue with philosophical thought; this has enabled her to produce various syntheses between faith and reason. The development of the Church's social teaching represents such a synthesis with regard to social issues; this teaching is called to be enriched by taking up new challenges.

64. Furthermore, although this Encyclical welcomes dialogue with everyone so that together we can seek paths of liberation, I would like from the outset to show how faith convictions can offer Christians, and some other believers as well, ample motivation to care for nature and for the most vulnerable of their brothers and sisters. If the simple fact of being human moves people to care for the environment of which they are a part, Christians in their turn "realize that their responsibility within creation, and their duty towards nature and the Creator, are an essential part of their faith".[36] It is good for humanity and the world at large when we believers better recognize the ecological commitments which stem from our convictions.

II. THE WISDOM OF THE BIBLICAL ACCOUNTS

65. Without repeating the entire theology of creation, we can ask what the great biblical narratives say about the relationship of human beings with the world. In the first creation account in the Book of Genesis, God's plan includes creating humanity. After the creation of man and woman, "God saw everything that he had made, and behold it was *very good*" (*Gen* 1:31). The Bible teaches that every man and woman is created out of love and made

---

[36] JOHN PAUL II, *Message for the 1990 World Day of Peace*, 15: AAS 82 (1990), 156.

in God's image and likeness (cf. *Gen* 1:26). This shows us the immense dignity of each person, "who is not just something, but someone. He is capable of self-knowledge, of self-possession and of freely giving himself and entering into communion with other persons".[37] Saint John Paul II stated that the special love of the Creator for each human being "confers upon him or her an infinite dignity".[38] Those who are committed to defending human dignity can find in the Christian faith the deepest reasons for this commitment. How wonderful is the certainty that each human life is not adrift in the midst of hopeless chaos, in a world ruled by pure chance or endlessly recurring cycles! The Creator can say to each one of us: "Before I formed you in the womb, I knew you" (*Jer* 1:5). We were conceived in the heart of God, and for this reason "each of us is the result of a thought of God. Each of us is willed, each of us is loved, each of us is necessary".[39]

66. The creation accounts in the book of Genesis contain, in their own symbolic and narrative language, profound teachings about human existence and its historical reality. They suggest that human life is grounded in three fundamental and closely intertwined relationships: with God, with our neighbour and with the earth itself. According to the Bible, these three vital relationships have been broken, both outwardly and within us. This rupture is sin. The harmony between the Creator, humanity and creation as a whole was disrupted by our presuming to take the place of God and refusing to acknowledge our creaturely limitations. This in turn distorted our mandate to "have dominion" over the earth (cf. *Gen* 1:28), to "till it and keep it" (*Gen* 2:15). As a result, the originally harmonious relationship between human beings and nature became conflictual (cf. *Gen* 3:17-19). It is significant that the harmony which Saint Francis of Assisi experienced with all

---

[37] *Catechism of the Catholic Church*, 357.

[38] *Angelus* in Osnabrück (Germany) with the disabled, 16 November 1980: *Insegnamenti* 3/2 (1980), 1232.

[39] BENEDICT XVI, *Homily for the Solemn Inauguration of the Petrine Ministry* (24 April 2005): AAS 97 (2005), 711.

creatures was seen as a healing of that rupture. Saint Bonaventure held that, through universal reconciliation with every creature, Saint Francis in some way returned to the state of original innocence.[40] This is a far cry from our situation today, where sin is manifest in all its destructive power in wars, the various forms of violence and abuse, the abandonment of the most vulnerable, and attacks on nature.

67. We are not God. The earth was here before us and it has been given to us. This allows us to respond to the charge that Judaeo-Christian thinking, on the basis of the Genesis account which grants man "dominion" over the earth (cf. *Gen* 1:28), has encouraged the unbridled exploitation of nature by painting him as domineering and destructive by nature. This is not a correct interpretation of the Bible as understood by the Church. Although it is true that we Christians have at times incorrectly interpreted the Scriptures, nowadays we must forcefully reject the notion that our being created in God's image and given dominion over the earth justifies absolute domination over other creatures. The biblical texts are to be read in their context, with an appropriate hermeneutic, recognizing that they tell us to "till and keep" the garden of the world (cf. *Gen* 2:15). "Tilling" refers to cultivating, ploughing or working, while "keeping" means caring, protecting, overseeing and preserving. This implies a relationship of mutual responsibility between human beings and nature. Each community can take from the bounty of the earth whatever it needs for subsistence, but it also has the duty to protect the earth and to ensure its fruitfulness for coming generations. "The earth is the Lord's" (*Ps* 24:1); to him belongs "the earth with all that is within it" (*Dt* 10:14). Thus God rejects every claim to absolute ownership: "The land shall not be sold in perpetuity, for the land is mine; for you are strangers and sojourners with me" (*Lev* 25:23).

---

[40] Cf. BONAVENTURE, *The Major Legend of Saint Francis*, VIII, 1, in *Francis of Assisi: Early Documents*, vol. 2, New York-London-Manila, 2000, 586.

68. This responsibility for God's earth means that human beings, endowed with intelligence, must respect the laws of nature and the delicate equilibria existing between the creatures of this world, for "he commanded and they were created; and he established them for ever and ever; he fixed their bounds and he set a law which cannot pass away" (*Ps* 148:5b-6). The laws found in the Bible dwell on relationships, not only among individuals but also with other living beings. "You shall not see your brother's donkey or his ox fallen down by the way and withhold your help. . . . If you chance to come upon a bird's nest in any tree or on the ground, with young ones or eggs and the mother sitting upon the young or upon the eggs; you shall not take the mother with the young" (*Dt* 22:4, 6). Along these same lines, rest on the seventh day is meant not only for human beings, but also so "that your ox and your donkey may have rest" (*Ex* 23:12). Clearly, the Bible has no place for a tyrannical anthropocentrism unconcerned for other creatures.

69. Together with our obligation to use the earth's goods responsibly, we are called to recognize that other living beings have a value of their own in God's eyes: "by their mere existence they bless him and give him glory",[41] and indeed, "the Lord rejoices in all his works" (*Ps* 104:31). By virtue of our unique dignity and our gift of intelligence, we are called to respect creation and its inherent laws, for "the Lord by wisdom founded the earth" (*Prov* 3:19). In our time, the Church does not simply state that other creatures are completely subordinated to the good of human beings, as if they have no worth in themselves and can be treated as we wish. The German bishops have taught that, where other creatures are concerned, "we can speak of the priority of *being* over that of *being useful*".[42] The Catechism clearly and forcefully criticizes a distorted anthropocentrism: "Each creature possesses its own particular goodness and perfection. . . . Each of the various

---

[41] *Catechism of the Catholic Church*, 2416.

[42] GERMAN BISHOPS' CONFERENCE, *Zukunft der Schöpfung—Zukunft der Menschheit. Einklärung der Deutschen Bischofskonferenz zu Fragen der Umwelt und der Energieversorgung* (1980), II, 2.

creatures, willed in its own being, reflects in its own way a ray of God's infinite wisdom and goodness. Man must therefore respect the particular goodness of every creature, to avoid any disordered use of things".[43]

70. In the story of Cain and Abel, we see how envy led Cain to commit the ultimate injustice against his brother, which in turn ruptured the relationship between Cain and God, and between Cain and the earth from which he was banished. This is seen clearly in the dramatic exchange between God and Cain. God asks: "Where is Abel, your brother?" Cain answers that he does not know, and God persists: "What have you done? The voice of your brother's blood is crying to me from the ground. And now you are cursed from the ground" (*Gen* 4:9-11). Disregard for the duty to cultivate and maintain a proper relationship with my neighbour, for whose care and custody I am responsible, ruins my relationship with my own self, with others, with God and with the earth. When all these relationships are neglected, when justice no longer dwells in the land, the Bible tells us that life itself is endangered. We see this in the story of Noah, where God threatens to do away with humanity because of its constant failure to fulfil the requirements of justice and peace: "I have determined to make an end of all flesh; for the earth is filled with violence through them" (*Gen* 6:13). These ancient stories, full of symbolism, bear witness to a conviction which we today share, that everything is interconnected, and that genuine care for our own lives and our relationships with nature is inseparable from fraternity, justice and faithfulness to others.

71. Although "the wickedness of man was great in the earth" (*Gen* 6:5) and the Lord "was sorry that he had made man on the earth" (*Gen* 6:6), nonetheless, through Noah, who remained innocent and just, God decided to open a path of salvation. In this way he gave humanity the chance of a new beginning. All it takes is one good person to restore hope! The biblical tradition clearly shows that this renewal entails recovering and respecting the rhythms

---

[43] *Catechism of the Catholic Church*, 339.

inscribed in nature by the hand of the Creator. We see this, for example, in the law of the Sabbath. On the seventh day, God rested from all his work. He commanded Israel to set aside each seventh day as a day of rest, a *Sabbath* (cf. *Gen* 2:2-3; *Ex* 16:23; 20:10). Similarly, every seven years, a sabbatical year was set aside for Israel, a complete rest for the land (cf. *Lev* 25:1-4), when sowing was forbidden and one reaped only what was necessary to live on and to feed one's household (cf. *Lev* 25:4-6). Finally, after seven weeks of years, which is to say forty-nine years, the Jubilee was celebrated as a year of general forgiveness and "liberty throughout the land for all its inhabitants" (cf. *Lev* 25:10). This law came about as an attempt to ensure balance and fairness in their relationships with others and with the land on which they lived and worked. At the same time, it was an acknowledgment that the gift of the earth with its fruits belongs to everyone. Those who tilled and kept the land were obliged to share its fruits, especially with the poor, with widows, orphans and foreigners in their midst: "When you reap the harvest of your land, you shall not reap your field to its very border, neither shall you gather the gleanings after the harvest. And you shall not strip your vineyard bare, neither shall you gather the fallen grapes of your vineyard; you shall leave them for the poor and for the sojourner" (*Lev* 19:9-10).

72. The Psalms frequently exhort us to praise God the Creator, "who spread out the earth on the waters, for his steadfast love endures for ever" (*Ps* 136:6). They also invite other creatures to join us in this praise: "Praise him, sun and moon, praise him, all you shining stars! Praise him, you highest heavens, and you waters above the heavens! Let them praise the name of the Lord, for he commanded and they were created" (*Ps* 148:3-5). We do not only exist by God's mighty power; we also live with him and beside him. This is why we adore him.

73. The writings of the prophets invite us to find renewed strength in times of trial by contemplating the all-powerful God who created the universe. Yet God's infinite power does not lead us to flee

his fatherly tenderness, because in him affection and strength are joined. Indeed, all sound spirituality entails both welcoming divine love and adoration, confident in the Lord because of his infinite power. In the Bible, the God who liberates and saves is the same God who created the universe, and these two divine ways of acting are intimately and inseparably connected: "Ah Lord God! It is you who made the heavens and the earth by your great power and by your outstretched arm! Nothing is too hard for you. . . . You brought your people Israel out of the land of Egypt with signs and wonders" (*Jer* 32:17, 21). "The Lord is the everlasting God, the Creator of the ends of the earth. He does not faint or grow weary; his understanding is unsearchable. He gives power to the faint, and strengthens the powerless" (*Is* 40:28b-29).

74. The experience of the Babylonian captivity provoked a spiritual crisis which led to deeper faith in God. Now his creative omnipotence was given pride of place in order to exhort the people to regain their hope in the midst of their wretched predicament. Centuries later, in another age of trial and persecution, when the Roman Empire was seeking to impose absolute dominion, the faithful would once again find consolation and hope in a growing trust in the all-powerful God: "Great and wonderful are your deeds, O Lord God the Almighty! Just and true are your ways!" (*Rev* 15:3). The God who created the universe out of nothing can also intervene in this world and overcome every form of evil. Injustice is not invincible.

75. A spirituality which forgets God as all-powerful and Creator is not acceptable. That is how we end up worshipping earthly powers, or ourselves usurping the place of God, even to the point of claiming an unlimited right to trample his creation underfoot. The best way to restore men and women to their rightful place, putting an end to their claim to absolute dominion over the earth, is to speak once more of the figure of a Father who creates and who alone owns the world. Otherwise, human beings will always try to impose their own laws and interests on reality.

III. THE MYSTERY OF THE UNIVERSE

76. In the Judaeo-Christian tradition, the word "creation" has a broader meaning than "nature", for it has to do with God's loving plan in which every creature has its own value and significance. Nature is usually seen as a system which can be studied, understood and controlled, whereas creation can only be understood as a gift from the outstretched hand of the Father of all, and as a reality illuminated by the love which calls us together into universal communion.

77. "By the word of the Lord the heavens were made" (*Ps* 33:6). This tells us that the world came about as the result of a decision, not from chaos or chance, and this exalts it all the more. The creating word expresses a free choice. The universe did not emerge as the result of arbitrary omnipotence, a show of force or a desire for self-assertion. Creation is of the order of love. God's love is the fundamental moving force in all created things: "For you love all things that exist, and detest none of the things that you have made; for you would not have made anything if you had hated it" (*Wis* 11:24). Every creature is thus the object of the Father's tenderness, who gives it its place in the world. Even the fleeting life of the least of beings is the object of his love, and in its few seconds of existence, God enfolds it with his affection. Saint Basil the Great described the Creator as "goodness without measure",[44] while Dante Alighieri spoke of "the love which moves the sun and the stars".[45] Consequently, we can ascend from created things "to the greatness of God and to his loving mercy".[46]

78. At the same time, Judaeo-Christian thought demythologized nature. While continuing to admire its grandeur and immensity, it no longer saw nature as divine. In doing so, it emphasizes all the more our human responsibility for nature. This rediscovery of

---

[44] *Hom. in Hexaemeron*, I, 2, 10: PG 29, 9.

[45] *The Divine Comedy, Paradiso*, Canto XXXIII, 145.

[46] BENEDICT XVI, *Catechesis* (9 November 2005), 3: *Insegnamenti* 1 (2005), 768.

nature can never be at the cost of the freedom and responsibility of human beings who, as part of the world, have the duty to cultivate their abilities in order to protect it and develop its potential. If we acknowledge the value and the fragility of nature and, at the same time, our God-given abilities, we can finally leave behind the modern myth of unlimited material progress. A fragile world, entrusted by God to human care, challenges us to devise intelligent ways of directing, developing and limiting our power.

79. In this universe, shaped by open and intercommunicating systems, we can discern countless forms of relationship and participation. This leads us to think of the whole as open to God's transcendence, within which it develops. Faith allows us to interpret the meaning and the mysterious beauty of what is unfolding. We are free to apply our intelligence towards things evolving positively, or towards adding new ills, new causes of suffering and real setbacks. This is what makes for the excitement and drama of human history, in which freedom, growth, salvation and love can blossom, or lead towards decadence and mutual destruction. The work of the Church seeks not only to remind everyone of the duty to care for nature, but at the same time "she must above all protect mankind from self-destruction".[47]

80. Yet God, who wishes to work with us and who counts on our cooperation, can also bring good out of the evil we have done. "The Holy Spirit can be said to possess an infinite creativity, proper to the divine mind, which knows how to loosen the knots of human affairs, including the most complex and inscrutable".[48] Creating a world in need of development, God in some way sought to limit himself in such a way that many of the things we think of as evils, dangers or sources of suffering, are in reality part of the pains of childbirth which he uses to draw us into the act of

---

[47] ID., Encyclical Letter *Caritas in Veritate* (29 June 2009), 51: AAS 101 (2009), 687.

[48] JOHN PAUL II, *Catechesis* (24 April 1991), 6: *Insegnamenti* 14 (1991), 856.

cooperation with the Creator.[49] God is intimately present to each being, without impinging on the autonomy of his creature, and this gives rise to the rightful autonomy of earthly affairs.[50] His divine presence, which ensures the subsistence and growth of each being, "continues the work of creation".[51] The Spirit of God has filled the universe with possibilities and therefore, from the very heart of things, something new can always emerge: "Nature is nothing other than a certain kind of art, namely God's art, impressed upon things, whereby those things are moved to a determinate end. It is as if a shipbuilder were able to give timbers the wherewithal to move themselves to take the form of a ship".[52]

81. Human beings, even if we postulate a process of evolution, also possess a uniqueness which cannot be fully explained by the evolution of other open systems. Each of us has his or her own personal identity and is capable of entering into dialogue with others and with God himself. Our capacity to reason, to develop arguments, to be inventive, to interpret reality and to create art, along with other not yet discovered capacities, are signs of a uniqueness which transcends the spheres of physics and biology. The sheer novelty involved in the emergence of a personal being within a material universe presupposes a direct action of God and a particular call to life and to relationship on the part of a "Thou" who addresses himself to another "thou". The biblical accounts of creation invite us to see each human being as a subject who can never be reduced to the status of an object.

82. Yet it would also be mistaken to view other living beings as mere objects subjected to arbitrary human domination. When

---

[49] The Catechism explains that God wished to create a world which is "journeying towards its ultimate perfection", and that this implies the presence of imperfection and physical evil; cf. *Catechism of the Catholic Church*, 310.

[50] Cf. SECOND VATICAN ECUMENICAL COUNCIL, Pastoral Constitution on the Church in the Modern World *Gaudium et Spes*, 36.

[51] THOMAS AQUINAS, *Summa Theologiae*, I, q. 104, art. 1 ad 4.

[52] ID., *In octo libros Physicorum Aristotelis expositio*, Lib. II, lectio 14.

nature is viewed solely as a source of profit and gain, this has serious consequences for society. This vision of "might is right" has engendered immense inequality, injustice and acts of violence against the majority of humanity, since resources end up in the hands of the first comer or the most powerful: the winner takes all. Completely at odds with this model are the ideals of harmony, justice, fraternity and peace as proposed by Jesus. As he said of the powers of his own age: "You know that the rulers of the Gentiles lord it over them, and their great men exercise authority over them. It shall not be so among you; but whoever would be great among you must be your servant" (*Mt* 20:25-26).

83. The ultimate destiny of the universe is in the fullness of God, which has already been attained by the risen Christ, the measure of the maturity of all things.[53] Here we can add yet another argument for rejecting every tyrannical and irresponsible domination of human beings over other creatures. The ultimate purpose of other creatures is not to be found in us. Rather, all creatures are moving forward with us and through us towards a common point of arrival, which is God, in that transcendent fullness where the risen Christ embraces and illumines all things. Human beings, endowed with intelligence and love, and drawn by the fullness of Christ, are called to lead all creatures back to their Creator.

IV. THE MESSAGE OF EACH CREATURE IN THE HARMONY OF CREATION

84. Our insistence that each human being is an image of God should not make us overlook the fact that each creature has its own purpose. None is superfluous. The entire material universe speaks of God's love, his boundless affection for us. Soil, water,

---

[53] Against this horizon we can set the contribution of Fr Teilhard de Chardin; cf. PAUL VI, *Address in a Chemical and Pharmaceutical Plant* (24 February 1966): *Insegnamenti* 4 (1966), 992-993; JOHN PAUL II, *Letter to the Reverend George Coyne* (1 June 1988): *Insegnamenti* 11/2 (1988), 1715; BENEDICT XVI, *Homily for the Celebration of Vespers in Aosta* (24 July 2009): *Insegnamenti* 5/2 (2009), 60.

mountains: everything is, as it were, a caress of God. The history of our friendship with God is always linked to particular places which take on an intensely personal meaning; we all remember places, and revisiting those memories does us much good. Anyone who has grown up in the hills or used to sit by the spring to drink, or played outdoors in the neighbourhood square; going back to these places is a chance to recover something of their true selves.

85. God has written a precious book, "whose letters are the multitude of created things present in the universe".[54] The Canadian bishops rightly pointed out that no creature is excluded from this manifestation of God: "From panoramic vistas to the tiniest living form, nature is a constant source of wonder and awe. It is also a continuing revelation of the divine".[55] The bishops of Japan, for their part, made a thought-provoking observation: "To sense each creature singing the hymn of its existence is to live joyfully in God's love and hope".[56] This contemplation of creation allows us to discover in each thing a teaching which God wishes to hand on to us, since "for the believer, to contemplate creation is to hear a message, to listen to a paradoxical and silent voice".[57] We can say that "alongside revelation properly so-called, contained in sacred Scripture, there is a divine manifestation in the blaze of the sun and the fall of night".[58] Paying attention to this manifestation, we learn to see ourselves in relation to all other creatures: "I express myself in expressing the world; in my effort to decipher the sacredness of the world, I explore my own".[59]

---

[54] JOHN PAUL II, *Catechesis* (30 January 2002), 6: *Insegnamenti* 25/1 (2002), 140.

[55] CANADIAN CONFERENCE OF CATHOLIC BISHOPS, SOCIAL AFFAIRS COMMISSION, Pastoral Letter *You Love All that Exists . . . All Things are Yours, God, Lover of Life"* (4 October 2003), 1.

[56] CATHOLIC BISHOPS' CONFERENCE OF JAPAN, *Reverence for Life. A Message for the Twenty-First Century* (1 January 2000), 89.

[57] JOHN PAUL II, *Catechesis* (26 January 2000), 5: *Insegnamenti* 23/1 (2000), 123.

[58] ID., *Catechesis* (2 August 2000), 3: *Insegnamenti* 23/2 (2000), 112.

[59] PAUL RICOEUR, *Philosophie de la Volonté, t. II: Finitude et Culpabilité*, Paris, 2009, 216.

86. The universe as a whole, in all its manifold relationships, shows forth the inexhaustible riches of God. Saint Thomas Aquinas wisely noted that multiplicity and variety "come from the intention of the first agent" who willed that "what was wanting to one in the representation of the divine goodness might be supplied by another",[60] inasmuch as God's goodness "could not be represented fittingly by any one creature".[61] Hence we need to grasp the variety of things in their multiple relationships.[62] We understand better the importance and meaning of each creature if we contemplate it within the entirety of God's plan. As the Catechism teaches: "God wills the interdependence of creatures. The sun and the moon, the cedar and the little flower, the eagle and the sparrow: the spectacle of their countless diversities and inequalities tells us that no creature is self-sufficient. Creatures exist only in dependence on each other, to complete each other, in the service of each other".[63]

87. When we can see God reflected in all that exists, our hearts are moved to praise the Lord for all his creatures and to worship him in union with them. This sentiment finds magnificent expression in the hymn of Saint Francis of Assisi:

> Praised be you, my Lord, with all your creatures,
> especially Sir Brother Sun,
> who is the day and through whom you give us
>   light.
> And he is beautiful and radiant with great splen-
>   dour;
> and bears a likeness of you, Most High.
> Praised be you, my Lord, through Sister Moon
>   and the stars,

---

[60] *Summa Theologiae*, I, q. 47, art. 1.
[61] Ibid.
[62] Cf. ibid., art. 2, ad 1; art. 3.
[63] *Catechism of the Catholic Church*, 340.

> in heaven you formed them clear and precious
>   and beautiful.
> Praised be you, my Lord, through Brother Wind,
> and through the air, cloudy and serene, and every
>   kind of weather
> through whom you give sustenance to your
>   creatures.
> Praised be you, my Lord, through Sister Water,
> who is very useful and humble and precious and
>   chaste.
> Praised be you, my Lord, through Brother Fire,
> through whom you light the night,
> and he is beautiful and playful and robust and
>   strong.[64]

88. The bishops of Brazil have pointed out that nature as a whole not only manifests God but is also a locus of his presence. The Spirit of life dwells in every living creature and calls us to enter into relationship with him.[65] Discovering this presence leads us to cultivate the "ecological virtues".[66] This is not to forget that there is an infinite distance between God and the things of this world, which do not possess his fullness. Otherwise, we would not be doing the creatures themselves any good either, for we would be failing to acknowledge their right and proper place. We would end up unduly demanding of them something which they, in their smallness, cannot give us.

V. A UNIVERSAL COMMUNION

89. The created things of this world are not free of ownership: "For they are yours, O Lord, who love the living" (*Wis* 11:26). This is

---

[64] *Canticle of the Creatures*, in *Francis of Assisi: Early Documents*, New York-London-Manila, 1999, 113-114.

[65] Cf. NATIONAL CONFERENCE OF THE BISHOPS OF BRAZIL, *A Igreja e a Questão Ecológica,* 1992, 53-54.

[66] Ibid., 61.

the basis of our conviction that, as part of the universe, called into being by one Father, all of us are linked by unseen bonds and together form a kind of universal family, a sublime communion which fills us with a sacred, affectionate and humble respect. Here I would reiterate that "God has joined us so closely to the world around us that we can feel the desertification of the soil almost as a physical ailment, and the extinction of a species as a painful disfigurement".[67]

90. This is not to put all living beings on the same level nor to deprive human beings of their unique worth and the tremendous responsibility it entails. Nor does it imply a divinization of the earth which would prevent us from working on it and protecting it in its fragility. Such notions would end up creating new imbalances which would deflect us from the reality which challenges us.[68] At times we see an obsession with denying any pre-eminence to the human person; more zeal is shown in protecting other species than in defending the dignity which all human beings share in equal measure. Certainly, we should be concerned lest other living beings be treated irresponsibly. But we should be particularly indignant at the enormous inequalities in our midst, whereby we continue to tolerate some considering themselves more worthy than others. We fail to see that some are mired in desperate and degrading poverty, with no way out, while others have not the faintest idea of what to do with their possessions, vainly showing off their supposed superiority and leaving behind them so much waste which, if it were the case everywhere, would destroy the planet. In practice, we continue to tolerate that some consider themselves more human than others, as if they had been born with greater rights.

91. A sense of deep communion with the rest of nature cannot be real if our hearts lack tenderness, compassion and concern for our fellow human beings. It is clearly inconsistent to combat trafficking

---

[67] Apostolic Exhortation *Evangelii Gaudium* (24 November 2013), 215: AAS 105 (2013), 1109.

[68] Cf. BENEDICT XVI, Encyclical Letter *Caritas in Veritate* (29 June 2009), 14: AAS 101 (2009), 650.

in endangered species while remaining completely indifferent to human trafficking, unconcerned about the poor, or undertaking to destroy another human being deemed unwanted. This compromises the very meaning of our struggle for the sake of the environment. It is no coincidence that, in the canticle in which Saint Francis praises God for his creatures, he goes on to say: "Praised be you my Lord, through those who give pardon for your love". Everything is connected. Concern for the environment thus needs to be joined to a sincere love for our fellow human beings and an unwavering commitment to resolving the problems of society.

92. Moreover, when our hearts are authentically open to universal communion, this sense of fraternity excludes nothing and no one. It follows that our indifference or cruelty towards fellow creatures of this world sooner or later affects the treatment we mete out to other human beings. We have only one heart, and the same wretchedness which leads us to mistreat an animal will not be long in showing itself in our relationships with other people. Every act of cruelty towards any creature is "contrary to human dignity".[69] We can hardly consider ourselves to be fully loving if we disregard any aspect of reality: "Peace, justice and the preservation of creation are three absolutely interconnected themes, which cannot be separated and treated individually without once again falling into reductionism".[70] Everything is related, and we human beings are united as brothers and sisters on a wonderful pilgrimage, woven together by the love God has for each of his creatures and which also unites us in fond affection with brother sun, sister moon, brother river and mother earth.

VI. THE COMMON DESTINATION OF GOODS

93. Whether believers or not, we are agreed today that the earth is essentially a shared inheritance, whose fruits are meant to benefit

---

[69] *Catechism of the Catholic Church*, 2418.

[70] CONFERENCE OF DOMINICAN BISHOPS, Pastoral Letter *Sobre la relación del hombre con la naturaleza* (21 January 1987).

everyone. For believers, this becomes a question of fidelity to the Creator, since God created the world for everyone. Hence every ecological approach needs to incorporate a social perspective which takes into account the fundamental rights of the poor and the underprivileged. The principle of the subordination of private property to the universal destination of goods, and thus the right of everyone to their use, is a golden rule of social conduct and "the first principle of the whole ethical and social order".[71] The Christian tradition has never recognized the right to private property as absolute or inviolable, and has stressed the social purpose of all forms of private property. Saint John Paul II forcefully reaffirmed this teaching, stating that "God gave the earth to the whole human race for the sustenance of all its members, *without excluding or favouring anyone*".[72] These are strong words. He noted that "a type of development which did not respect and promote human rights—personal and social, economic and political, including the rights of nations and of peoples—would not be really worthy of man".[73] He clearly explained that "the Church does indeed defend the legitimate right to private property, but she also teaches no less clearly that there is always a social mortgage on all private property, in order that goods may serve the general purpose that God gave them".[74] Consequently, he maintained, "it is not in accord with God's plan that this gift be used in such a way that its benefits favour only a few".[75] This calls into serious question the unjust habits of a part of humanity.[76]

---

[71] JOHN PAUL II, Encyclical Letter *Laborem Exercens* (14 September 1981), 19: AAS 73 (1981), 626.

[72] Encyclical Letter *Centesimus Annus* (1 May 1991), 31: AAS 83 (1991), 831.

[73] Encyclical Letter *Sollicitudo Rei Socialis* (30 December 1987), 33: AAS 80 (1988), 557.

[74] *Address to Indigenous and Rural People,* Cuilapán, Mexico (29 January 1979), 6: AAS 71 (1979), 209.

[75] *Homily at Mass for Farmers,* Recife, Brazil (7 July 1980): AAS 72 (1980), 926.

[76] Cf. *Message for the 1990 World Day of Peace*, 8: AAS 82 (1990), 152.

94. The rich and the poor have equal dignity, for "the Lord is the maker of them all" (*Prov* 22:2). "He himself made both small and great" (*Wis* 6:7), and "he makes his sun rise on the evil and on the good" (*Mt* 5:45). This has practical consequences, such as those pointed out by the bishops of Paraguay: "Every *campesino* has a natural right to possess a reasonable allotment of land where he can establish his home, work for subsistence of his family and a secure life. This right must be guaranteed so that its exercise is not illusory but real. That means that apart from the ownership of property, rural people must have access to means of technical education, credit, insurance, and markets".[77]

95. The natural environment is a collective good, the patrimony of all humanity and the responsibility of everyone. If we make something our own, it is only to administer it for the good of all. If we do not, we burden our consciences with the weight of having denied the existence of others. That is why the New Zealand bishops asked what the commandment "Thou shall not kill" means when "twenty percent of the world's population consumes resources at a rate that robs the poor nations and future generations of what they need to survive".[78]

VII. THE GAZE OF JESUS

96. Jesus took up the biblical faith in God the Creator, emphasizing a fundamental truth: God is Father (cf. *Mt* 11:25). In talking with his disciples, Jesus would invite them to recognize the paternal relationship God has with all his creatures. With moving tenderness he would remind them that each one of them is important in God's eyes: "Are not five sparrows sold for two pennies? And not one of them is forgotten before God" (*Lk* 12:6). "Look at the birds

---

[77] PARAGUAYAN BISHOPS' CONFERENCE, Pastoral Letter *El campesino paraguayo y la tierra* (12 June 1983), 2, 4, d.

[78] NEW ZEALAND CATHOLIC BISHOPS CONFERENCE, *Statement on Environmental Issues* (1 September 2006).

of the air: they neither sow nor reap nor gather into barns, and yet your heavenly Father feeds them" (*Mt* 6:26).

97. The Lord was able to invite others to be attentive to the beauty that there is in the world because he himself was in constant touch with nature, lending it an attention full of fondness and wonder. As he made his way throughout the land, he often stopped to contemplate the beauty sown by his Father, and invited his disciples to perceive a divine message in things: "Lift up your eyes, and see how the fields are already white for harvest" (*Jn* 4:35). "The kingdom of God is like a grain of mustard seed which a man took and sowed in his field; it is the smallest of all seeds, but once it has grown, it is the greatest of plants" (*Mt* 13:31-32).

98. Jesus lived in full harmony with creation, and others were amazed: "What sort of man is this, that even the winds and the sea obey him?" (*Mt* 8:27). His appearance was not that of an ascetic set apart from the world, nor of an enemy to the pleasant things of life. Of himself he said: "The Son of Man came eating and drinking and they say, 'Look, a glutton and a drunkard!'" (*Mt* 11:19). He was far removed from philosophies which despised the body, matter and the things of the world. Such unhealthy dualisms, nonetheless, left a mark on certain Christian thinkers in the course of history and disfigured the Gospel. Jesus worked with his hands, in daily contact with the matter created by God, to which he gave form by his craftsmanship. It is striking that most of his life was dedicated to this task in a simple life which awakened no admiration at all: "Is not this the carpenter, the son of Mary?" (*Mk* 6:3). In this way he sanctified human labour and endowed it with a special significance for our development. As Saint John Paul II taught, "by enduring the toil of work in union with Christ crucified for us, man in a way collaborates with the Son of God for the redemption of humanity".[79]

---

[79] Encyclical Letter *Laborem Exercens* (14 September 1981), 27: AAS 73 (1981), 645.

99. In the Christian understanding of the world, the destiny of all creation is bound up with the mystery of Christ, present from the beginning: "All things have been created though him and for him" (*Col* 1:16).[80] The prologue of the Gospel of John (1:1-18) reveals Christ's creative work as the Divine Word (*Logos*). But then, unexpectedly, the prologue goes on to say that this same Word "became flesh" (*Jn* 1:14). One Person of the Trinity entered into the created cosmos, throwing in his lot with it, even to the cross. From the beginning of the world, but particularly through the incarnation, the mystery of Christ is at work in a hidden manner in the natural world as a whole, without thereby impinging on its autonomy.

100. The New Testament does not only tell us of the earthly Jesus and his tangible and loving relationship with the world. It also shows him risen and glorious, present throughout creation by his universal Lordship: "For in him all the fullness of God was pleased to dwell, and through him to reconcile to himself all things, whether on earth or in heaven, making peace by the blood of his cross" (*Col* 1:19-20). This leads us to direct our gaze to the end of time, when the Son will deliver all things to the Father, so that "God may be everything to every one" (*1 Cor* 15:28). Thus, the creatures of this world no longer appear to us under merely natural guise because the risen One is mysteriously holding them to himself and directing them towards fullness as their end. The very flowers of the field and the birds which his human eyes contemplated and admired are now imbued with his radiant presence.

CHAPTER THREE

THE HUMAN ROOTS OF THE ECOLOGICAL CRISIS

101. It would hardly be helpful to describe symptoms without acknowledging the human origins of the ecological crisis. A certain way of understanding human life and activity has gone awry, to

---

[80] Hence Saint Justin could speak of "seeds of the Word" in the world; cf. *II Apologia* 8, 1-2; 13, 3-6: PG 6, 457-458, 467.

the serious detriment of the world around us. Should we not pause and consider this? At this stage, I propose that we focus on the dominant technocratic paradigm and the place of human beings and of human action in the world.

I. TECHNOLOGY: CREATIVITY AND POWER

102. Humanity has entered a new era in which our technical prowess has brought us to a crossroads. We are the beneficiaries of two centuries of enormous waves of change: steam engines, railways, the telegraph, electricity, automobiles, aeroplanes, chemical industries, modern medicine, information technology and, more recently, the digital revolution, robotics, biotechnologies and nanotechnologies. It is right to rejoice in these advances and to be excited by the immense possibilities which they continue to open up before us, for "science and technology are wonderful products of a God-given human creativity".[81] The modification of nature for useful purposes has distinguished the human family from the beginning; technology itself "expresses the inner tension that impels man gradually to overcome material limitations".[82] Technology has remedied countless evils which used to harm and limit human beings. How can we not feel gratitude and appreciation for this progress, especially in the fields of medicine, engineering and communications? How could we not acknowledge the work of many scientists and engineers who have provided alternatives to make development sustainable?

103. Technoscience, when well directed, can produce important means of improving the quality of human life, from useful domestic appliances to great transportation systems, bridges, buildings and public spaces. It can also produce art and enable men and women immersed in the material world to "leap" into the world

---

[81] JOHN PAUL II, *Address to Scientists and Representatives of the United Nations University,* Hiroshima (25 February 1981), 3: AAS 73 (1981), 422.

[82] BENEDICT XVI, Encyclical Letter *Caritas in Veritate* (29 June 2009), 69: AAS 101 (2009), 702.

of beauty. Who can deny the beauty of an aircraft or a skyscraper? Valuable works of art and music now make use of new technologies. So, in the beauty intended by the one who uses new technical instruments and in the contemplation of such beauty, a quantum leap occurs, resulting in a fulfilment which is uniquely human.

104. Yet it must also be recognized that nuclear energy, biotechnology, information technology, knowledge of our DNA, and many other abilities which we have acquired, have given us tremendous power. More precisely, they have given those with the knowledge, and especially the economic resources to use them, an impressive dominance over the whole of humanity and the entire world. Never has humanity had such power over itself, yet nothing ensures that it will be used wisely, particularly when we consider how it is currently being used. We need but think of the nuclear bombs dropped in the middle of the twentieth century, or the array of technology which Nazism, Communism and other totalitarian regimes have employed to kill millions of people, to say nothing of the increasingly deadly arsenal of weapons available for modern warfare. In whose hands does all this power lie, or will it eventually end up? It is extremely risky for a small part of humanity to have it.

105. There is a tendency to believe that every increase in power means "an increase of 'progress' itself", an advance in "security, usefulness, welfare and vigour; . . . an assimilation of new values into the stream of culture",[83] as if reality, goodness and truth automatically flow from technological and economic power as such. The fact is that "contemporary man has not been trained to use power well",[84] because our immense technological development has not been accompanied by a development in human responsibility, values and conscience. Each age tends to have only a meagre awareness of its own limitations. It is possible that we do not grasp the gravity of the challenges now before us. "The risk is growing

---

[83] ROMANO GUARDINI, *Das Ende der Neuzeit*, 9th ed., Würzburg, 1965, 87 (English: *The End of the Modern World*, Wilmington, 1998, 82).
[84] Ibid.

day by day that man will not use his power as he should"; in effect, "power is never considered in terms of the responsibility of choice which is inherent in freedom" since its "only norms are taken from alleged necessity, from either utility or security".[85] But human beings are not completely autonomous. Our freedom fades when it is handed over to the blind forces of the unconscious, of immediate needs, of self-interest, and of violence. In this sense, we stand naked and exposed in the face of our ever-increasing power, lacking the wherewithal to control it. We have certain superficial mechanisms, but we cannot claim to have a sound ethics, a culture and spirituality genuinely capable of setting limits and teaching clear-minded self-restraint.

II. THE GLOBALIZATION OF THE
TECHNOCRATIC PARADIGM

106. The basic problem goes even deeper: it is the way that humanity has taken up technology and its development *according to an undifferentiated and one-dimensional paradigm*. This paradigm exalts the concept of a subject who, using logical and rational procedures, progressively approaches and gains control over an external object. This subject makes every effort to establish the scientific and experimental method, which in itself is already a technique of possession, mastery and transformation. It is as if the subject were to find itself in the presence of something formless, completely open to manipulation. Men and women have constantly intervened in nature, but for a long time this meant being in tune with and respecting the possibilities offered by the things themselves. It was a matter of receiving what nature itself allowed, as if from its own hand. Now, by contrast, we are the ones to lay our hands on things, attempting to extract everything possible from them while frequently ignoring or forgetting the reality in front of us. Human beings and material objects no longer extend a friendly hand to one another; the relationship has become confrontational. This has made it easy to accept the idea of infinite or unlimited

---

[85] Ibid., 87-88 (*The End of the Modern World*, 83).

growth, which proves so attractive to economists, financiers and experts in technology. It is based on the lie that there is an infinite supply of the earth's goods, and this leads to the planet being squeezed dry beyond every limit. It is the false notion that "an infinite quantity of energy and resources are available, that it is possible to renew them quickly, and that the negative effects of the exploitation of the natural order can be easily absorbed".[86]

107. It can be said that many problems of today's world stem from the tendency, at times unconscious, to make the method and aims of science and technology an epistemological paradigm which shapes the lives of individuals and the workings of society. The effects of imposing this model on reality as a whole, human and social, are seen in the deterioration of the environment, but this is just one sign of a reductionism which affects every aspect of human and social life. We have to accept that technological products are not neutral, for they create a framework which ends up conditioning lifestyles and shaping social possibilities along the lines dictated by the interests of certain powerful groups. Decisions which may seem purely instrumental are in reality decisions about the kind of society we want to build.

108. The idea of promoting a different cultural paradigm and employing technology as a mere instrument is nowadays inconceivable. The technological paradigm has become so dominant that it would be difficult to do without its resources and even more difficult to utilize them without being dominated by their internal logic. It has become countercultural to choose a lifestyle whose goals are even partly independent of technology, of its costs and its power to globalize and make us all the same. Technology tends to absorb everything into its ironclad logic, and those who are surrounded with technology "know full well that it moves forward in the final analysis neither for profit nor for the well-being of the

---

[86] PONTIFICAL COUNCIL FOR JUSTICE AND PEACE, *Compendium of the Social Doctrine of the Church*, 462.

human race", that "in the most radical sense of the term power is its motive—a lordship over all".[87] As a result, "man seizes hold of the naked elements of both nature and human nature".[88] Our capacity to make decisions, a more genuine freedom and the space for each one's alternative creativity are diminished.

109. The technocratic paradigm also tends to dominate economic and political life. The economy accepts every advance in technology with a view to profit, without concern for its potentially negative impact on human beings. Finance overwhelms the real economy. The lessons of the global financial crisis have not been assimilated, and we are learning all too slowly the lessons of environmental deterioration. Some circles maintain that current economics and technology will solve all environmental problems, and argue, in popular and non-technical terms, that the problems of global hunger and poverty will be resolved simply by market growth. They are less concerned with certain economic theories which today scarcely anybody dares defend, than with their actual operation in the functioning of the economy. They may not affirm such theories with words, but nonetheless support them with their deeds by showing no interest in more balanced levels of production, a better distribution of wealth, concern for the environment and the rights of future generations. Their behaviour shows that for them maximizing profits is enough. Yet by itself the market cannot guarantee integral human development and social inclusion.[89] At the same time, we have "a sort of 'superdevelopment' of a wasteful and consumerist kind which forms an unacceptable contrast with the ongoing situations of dehumanizing deprivation",[90] while we are all too slow in developing economic institutions and social initiatives which can give the poor regular access to basic resources.

[87] ROMANO GUARDINI, *Das Ende der Neuzeit*, 63-64 (*The End of the Modern World*, 56).

[88] Ibid., 64 (*The End of the Modern World*, 56).

[89] Cf. BENEDICT XVI, Encyclical Letter *Caritas in Veritate* (29 June 2009), 35: AAS 101 (2009), 671.

[90] Ibid., 22: p. 657.

We fail to see the deepest roots of our present failures, which have to do with the direction, goals, meaning and social implications of technological and economic growth.

110. The specialization which belongs to technology makes it difficult to see the larger picture. The fragmentation of knowledge proves helpful for concrete applications, and yet it often leads to a loss of appreciation for the whole, for the relationships between things, and for the broader horizon, which then becomes irrelevant. This very fact makes it hard to find adequate ways of solving the more complex problems of today's world, particularly those regarding the environment and the poor; these problems cannot be dealt with from a single perspective or from a single set of interests. A science which would offer solutions to the great issues would necessarily have to take into account the data generated by other fields of knowledge, including philosophy and social ethics; but this is a difficult habit to acquire today. Nor are there genuine ethical horizons to which one can appeal. Life gradually becomes a surrender to situations conditioned by technology, itself viewed as the principal key to the meaning of existence. In the concrete situation confronting us, there are a number of symptoms which point to what is wrong, such as environmental degradation, anxiety, a loss of the purpose of life and of community living. Once more we see that "realities are more important than ideas".[91]

111. Ecological culture cannot be reduced to a series of urgent and partial responses to the immediate problems of pollution, environmental decay and the depletion of natural resources. There needs to be a distinctive way of looking at things, a way of thinking, policies, an educational programme, a lifestyle and a spirituality which together generate resistance to the assault of the technocratic paradigm. Otherwise, even the best ecological initiatives can find themselves caught up in the same globalized logic.

---

[91] Apostolic Exhortation *Evangelii Gaudium* (24 November 2013), 231: AAS 105 (2013), 1114.

To seek only a technical remedy to each environmental problem which comes up is to separate what is in reality interconnected and to mask the true and deepest problems of the global system.

112. Yet we can once more broaden our vision. We have the freedom needed to limit and direct technology; we can put it at the service of another type of progress, one which is healthier, more human, more social, more integral. Liberation from the dominant technocratic paradigm does in fact happen sometimes, for example, when cooperatives of small producers adopt less polluting means of production, and opt for a non-consumerist model of life, recreation and community. Or when technology is directed primarily to resolving people's concrete problems, truly helping them live with more dignity and less suffering. Or indeed when the desire to create and contemplate beauty manages to overcome reductionism through a kind of salvation which occurs in beauty and in those who behold it. An authentic humanity, calling for a new synthesis, seems to dwell in the midst of our technological culture, almost unnoticed, like a mist seeping gently beneath a closed door. Will the promise last, in spite of everything, with all that is authentic rising up in stubborn resistance?

113. There is also the fact that people no longer seem to believe in a happy future; they no longer have blind trust in a better tomorrow based on the present state of the world and our technical abilities. There is a growing awareness that scientific and technological progress cannot be equated with the progress of humanity and history, a growing sense that the way to a better future lies elsewhere. This is not to reject the possibilities which technology continues to offer us. But humanity has changed profoundly, and the accumulation of constant novelties exalts a superficiality which pulls us in one direction. It becomes difficult to pause and recover depth in life. If architecture reflects the spirit of an age, our megastructures and drab apartment blocks express the spirit of globalized technology, where a constant flood of new products coexists with a tedious monotony. Let us refuse to resign ourselves to this,

and continue to wonder about the purpose and meaning of everything. Otherwise we would simply legitimate the present situation and need new forms of escapism to help us endure the emptiness.

114. All of this shows the urgent need for us to move forward in a bold cultural revolution. Science and technology are not neutral; from the beginning to the end of a process, various intentions and possibilities are in play and can take on distinct shapes. Nobody is suggesting a return to the Stone Age, but we do need to slow down and look at reality in a different way, to appropriate the positive and sustainable progress which has been made, but also to recover the values and the great goals swept away by our unrestrained delusions of grandeur.

III. THE CRISIS AND EFFECTS
OF MODERN ANTHROPOCENTRISM

115. Modern anthropocentrism has paradoxically ended up prizing technical thought over reality, since "the technological mind sees nature as an insensate order, as a cold body of facts, as a mere 'given', as an object of utility, as raw material to be hammered into useful shape; it views the cosmos similarly as a mere 'space' into which objects can be thrown with complete indifference".[92] The intrinsic dignity of the world is thus compromised. When human beings fail to find their true place in this world, they misunderstand themselves and end up acting against themselves: "Not only has God given the earth to man, who must use it with respect for the original good purpose for which it was given, but, man too is God's gift to man. He must therefore respect the natural and moral structure with which he has been endowed".[93]

116. Modernity has been marked by an excessive anthropocentrism which today, under another guise, continues to stand in the way

---

[92] ROMANO GUARDINI, *Das Ende der Neuzeit*, 63 (*The End of the Modern World*, 55).

[93] JOHN PAUL II, Encyclical Letter *Centesimus Annus* (1 May 1991), 38: AAS 83 (1991), 841.

of shared understanding and of any effort to strengthen social bonds. The time has come to pay renewed attention to reality and the limits it imposes; this in turn is the condition for a more sound and fruitful development of individuals and society. An inadequate presentation of Christian anthropology gave rise to a wrong understanding of the relationship between human beings and the world. Often, what was handed on was a Promethean vision of mastery over the world, which gave the impression that the protection of nature was something that only the faint-hearted cared about. Instead, our "dominion" over the universe should be understood more properly in the sense of responsible stewardship.[94]

117. Neglecting to monitor the harm done to nature and the environmental impact of our decisions is only the most striking sign of a disregard for the message contained in the structures of nature itself. When we fail to acknowledge as part of reality the worth of a poor person, a human embryo, a person with disabilities—to offer just a few examples—it becomes difficult to hear the cry of nature itself; everything is connected. Once the human being declares independence from reality and behaves with absolute dominion, the very foundations of our life begin to crumble, for "instead of carrying out his role as a cooperator with God in the work of creation, man sets himself up in place of God and thus ends up provoking a rebellion on the part of nature".[95]

118. This situation has led to a constant schizophrenia, wherein a technocracy which sees no intrinsic value in lesser beings coexists with the other extreme, which sees no special value in human beings. But one cannot prescind from humanity. There can be no renewal of our relationship with nature without a renewal of humanity itself. There can be no ecology without an adequate anthropology. When the human person is considered as simply

---

[94] Cf. *Love for Creation. An Asian Response to the Ecological Crisis*, Declaration of the Colloquium sponsored by the Federation of Asian Bishops' Conferences (Tagatay, 31 January-5 February 1993), 3.3.2.

[95] JOHN PAUL II, Encyclical Letter *Centesimus Annus* (1 May 1991), 37: AAS 83 (1991), 840.

one being among others, the product of chance or physical determinism, then "our overall sense of responsibility wanes".[96] A misguided anthropocentrism need not necessarily yield to "biocentrism", for that would entail adding yet another imbalance, failing to solve present problems and adding new ones. Human beings cannot be expected to feel responsibility for the world unless, at the same time, their unique capacities of knowledge, will, freedom and responsibility are recognized and valued.

119. Nor must the critique of a misguided anthropocentrism underestimate the importance of interpersonal relations. If the present ecological crisis is one small sign of the ethical, cultural and spiritual crisis of modernity, we cannot presume to heal our relationship with nature and the environment without healing all fundamental human relationships. Christian thought sees human beings as possessing a particular dignity above other creatures; it thus inculcates esteem for each person and respect for others. Our openness to others, each of whom is a "thou" capable of knowing, loving and entering into dialogue, remains the source of our nobility as human persons. A correct relationship with the created world demands that we not weaken this social dimension of openness to others, much less the transcendent dimension of our openness to the "Thou" of God. Our relationship with the environment can never be isolated from our relationship with others and with God. Otherwise, it would be nothing more than romantic individualism dressed up in ecological garb, locking us into a stifling immanence.

120. Since everything is interrelated, concern for the protection of nature is also incompatible with the justification of abortion. How can we genuinely teach the importance of concern for other vulnerable beings, however troublesome or inconvenient they may be, if we fail to protect a human embryo, even when its presence is uncomfortable and creates difficulties? "If personal and social sensitivity towards the acceptance of the new life is lost,

---

[96] BENEDICT XVI, *Message for the 2010 World Day of Peace*, 2: AAS 102 (2010), 41.

then other forms of acceptance that are valuable for society also wither away".[97]

121. We need to develop a new synthesis capable of overcoming the false arguments of recent centuries. Christianity, in fidelity to its own identity and the rich deposit of truth which it has received from Jesus Christ, continues to reflect on these issues in fruitful dialogue with changing historical situations. In doing so, it reveals its eternal newness.[98]

Practical relativism

122. A misguided anthropocentrism leads to a misguided lifestyle. In the Apostolic Exhortation *Evangelii Gaudium,* I noted that the practical relativism typical of our age is "even more dangerous than doctrinal relativism".[99] When human beings place themselves at the centre, they give absolute priority to immediate convenience and all else becomes relative. Hence we should not be surprised to find, in conjunction with the omnipresent technocratic paradigm and the cult of unlimited human power, the rise of a relativism which sees everything as irrelevant unless it serves one's own immediate interests. There is a logic in all this whereby different attitudes can feed on one another, leading to environmental degradation and social decay.

123. The culture of relativism is the same disorder which drives one person to take advantage of another, to treat others as mere objects, imposing forced labour on them or enslaving them to pay their debts. The same kind of thinking leads to the sexual exploitation of children and abandonment of the elderly who no longer serve our interests. It is also the mindset of those who

---

[97] ID., Encyclical Letter *Caritas in Veritate* (29 June 2009), 28: AAS 101 (2009), 663.

[98] Cf. VINCENT OF LERINS, *Commonitorium Primum*, ch. 23: PL 50, 688: "Ut annis scilicet consolidetur, dilatetur tempore, sublimetur aetate".

[99] No. 80: AAS 105 (2013), 1053.

say: Let us allow the invisible forces of the market to regulate the economy, and consider their impact on society and nature as collateral damage. In the absence of objective truths or sound principles other than the satisfaction of our own desires and immediate needs, what limits can be placed on human trafficking, organized crime, the drug trade, commerce in blood diamonds and the fur of endangered species? Is it not the same relativistic logic which justifies buying the organs of the poor for resale or use in experimentation, or eliminating children because they are not what their parents wanted? This same "use and throw away" logic generates so much waste, because of the disordered desire to consume more than what is really necessary. We should not think that political efforts or the force of law will be sufficient to prevent actions which affect the environment because, when the culture itself is corrupt and objective truth and universally valid principles are no longer upheld, then laws can only be seen as arbitrary impositions or obstacles to be avoided.

The need to protect employment

124. Any approach to an integral ecology, which by definition does not exclude human beings, needs to take account of the value of labour, as Saint John Paul II wisely noted in his Encyclical *Laborem Exercens*. According to the biblical account of creation, God placed man and woman in the garden he had created (cf. *Gen* 2:15) not only to preserve it ("keep") but also to make it fruitful ("till"). Labourers and craftsmen thus "maintain the fabric of the world" (*Sir* 38:34). Developing the created world in a prudent way is the best way of caring for it, as this means that we ourselves become the instrument used by God to bring out the potential which he himself inscribed in things: "The Lord created medicines out of the earth, and a sensible man will not despise them" (*Sir* 38:4).

125. If we reflect on the proper relationship between human beings and the world around us, we see the need for a correct

understanding of work; if we talk about the relationship between human beings and things, the question arises as to the meaning and purpose of all human activity. This has to do not only with manual or agricultural labour but with any activity involving a modification of existing reality, from producing a social report to the design of a technological development. Underlying every form of work is a concept of the relationship which we can and must have with what is other than ourselves. Together with the awe-filled contemplation of creation which we find in Saint Francis of Assisi, the Christian spiritual tradition has also developed a rich and balanced understanding of the meaning of work, as, for example, in the life of Blessed Charles de Foucauld and his followers.

126. We can also look to the great tradition of monasticism. Originally, it was a kind of flight from the world, an escape from the decadence of the cities. The monks sought the desert, convinced that it was the best place for encountering the presence of God. Later, Saint Benedict of Norcia proposed that his monks live in community, combining prayer and spiritual reading with manual labour (*ora et labora*). Seeing manual labour as spiritually meaningful proved revolutionary. Personal growth and sanctification came to be sought in the interplay of recollection and work. This way of experiencing work makes us more protective and respectful of the environment; it imbues our relationship to the world with a healthy sobriety.

127. We are convinced that "man is the source, the focus and the aim of all economic and social life".[100] Nonetheless, once our human capacity for contemplation and reverence is impaired, it becomes easy for the meaning of work to be misunderstood.[101] We need to remember that men and women have "the capacity to improve their lot, to further their moral growth and to develop

---

[100] SECOND VATICAN ECUMENICAL COUNCIL, Pastoral Constitution on the Church in the Modern World *Gaudium et Spes*, 63.

[101] Cf. JOHN PAUL II, Encyclical Letter *Centesimus Annus* (1 May 1991), 37: AAS 83 (1991), 840.

their spiritual endowments".[102] Work should be the setting for this rich personal growth, where many aspects of life enter into play: creativity, planning for the future, developing our talents, living out our values, relating to others, giving glory to God. It follows that, in the reality of today's global society, it is essential that "we continue to prioritize the goal of access to steady employment for everyone",[103] no matter the limited interests of business and dubious economic reasoning.

128. We were created with a vocation to work. The goal should not be that technological progress increasingly replace human work, for this would be detrimental to humanity. Work is a necessity, part of the meaning of life on this earth, a path to growth, human development and personal fulfilment. Helping the poor financially must always be a provisional solution in the face of pressing needs. The broader objective should always be to allow them a dignified life through work. Yet the orientation of the economy has favoured a kind of technological progress in which the costs of production are reduced by laying off workers and replacing them with machines. This is yet another way in which we can end up working against ourselves. The loss of jobs also has a negative impact on the economy "through the progressive erosion of social capital: the network of relationships of trust, dependability, and respect for rules, all of which are indispensable for any form of civil coexistence".[104] In other words, "human costs always include economic costs, and economic dysfunctions always involve human costs".[105] To stop investing in people, in order to gain greater short-term financial gain, is bad business for society.

129. In order to continue providing employment, it is imperative to promote an economy which favours productive diversity and

---

[102] PAUL VI, Encyclical Letter *Populorum Progressio* (26 March 1967), 34: AAS 59 (1967), 274.

[103] BENEDICT XVI, Encyclical Letter *Caritas in Veritate* (29 June 2009), 32: AAS 101 (2009), 666.

[104] Ibid.

[105] Ibid.

business creativity. For example, there is a great variety of small-scale food production systems which feed the greater part of the world's peoples, using a modest amount of land and producing less waste, be it in small agricultural parcels, in orchards and gardens, hunting and wild harvesting or local fishing. Economies of scale, especially in the agricultural sector, end up forcing smallholders to sell their land or to abandon their traditional crops. Their attempts to move to other, more diversified, means of production prove fruitless because of the difficulty of linkage with regional and global markets, or because the infrastructure for sales and transport is geared to larger businesses. Civil authorities have the right and duty to adopt clear and firm measures in support of small producers and differentiated production. To ensure economic freedom from which all can effectively benefit, restraints occasionally have to be imposed on those possessing greater resources and financial power. To claim economic freedom while real conditions bar many people from actual access to it, and while possibilities for employment continue to shrink, is to practise a doublespeak which brings politics into disrepute. Business is a noble vocation, directed to producing wealth and improving our world. It can be a fruitful source of prosperity for the areas in which it operates, especially if it sees the creation of jobs as an essential part of its service to the common good.

New biological technologies

130. In the philosophical and theological vision of the human being and of creation which I have presented, it is clear that the human person, endowed with reason and knowledge, is not an external factor to be excluded. While human intervention on plants and animals is permissible when it pertains to the necessities of human life, the *Catechism of the Catholic Church* teaches that experimentation on animals is morally acceptable only "if it remains within reasonable limits [and] contributes to caring for or saving human lives".[106] The *Catechism* firmly states that human power has

---

[106] *Catechism of the Catholic Church*, 2417.

limits and that "it is contrary to human dignity to cause animals to suffer or die needlessly".[107] All such use and experimentation "requires a religious respect for the integrity of creation".[108]

131. Here I would recall the balanced position of Saint John Paul II, who stressed the benefits of scientific and technological progress as evidence of "the nobility of the human vocation to participate responsibly in God's creative action", while also noting that "we cannot interfere in one area of the ecosystem without paying due attention to the consequences of such interference in other areas".[109] He made it clear that the Church values the benefits which result "from the study and applications of molecular biology, supplemented by other disciplines such as genetics, and its technological application in agriculture and industry".[110] But he also pointed out that this should not lead to "indiscriminate genetic manipulation"[111] which ignores the negative effects of such interventions. Human creativity cannot be suppressed. If an artist cannot be stopped from using his or her creativity, neither should those who possess particular gifts for the advancement of science and technology be prevented from using their God-given talents for the service of others. We need constantly to rethink the goals, effects, overall context and ethical limits of this human activity, which is a form of power involving considerable risks.

132. This, then, is the correct framework for any reflection concerning human intervention on plants and animals, which at present includes genetic manipulation by biotechnology for the sake of exploiting the potential present in material reality. The respect owed by faith to reason calls for close attention to what the biological sciences, through research uninfluenced by economic interests, can teach us about biological structures, their possibilities and their

---

[107] Ibid., 2418.

[108] Ibid., 2415.

[109] *Message for the 1990 World Day of Peace*, 6: AAS 82 (1990), 150.

[110] *Address to the Pontifical Academy of Sciences* (3 October 1981), 3: *Insegnamenti* 4/2 (1981), 333.

[111] *Message for the 1990 World Day of Peace*, 7: AAS 82 (1990), 151.

mutations. Any legitimate intervention will act on nature only in order "to favour its development in its own line, that of creation, as intended by God".[112]

133. It is difficult to make a general judgement about genetic modification (GM), whether vegetable or animal, medical or agricultural, since these vary greatly among themselves and call for specific considerations. The risks involved are not always due to the techniques used, but rather to their improper or excessive application. Genetic mutations, in fact, have often been, and continue to be, caused by nature itself. Nor are mutations caused by human intervention a modern phenomenon. The domestication of animals, the crossbreeding of species and other older and universally accepted practices can be mentioned as examples. We need but recall that scientific developments in GM cereals began with the observation of natural bacteria which spontaneously modified plant genomes. In nature, however, this process is slow and cannot be compared to the fast pace induced by contemporary technological advances, even when the latter build upon several centuries of scientific progress.

134. Although no conclusive proof exists that GM cereals may be harmful to human beings, and in some regions their use has brought about economic growth which has helped to resolve problems, there remain a number of significant difficulties which should not be underestimated. In many places, following the introduction of these crops, productive land is concentrated in the hands of a few owners due to "the progressive disappearance of small producers, who, as a consequence of the loss of the exploited lands, are obliged to withdraw from direct production".[113] The most vulnerable of these become temporary labourers, and many rural workers end up moving to poverty-stricken urban areas. The

---

[112] JOHN PAUL II, *Address to the 35th General Assembly of the World Medical Association* (29 October 1983), 6: AAS 76 (1984), 394.

[113] EPISCOPAL COMMISSION FOR PASTORAL CONCERNS IN ARGENTINA, *Una tierra para todos* (June 2005), 19.

expansion of these crops has the effect of destroying the complex network of ecosystems, diminishing the diversity of production and affecting regional economies, now and in the future. In various countries, we see an expansion of oligopolies for the production of cereals and other products needed for their cultivation. This dependency would be aggravated were the production of infertile seeds to be considered; the effect would be to force farmers to purchase them from larger producers.

135. Certainly, these issues require constant attention and a concern for their ethical implications. A broad, responsible scientific and social debate needs to take place, one capable of considering all the available information and of calling things by their name. It sometimes happens that complete information is not put on the table; a selection is made on the basis of particular interests, be they politico-economic or ideological. This makes it difficult to reach a balanced and prudent judgement on different questions, one which takes into account all the pertinent variables. Discussions are needed in which all those directly or indirectly affected (farmers, consumers, civil authorities, scientists, seed producers, people living near fumigated fields, and others) can make known their problems and concerns, and have access to adequate and reliable information in order to make decisions for the common good, present and future. This is a complex environmental issue; it calls for a comprehensive approach which would require, at the very least, greater efforts to finance various lines of independent, interdisciplinary research capable of shedding new light on the problem.

136. On the other hand, it is troubling that, when some ecological movements defend the integrity of the environment, rightly demanding that certain limits be imposed on scientific research, they sometimes fail to apply those same principles to human life. There is a tendency to justify transgressing all boundaries when experimentation is carried out on living human embryos. We forget that the inalienable worth of a human being transcends his or her degree of development. In the same way, when technology

disregards the great ethical principles, it ends up considering any practice whatsoever as licit. As we have seen in this chapter, a technology severed from ethics will not easily be able to limit its own power.

CHAPTER FOUR

INTEGRAL ECOLOGY

137. Since everything is closely interrelated, and today's problems call for a vision capable of taking into account every aspect of the global crisis, I suggest that we now consider some elements of an *integral ecology*, one which clearly respects its human and social dimensions.

I. ENVIRONMENTAL, ECONOMIC AND SOCIAL ECOLOGY

138. Ecology studies the relationship between living organisms and the environment in which they develop. This necessarily entails reflection and debate about the conditions required for the life and survival of society, and the honesty needed to question certain models of development, production and consumption. It cannot be emphasized enough how everything is interconnected. Time and space are not independent of one another, and not even atoms or subatomic particles can be considered in isolation. Just as the different aspects of the planet—physical, chemical and biological—are interrelated, so too living species are part of a network which we will never fully explore and understand. A good part of our genetic code is shared by many living beings. It follows that the fragmentation of knowledge and the isolation of bits of information can actually become a form of ignorance, unless they are integrated into a broader vision of reality.

139. When we speak of the "environment", what we really mean is a relationship existing between nature and the society which lives in it. Nature cannot be regarded as something separate from

ourselves or as a mere setting in which we live. We are part of nature, included in it and thus in constant interaction with it. Recognizing the reasons why a given area is polluted requires a study of the workings of society, its economy, its behaviour patterns, and the ways it grasps reality. Given the scale of change, it is no longer possible to find a specific, discrete answer for each part of the problem. It is essential to seek comprehensive solutions which consider the interactions within natural systems themselves and with social systems. We are faced not with two separate crises, one environmental and the other social, but rather with one complex crisis which is both social and environmental. Strategies for a solution demand an integrated approach to combating poverty, restoring dignity to the excluded, and at the same time protecting nature.

140. Due to the number and variety of factors to be taken into account when determining the environmental impact of a concrete undertaking, it is essential to give researchers their due role, to facilitate their interaction, and to ensure broad academic freedom. Ongoing research should also give us a better understanding of how different creatures relate to one another in making up the larger units which today we term "ecosystems". We take these systems into account not only to determine how best to use them, but also because they have an intrinsic value independent of their usefulness. Each organism, as a creature of God, is good and admirable in itself; the same is true of the harmonious ensemble of organisms existing in a defined space and functioning as a system. Although we are often not aware of it, we depend on these larger systems for our own existence. We need only recall how ecosystems interact in dispersing carbon dioxide, purifying water, controlling illnesses and epidemics, forming soil, breaking down waste, and in many other ways which we overlook or simply do not know about. Once they become conscious of this, many people realize that we live and act on the basis of a reality which has previously been given to us, which precedes our existence and our abilities. So, when we speak of "sustainable use", consideration must always be given to each ecosystem's regenerative ability in its different areas and aspects.

141. Economic growth, for its part, tends to produce predictable reactions and a certain standardization with the aim of simplifying procedures and reducing costs. This suggests the need for an "economic ecology" capable of appealing to a broader vision of reality. The protection of the environment is in fact "an integral part of the development process and cannot be considered in isolation from it".[114] We urgently need a humanism capable of bringing together the different fields of knowledge, including economics, in the service of a more integral and integrating vision. Today, the analysis of environmental problems cannot be separated from the analysis of human, family, work-related and urban contexts, nor from how individuals relate to themselves, which leads in turn to how they relate to others and to the environment. There is an interrelation between ecosystems and between the various spheres of social interaction, demonstrating yet again that "the whole is greater than the part".[115]

142. If everything is related, then the health of a society's institutions has consequences for the environment and the quality of human life. "Every violation of solidarity and civic friendship harms the environment".[116] In this sense, social ecology is necessarily institutional, and gradually extends to the whole of society, from the primary social group, the family, to the wider local, national and international communities. Within each social stratum, and between them, institutions develop to regulate human relationships. Anything which weakens those institutions has negative consequences, such as injustice, violence and loss of freedom. A number of countries have a relatively low level of institutional effectiveness, which results in greater problems for their people while benefiting those who profit from this situation. Whether in the administration of the state, the various levels of civil society,

---

[114] *Rio Declaration on Environment and Development* (14 June 1992), Principle 4.

[115] Apostolic Exhortation *Evangelii Gaudium* (24 November 2013), 237: AAS 105 (2013), 1116.

[116] BENEDICT XVI, Encyclical Letter *Caritas in Veritate* (29 June 2009), 51: AAS 101 (2009), 687.

or relationships between individuals themselves, lack of respect for the law is becoming more common. Laws may be well framed yet remain a dead letter. Can we hope, then, that in such cases, legislation and regulations dealing with the environment will really prove effective? We know, for example, that countries which have clear legislation about the protection of forests continue to keep silent as they watch laws repeatedly being broken. Moreover, what takes place in any one area can have a direct or indirect influence on other areas. Thus, for example, drug use in affluent societies creates a continual and growing demand for products imported from poorer regions, where behaviour is corrupted, lives are destroyed, and the environment continues to deteriorate.

II. CULTURAL ECOLOGY

143. Together with the patrimony of nature, there is also an historic, artistic and cultural patrimony which is likewise under threat. This patrimony is a part of the shared identity of each place and a foundation upon which to build a habitable city. It is not a matter of tearing down and building new cities, supposedly more respectful of the environment yet not always more attractive to live in. Rather, there is a need to incorporate the history, culture and architecture of each place, thus preserving its original identity. Ecology, then, also involves protecting the cultural treasures of humanity in the broadest sense. More specifically, it calls for greater attention to local cultures when studying environmental problems, favouring a dialogue between scientific-technical language and the language of the people. Culture is more than what we have inherited from the past; it is also, and above all, a living, dynamic and participatory present reality, which cannot be excluded as we rethink the relationship between human beings and the environment.

144. A consumerist vision of human beings, encouraged by the mechanisms of today's globalized economy, has a levelling effect on cultures, diminishing the immense variety which is the heritage of all humanity. Attempts to resolve all problems through uniform

regulations or technical interventions can lead to overlooking the complexities of local problems which demand the active participation of all members of the community. New processes taking shape cannot always fit into frameworks imported from outside; they need to be based in the local culture itself. As life and the world are dynamic realities, so our care for the world must also be flexible and dynamic. Merely technical solutions run the risk of addressing symptoms and not the more serious underlying problems. There is a need to respect the rights of peoples and cultures, and to appreciate that the development of a social group presupposes an historical process which takes place within a cultural context and demands the constant and active involvement of local people *from within their proper culture.* Nor can the notion of the quality of life be imposed from without, for quality of life must be understood within the world of symbols and customs proper to each human group.

145. Many intensive forms of environmental exploitation and degradation not only exhaust the resources which provide local communities with their livelihood, but also undo the social structures which, for a long time, shaped cultural identity and their sense of the meaning of life and community. The disappearance of a culture can be just as serious, or even more serious, than the disappearance of a species of plant or animal. The imposition of a dominant lifestyle linked to a single form of production can be just as harmful as the altering of ecosystems.

146. In this sense, it is essential to show special care for indigenous communities and their cultural traditions. They are not merely one minority among others, but should be the principal dialogue partners, especially when large projects affecting their land are proposed. For them, land is not a commodity but rather a gift from God and from their ancestors who rest there, a sacred space with which they need to interact if they are to maintain their identity and values. When they remain on their land, they themselves care for it best. Nevertheless, in various parts of the world, pressure is being put on them to abandon their homelands to make

room for agricultural or mining projects which are undertaken without regard for the degradation of nature and culture.

III. ECOLOGY OF DAILY LIFE

147. Authentic development includes efforts to bring about an integral improvement in the quality of human life, and this entails considering the setting in which people live their lives. These settings influence the way we think, feel and act. In our rooms, our homes, our workplaces and neighbourhoods, we use our environment as a way of expressing our identity. We make every effort to adapt to our environment, but when it is disorderly, chaotic or saturated with noise and ugliness, such overstimulation makes it difficult to find ourselves integrated and happy.

148. An admirable creativity and generosity is shown by persons and groups who respond to environmental limitations by alleviating the adverse effects of their surroundings and learning to orient their lives amid disorder and uncertainty. For example, in some places, where the façades of buildings are derelict, people show great care for the interior of their homes, or find contentment in the kindness and friendliness of others. A wholesome social life can light up a seemingly undesirable environment. At times a commendable human ecology is practised by the poor despite numerous hardships. The feeling of asphyxiation brought on by densely populated residential areas is countered if close and warm relationships develop, if communities are created, if the limitations of the environment are compensated for in the interior of each person who feels held within a network of solidarity and belonging. In this way, any place can turn from being a hell on earth into the setting for a dignified life.

149. The extreme poverty experienced in areas lacking harmony, open spaces or potential for integration, can lead to incidents of brutality and to exploitation by criminal organizations. In the unstable neighbourhoods of mega-cities, the daily experience of overcrowding and social anonymity can create a sense of

uprootedness which spawns antisocial behaviour and violence. Nonetheless, I wish to insist that love always proves more powerful. Many people in these conditions are able to weave bonds of belonging and togetherness which convert overcrowding into an experience of community in which the walls of the ego are torn down and the barriers of selfishness overcome. This experience of a communitarian salvation often generates creative ideas for the improvement of a building or a neighbourhood.[117]

150. Given the interrelationship between living space and human behaviour, those who design buildings, neighbourhoods, public spaces and cities, ought to draw on the various disciplines which help us to understand people's thought processes, symbolic language and ways of acting. It is not enough to seek the beauty of design. More precious still is the service we offer to another kind of beauty: people's quality of life, their adaptation to the environment, encounter and mutual assistance. Here too, we see how important it is that urban planning always take into consideration the views of those who will live in these areas.

151. There is also a need to protect those common areas, visual landmarks and urban landscapes which increase our sense of belonging, of rootedness, of "feeling at home" within a city which includes us and brings us together. It is important that the different parts of a city be well integrated and that those who live there have a sense of the whole, rather than being confined to one neighbourhood and failing to see the larger city as space which they share with others. Interventions which affect the urban or rural landscape should take into account how various elements combine to form a whole which is perceived by its inhabitants as a coherent and meaningful framework for their lives. Others will then no longer

---

[117] Some authors have emphasized the values frequently found, for example, in the *villas*, *chabolas* or *favelas* of Latin America: cf. JUAN CARLOS SCANNONE, S.J., "La irrupción del pobre y la lógica de la gratuidad", in JUAN CARLOS SCANNONE and MARCELO PERINE (eds.), *Irrupción del pobre y que hacer filosófico. Hacia una nueva racionalidad,* Buenos Aires, 1993, 225-230.

be seen as strangers, but as part of a "we" which all of us are working to create. For this same reason, in both urban and rural settings, it is helpful to set aside some places which can be preserved and protected from constant changes brought by human intervention.

152. Lack of housing is a grave problem in many parts of the world, both in rural areas and in large cities, since state budgets usually cover only a small portion of the demand. Not only the poor, but many other members of society as well, find it difficult to own a home. Having a home has much to do with a sense of personal dignity and the growth of families. This is a major issue for human ecology. In some places, where makeshift shanty towns have sprung up, this will mean developing those neighbourhoods rather than razing or displacing them. When the poor live in unsanitary slums or in dangerous tenements, "in cases where it is necessary to relocate them, in order not to heap suffering upon suffering, adequate information needs to be given beforehand, with choices of decent housing offered, and the people directly involved must be part of the process".[118] At the same time, creativity should be shown in integrating rundown neighbourhoods into a welcoming city: "How beautiful those cities which overcome paralyzing mistrust, integrate those who are different and make this very integration a new factor of development! How attractive are those cities which, even in their architectural design, are full of spaces which connect, relate and favour the recognition of others!"[119]

153. The quality of life in cities has much to do with systems of transport, which are often a source of much suffering for those who use them. Many cars, used by one or more people, circulate in cities, causing traffic congestion, raising the level of pollution, and consuming enormous quantities of non-renewable energy. This makes it necessary to build more roads and parking areas which

---

[118] PONTIFICAL COUNCIL FOR JUSTICE AND PEACE, *Compendium of the Social Doctrine of the Church*, 482.

[119] Apostolic Exhortation *Evangelii Gaudium* (24 November 2013), 210: AAS 105 (2013), 1107.

spoil the urban landscape. Many specialists agree on the need to give priority to public transportation. Yet some measures needed will not prove easily acceptable to society unless substantial improvements are made in the systems themselves, which in many cities force people to put up with undignified conditions due to crowding, inconvenience, infrequent service and lack of safety.

154. Respect for our dignity as human beings often jars with the chaotic realities that people have to endure in city life. Yet this should not make us overlook the abandonment and neglect also experienced by some rural populations which lack access to essential services and where some workers are reduced to conditions of servitude, without rights or even the hope of a more dignified life.

155. Human ecology also implies another profound reality: the relationship between human life and the moral law, which is inscribed in our nature and is necessary for the creation of a more dignified environment. Pope Benedict XVI spoke of an "ecology of man", based on the fact that "man too has a nature that he must respect and that he cannot manipulate at will".[120] It is enough to recognize that our body itself establishes us in a direct relationship with the environment and with other living beings. The acceptance of our bodies as God's gift is vital for welcoming and accepting the entire world as a gift from the Father and our common home, whereas thinking that we enjoy absolute power over our own bodies turns, often subtly, into thinking that we enjoy absolute power over creation. Learning to accept our body, to care for it and to respect its fullest meaning, is an essential element of any genuine human ecology. Also, valuing one's own body in its femininity or masculinity is necessary if I am going to be able to recognize myself in an encounter with someone who is different. In this way we can joyfully accept the specific gifts of another man or woman, the work of God the Creator, and find mutual enrichment. It is not

---

[120] *Address to the German Bundestag*, Berlin (22 September 2011): AAS 103 (2011), 668.

a healthy attitude which would seek "to cancel out sexual difference because it no longer knows how to confront it".[121]

IV. THE PRINCIPLE OF THE COMMON GOOD

156. An integral ecology is inseparable from the notion of the common good, a central and unifying principle of social ethics. The common good is "the sum of those conditions of social life which allow social groups and their individual members relatively thorough and ready access to their own fulfilment".[122]

157. Underlying the principle of the common good is respect for the human person as such, endowed with basic and inalienable rights ordered to his or her integral development. It has also to do with the overall welfare of society and the development of a variety of intermediate groups, applying the principle of subsidiarity. Outstanding among those groups is the family, as the basic cell of society. Finally, the common good calls for social peace, the stability and security provided by a certain order which cannot be achieved without particular concern for distributive justice; whenever this is violated, violence always ensues. Society as a whole, and the state in particular, are obliged to defend and promote the common good.

158. In the present condition of global society, where injustices abound and growing numbers of people are deprived of basic human rights and considered expendable, the principle of the common good immediately becomes, logically and inevitably, a summons to solidarity and a preferential option for the poorest of our brothers and sisters. This option entails recognizing the implications of the universal destination of the world's goods, but, as

---

[121] *Catechesis* (15 April 2015): *L'Osservatore Romano*, 16 April 2015, p. 8.

[122] SECOND VATICAN ECUMENICAL COUNCIL, Pastoral Constitution on the Church in the Modern World *Gaudium et Spes*, 26.

I mentioned in the Apostolic Exhortation *Evangelii Gaudium*,[123] it demands before all else an appreciation of the immense dignity of the poor in the light of our deepest convictions as believers. We need only look around us to see that, today, this option is in fact an ethical imperative essential for effectively attaining the common good.

V. JUSTICE BETWEEN THE GENERATIONS

159. The notion of the common good also extends to future generations. The global economic crises have made painfully obvious the detrimental effects of disregarding our common destiny, which cannot exclude those who come after us. We can no longer speak of sustainable development apart from intergenerational solidarity. Once we start to think about the kind of world we are leaving to future generations, we look at things differently; we realize that the world is a gift which we have freely received and must share with others. Since the world has been given to us, we can no longer view reality in a purely utilitarian way, in which efficiency and productivity are entirely geared to our individual benefit. Intergenerational solidarity is not optional, but rather a basic question of justice, since the world we have received also belongs to those who will follow us. The Portuguese bishops have called upon us to acknowledge this obligation of justice: "The environment is part of a logic of receptivity. It is on loan to each generation, which must then hand it on to the next".[124] An integral ecology is marked by this broader vision.

160. What kind of world do we want to leave to those who come after us, to children who are now growing up? This question not only concerns the environment in isolation; the issue cannot be approached piecemeal. When we ask ourselves what kind of world we want to leave behind, we think in the first place of its general

---

[123] Cf. Nos. 186-201: AAS 105 (2013), 1098-1105.
[124] PORTUGUESE BISHOPS' CONFERENCE, Pastoral Letter *Responsabilidade Solidária pelo Bem Comum* (15 September 2003), 20.

direction, its meaning and its values. Unless we struggle with these deeper issues, I do not believe that our concern for ecology will produce significant results. But if these issues are courageously faced, we are led inexorably to ask other pointed questions: What is the purpose of our life in this world? Why are we here? What is the goal of our work and all our efforts? What need does the earth have of us? It is no longer enough, then, simply to state that we should be concerned for future generations. We need to see that what is at stake is our own dignity. Leaving an inhabitable planet to future generations is, first and foremost, up to us. The issue is one which dramatically affects us, for it has to do with the ultimate meaning of our earthly sojourn.

161. Doomsday predictions can no longer be met with irony or disdain. We may well be leaving to coming generations debris, desolation and filth. The pace of consumption, waste and environmental change has so stretched the planet's capacity that our contemporary lifestyle, unsustainable as it is, can only precipitate catastrophes, such as those which even now periodically occur in different areas of the world. The effects of the present imbalance can only be reduced by our decisive action, here and now. We need to reflect on our accountability before those who will have to endure the dire consequences.

162. Our difficulty in taking up this challenge seriously has much to do with an ethical and cultural decline which has accompanied the deterioration of the environment. Men and women of our postmodern world run the risk of rampant individualism, and many problems of society are connected with today's self-centred culture of instant gratification. We see this in the crisis of family and social ties and the difficulties of recognizing the other. Parents can be prone to impulsive and wasteful consumption, which then affects their children who find it increasingly difficult to acquire a home of their own and build a family. Furthermore, our inability to think seriously about future generations is linked to our inability to broaden the scope of our present interests and to give consideration to those who remain excluded from development. Let us not only

keep the poor of the future in mind, but also today's poor, whose life on this earth is brief and who cannot keep on waiting. Hence, "in addition to a fairer sense of intergenerational solidarity there is also an urgent moral need for a renewed sense of intragenerational solidarity".[125]

CHAPTER FIVE

LINES OF APPROACH AND ACTION

163. So far I have attempted to take stock of our present situation, pointing to the cracks in the planet that we inhabit as well as to the profoundly human causes of environmental degradation. Although the contemplation of this reality in itself has already shown the need for a change of direction and other courses of action, now we shall try to outline the major paths of dialogue which can help us escape the spiral of self-destruction which currently engulfs us.

I. DIALOGUE ON THE ENVIRONMENT IN THE INTERNATIONAL COMMUNITY

164. Beginning in the middle of the last century and overcoming many difficulties, there has been a growing conviction that our planet is a homeland and that humanity is one people living in a common home. An interdependent world not only makes us more conscious of the negative effects of certain lifestyles and models of production and consumption which affect us all; more importantly, it motivates us to ensure that solutions are proposed from a global perspective, and not simply to defend the interests of a few countries. Interdependence obliges us to think of *one world with a common plan*. Yet the same ingenuity which has brought about enormous technological progress has so far proved incapable of finding effective ways of dealing with grave environmental and social problems worldwide. A global consensus is essential

---

[125] BENEDICT XVI, *Message for the 2010 World Day of Peace*, 8: AAS 102 (2010), 45.

for confronting the deeper problems, which cannot be resolved by unilateral actions on the part of individual countries. Such a consensus could lead, for example, to planning a sustainable and diversified agriculture, developing renewable and less polluting forms of energy, encouraging a more efficient use of energy, promoting a better management of marine and forest resources, and ensuring universal access to drinking water.

165. We know that technology based on the use of highly polluting fossil fuels—especially coal, but also oil and, to a lesser degree, gas—needs to be progressively replaced without delay. Until greater progress is made in developing widely accessible sources of renewable energy, it is legitimate to choose the less harmful alternative or to find short-term solutions. But the international community has still not reached adequate agreements about the responsibility for paying the costs of this energy transition. In recent decades, environmental issues have given rise to considerable public debate and have elicited a variety of committed and generous civic responses. Politics and business have been slow to react in a way commensurate with the urgency of the challenges facing our world. Although the post-industrial period may well be remembered as one of the most irresponsible in history, nonetheless there is reason to hope that humanity at the dawn of the twenty-first century will be remembered for having generously shouldered its grave responsibilities.

166. Worldwide, the ecological movement has made significant advances, thanks also to the efforts of many organizations of civil society. It is impossible here to mention them all, or to review the history of their contributions. But thanks to their efforts, environmental questions have increasingly found a place on public agendas and encouraged more far-sighted approaches. This notwithstanding, recent World Summits on the environment have not lived up to expectations because, due to lack of political will, they were unable to reach truly meaningful and effective global agreements on the environment.

167. The 1992 Earth Summit in Rio de Janeiro is worth mentioning. It proclaimed that "human beings are at the centre of concerns for sustainable development".[126] Echoing the 1972 Stockholm Declaration, it enshrined international cooperation to care for the ecosystem of the entire earth, the obligation of those who cause pollution to assume its costs, and the duty to assess the environmental impact of given projects and works. It set the goal of limiting greenhouse gas concentration in the atmosphere, in an effort to reverse the trend of global warming. It also drew up an agenda with an action plan and a convention on biodiversity, and stated principles regarding forests. Although the summit was a real step forward, and prophetic for its time, its accords have been poorly implemented, due to the lack of suitable mechanisms for oversight, periodic review and penalties in cases of non-compliance. The principles which it proclaimed still await an efficient and flexible means of practical implementation.

168. Among positive experiences in this regard, we might mention, for example, the Basel Convention on hazardous wastes, with its system of reporting, standards and controls. There is also the binding Convention on international trade in endangered species of wild fauna and flora, which includes on-site visits for verifying effective compliance. Thanks to the Vienna Convention for the protection of the ozone layer and its implementation through the Montreal Protocol and amendments, the problem of the layer's thinning seems to have entered a phase of resolution.

169. As far as the protection of biodiversity and issues related to desertification are concerned, progress has been far less significant. With regard to climate change, the advances have been regrettably few. Reducing greenhouse gases requires honesty, courage and responsibility, above all on the part of those countries which are more powerful and pollute the most. The Conference of the United

---

[126] *Rio Declaration on Environment and Development* (14 June 1992), Principle 1.

Nations on Sustainable Development, "Rio+20" (Rio de Janeiro 2012), issued a wide-ranging but ineffectual outcome document. International negotiations cannot make significant progress due to positions taken by countries which place their national interests above the global common good. Those who will have to suffer the consequences of what we are trying to hide will not forget this failure of conscience and responsibility. Even as this Encyclical was being prepared, the debate was intensifying. We believers cannot fail to ask God for a positive outcome to the present discussions, so that future generations will not have to suffer the effects of our ill-advised delays.

170. Some strategies for lowering pollutant gas emissions call for the internationalization of environmental costs, which would risk imposing on countries with fewer resources burdensome commitments to reducing emissions comparable to those of the more industrialized countries. Imposing such measures penalizes those countries most in need of development. A further injustice is perpetrated under the guise of protecting the environment. Here also, the poor end up paying the price. Furthermore, since the effects of climate change will be felt for a long time to come, even if stringent measures are taken now, some countries with scarce resources will require assistance in adapting to the effects already being produced, which affect their economies. In this context, there is a need for common and differentiated responsibilities. As the bishops of Bolivia have stated, "the countries which have benefited from a high degree of industrialization, at the cost of enormous emissions of greenhouse gases, have a greater responsibility for providing a solution to the problems they have caused".[127]

171. The strategy of buying and selling "carbon credits" can lead to a new form of speculation which would not help reduce the emission of polluting gases worldwide. This system seems to

---

[127] BOLIVIAN BISHOPS' CONFERENCE, Pastoral Letter on the Environment and Human Development in Bolivia *El universo, don de Dios para la vida* (March 2012), 86.

provide a quick and easy solution under the guise of a certain commitment to the environment, but in no way does it allow for the radical change which present circumstances require. Rather, it may simply become a ploy which permits maintaining the excessive consumption of some countries and sectors.

172. For poor countries, the priorities must be to eliminate extreme poverty and to promote the social development of their people. At the same time, they need to acknowledge the scandalous level of consumption in some privileged sectors of their population and to combat corruption more effectively. They are likewise bound to develop less polluting forms of energy production, but to do so they require the help of countries which have experienced great growth at the cost of the ongoing pollution of the planet. Taking advantage of abundant solar energy will require the establishment of mechanisms and subsidies which allow developing countries access to technology transfer, technical assistance and financial resources, but in a way which respects their concrete situations, since "the compatibility of [infrastructures] with the context for which they have been designed is not always adequately assessed".[128] The costs of this would be low, compared to the risks of climate change. In any event, these are primarily ethical decisions, rooted in solidarity between all peoples.

173. Enforceable international agreements are urgently needed, since local authorities are not always capable of effective intervention. Relations between states must be respectful of each other's sovereignty, but must also lay down mutually agreed means of averting regional disasters which would eventually affect everyone. Global regulatory norms are needed to impose obligations and prevent unacceptable actions, for example, when powerful companies or countries dump contaminated waste or offshore polluting industries in other countries.

---

[128] PONTIFICAL COUNCIL FOR JUSTICE AND PEACE, *Energy, Justice and Peace,* IV, 1, Vatican City (2014), 53.

174. Let us also mention the system of governance of the oceans. International and regional conventions do exist, but fragmentation and the lack of strict mechanisms of regulation, control and penalization end up undermining these efforts. The growing problem of marine waste and the protection of the open seas represent particular challenges. What is needed, in effect, is an agreement on systems of governance for the whole range of so-called "global commons".

175. The same mindset which stands in the way of making radical decisions to reverse the trend of global warming also stands in the way of achieving the goal of eliminating poverty. A more responsible overall approach is needed to deal with both problems: the reduction of pollution and the development of poorer countries and regions. The twenty-first century, while maintaining systems of governance inherited from the past, is witnessing a weakening of the power of nation states, chiefly because the economic and financial sectors, being transnational, tends to prevail over the political. Given this situation, it is essential to devise stronger and more efficiently organized international institutions, with functionaries who are appointed fairly by agreement among national governments, and empowered to impose sanctions. As Benedict XVI has affirmed in continuity with the social teaching of the Church: "To manage the global economy; to revive economies hit by the crisis; to avoid any deterioration of the present crisis and the greater imbalances that would result; to bring about integral and timely disarmament, food security and peace; to guarantee the protection of the environment and to regulate migration: for all this, there is urgent need of a true world political authority, as my predecessor Blessed John XXIII indicated some years ago".[129] Diplomacy also takes on new importance in the work of developing international strategies which can anticipate serious problems affecting us all.

---

[129] BENEDICT XVI, Encyclical Letter *Caritas in Veritate* (29 June 2009), 67: AAS 101 (2009).

II. DIALOGUE FOR NEW NATIONAL
AND LOCAL POLICIES

176. There are not just winners and losers among countries, but within poorer countries themselves. Hence different responsibilities need to be identified. Questions related to the environment and economic development can no longer be approached only from the standpoint of differences between countries; they also call for greater attention to policies on the national and local levels.

177. Given the real potential for a misuse of human abilities, individual states can no longer ignore their responsibility for planning, coordination, oversight and enforcement within their respective borders. How can a society plan and protect its future amid constantly developing technological innovations? One authoritative source of oversight and coordination is the law, which lays down rules for admissible conduct in the light of the common good. The limits which a healthy, mature and sovereign society must impose are those related to foresight and security, regulatory norms, timely enforcement, the elimination of corruption, effective responses to undesired side-effects of production processes, and appropriate intervention where potential or uncertain risks are involved. There is a growing jurisprudence dealing with the reduction of pollution by business activities. But political and institutional frameworks do not exist simply to avoid bad practice, but also to promote best practice, to stimulate creativity in seeking new solutions and to encourage individual or group initiatives.

178. A politics concerned with immediate results, supported by consumerist sectors of the population, is driven to produce short-term growth. In response to electoral interests, governments are reluctant to upset the public with measures which could affect the level of consumption or create risks for foreign investment. The myopia of power politics delays the inclusion of a far-sighted environmental agenda within the overall agenda of governments. Thus

we forget that "time is greater than space",[130] that we are always more effective when we generate processes rather than holding on to positions of power. True statecraft is manifest when, in difficult times, we uphold high principles and think of the long-term common good. Political powers do not find it easy to assume this duty in the work of nation-building.

179. In some places, cooperatives are being developed to exploit renewable sources of energy which ensure local self-sufficiency and even the sale of surplus energy. This simple example shows that, while the existing world order proves powerless to assume its responsibilities, local individuals and groups can make a real difference. They are able to instil a greater sense of responsibility, a strong sense of community, a readiness to protect others, a spirit of creativity and a deep love for the land. They are also concerned about what they will eventually leave to their children and grand-children. These values are deeply rooted in indigenous peoples. Because the enforcement of laws is at times inadequate due to corruption, public pressure has to be exerted in order to bring about decisive political action. Society, through non-governmental organizations and intermediate groups, must put pressure on governments to develop more rigorous regulations, procedures and controls. Unless citizens control political power—national, regional and municipal—it will not be possible to control damage to the environment. Local legislation can be more effective, too, if agreements exist between neighbouring communities to support the same environmental policies.

180. There are no uniform recipes, because each country or region has its own problems and limitations. It is also true that political realism may call for transitional measures and technologies, so long as these are accompanied by the gradual framing and acceptance of binding commitments. At the same time, on the national and local levels, much still needs to be done, such as promoting

---

[130] Apostolic Exhortation *Evangelii Gaudium* (24 November 2013), 222: AAS 105 (2013), 1111.

ways of conserving energy. These would include favouring forms of industrial production with maximum energy efficiency and diminished use of raw materials, removing from the market products which are less energy efficient or more polluting, improving transport systems, and encouraging the construction and repair of buildings aimed at reducing their energy consumption and levels of pollution. Political activity on the local level could also be directed to modifying consumption, developing an economy of waste disposal and recycling, protecting certain species and planning a diversified agriculture and the rotation of crops. Agriculture in poorer regions can be improved through investment in rural infrastructures, a better organization of local or national markets, systems of irrigation, and the development of techniques of sustainable agriculture. New forms of cooperation and community organization can be encouraged in order to defend the interests of small producers and preserve local ecosystems from destruction. Truly, much can be done!

181. Here, continuity is essential, because policies related to climate change and environmental protection cannot be altered with every change of government. Results take time and demand immediate outlays which may not produce tangible effects within any one government's term. That is why, in the absence of pressure from the public and from civic institutions, political authorities will always be reluctant to intervene, all the more when urgent needs must be met. To take up these responsibilities and the costs they entail, politicians will inevitably clash with the mindset of short-term gain and results which dominates present-day economics and politics. But if they are courageous, they will attest to their God-given dignity and leave behind a testimony of selfless responsibility. A healthy politics is sorely needed, capable of reforming and coordinating institutions, promoting best practices and overcoming undue pressure and bureaucratic inertia. It should be added, though, that even the best mechanisms can break down when there are no worthy goals and values, or a genuine and profound humanism to serve as the basis of a noble and generous society.

III. DIALOGUE AND TRANSPARENCY
IN DECISION-MAKING

182. An assessment of the environmental impact of business ventures and projects demands transparent political processes involving a free exchange of views. On the other hand, the forms of corruption which conceal the actual environmental impact of a given project, in exchange for favours, usually produce specious agreements which fail to inform adequately and to allow for full debate.

183. Environmental impact assessment should not come after the drawing up of a business proposition or the proposal of a particular policy, plan or programme. It should be part of the process from the beginning, and be carried out in a way which is interdisciplinary, transparent and free of all economic or political pressure. It should be linked to a study of working conditions and possible effects on people's physical and mental health, on the local economy and on public safety. Economic returns can thus be forecast more realistically, taking into account potential scenarios and the eventual need for further investment to correct possible undesired effects. A consensus should always be reached between the different stakeholders, who can offer a variety of approaches, solutions and alternatives. The local population should have a special place at the table; they are concerned about their own future and that of their children, and can consider goals transcending immediate economic interest. We need to stop thinking in terms of "interventions" to save the environment in favour of policies developed and debated by all interested parties. The participation of the latter also entails being fully informed about such projects and their different risks and possibilities; this includes not just preliminary decisions but also various follow-up activities and continued monitoring. Honesty and truth are needed in scientific and political discussions; these should not be limited to the issue of whether or not a particular project is permitted by law.

184. In the face of possible risks to the environment which may affect the common good now and in the future, decisions must be made "based on a comparison of the risks and benefits foreseen for the various possible alternatives".[131] This is especially the case when a project may lead to a greater use of natural resources, higher levels of emission or discharge, an increase of refuse, or significant changes to the landscape, the habitats of protected species or public spaces. Some projects, if insufficiently studied, can profoundly affect the quality of life of an area due to very different factors such as unforeseen noise pollution, the shrinking of visual horizons, the loss of cultural values, or the effects of nuclear energy use. The culture of consumerism, which prioritizes short-term gain and private interest, can make it easy to rubber-stamp authorizations or to conceal information.

185. In any discussion about a proposed venture, a number of questions need to be asked in order to discern whether or not it will contribute to genuine integral development. What will it accomplish? Why? Where? When? How? For whom? What are the risks? What are the costs? Who will pay those costs and how? In this discernment, some questions must have higher priority. For example, we know that water is a scarce and indispensable resource and a fundamental right which conditions the exercise of other human rights. This indisputable fact overrides any other assessment of environmental impact on a region.

186. The Rio Declaration of 1992 states that "where there are threats of serious or irreversible damage, lack of full scientific certainty shall not be used as a pretext for postponing cost-effective measures"[132] which prevent environmental degradation. This precautionary principle makes it possible to protect those who

---

[131] PONTIFICAL COUNCIL FOR JUSTICE AND PEACE, *Compendium of the Social Doctrine of the Church*, 469.

[132] *Rio Declaration on the Environment and Development* (14 June 1992), Principle 15.

are most vulnerable and whose ability to defend their interests and to assemble incontrovertible evidence is limited. If objective information suggests that serious and irreversible damage may result, a project should be halted or modified, even in the absence of indisputable proof. Here the burden of proof is effectively reversed, since in such cases objective and conclusive demonstrations will have to be brought forward to demonstrate that the proposed activity will not cause serious harm to the environment or to those who inhabit it.

187. This does not mean being opposed to any technological innovations which can bring about an improvement in the quality of life. But it does mean that profit cannot be the sole criterion to be taken into account, and that, when significant new information comes to light, a reassessment should be made, with the involvement of all interested parties. The outcome may be a decision not to proceed with a given project, to modify it or to consider alternative proposals.

188. There are certain environmental issues where it is not easy to achieve a broad consensus. Here I would state once more that the Church does not presume to settle scientific questions or to replace politics. But I am concerned to encourage an honest and open debate so that particular interests or ideologies will not prejudice the common good.

IV. POLITICS AND ECONOMY IN DIALOGUE FOR HUMAN FULFILMENT

189. Politics must not be subject to the economy, nor should the economy be subject to the dictates of an efficiency-driven paradigm of technocracy. Today, in view of the common good, there is urgent need for politics and economics to enter into a frank dialogue in the service of life, especially human life. Saving banks at any cost, making the public pay the price, forgoing a firm commitment to reviewing and reforming the entire system, only reaffirms the absolute power of a financial system, a power which

has no future and will only give rise to new crises after a slow, costly and only apparent recovery. The financial crisis of 2007-08 provided an opportunity to develop a new economy, more attentive to ethical principles, and new ways of regulating speculative financial practices and virtual wealth. But the response to the crisis did not include rethinking the outdated criteria which continue to rule the world. Production is not always rational, and is usually tied to economic variables which assign to products a value that does not necessarily correspond to their real worth. This frequently leads to an overproduction of some commodities, with unnecessary impact on the environment and with negative results on regional economies.[133] The financial bubble also tends to be a productive bubble. The problem of the real economy is not confronted with vigour, yet it is the real economy which makes diversification and improvement in production possible, helps companies to function well, and enables small and medium businesses to develop and create employment.

190. Here too, it should always be kept in mind that "environmental protection cannot be assured solely on the basis of financial calculations of costs and benefits. The environment is one of those goods that cannot be adequately safeguarded or promoted by market forces".[134] Once more, we need to reject a magical conception of the market, which would suggest that problems can be solved simply by an increase in the profits of companies or individuals. Is it realistic to hope that those who are obsessed with maximizing profits will stop to reflect on the environmental damage which they will leave behind for future generations? Where profits alone count, there can be no thinking about the rhythms of nature, its phases of decay and regeneration, or the complexity of ecosystems which may be gravely upset by human intervention. Moreover,

---

[133] Cf. MEXICAN BISHOPS' CONFERENCE, EPISCOPAL COMMISSION FOR PASTORAL AND SOCIAL CONCERNS, *Jesucristo, vida y esperanza de los indigenas e campesinos* (14 January 2008).

[134] PONTIFICAL COUNCIL FOR JUSTICE AND PEACE, *Compendium of the Social Doctrine of the Church*, 470.

biodiversity is considered at most a deposit of economic resources available for exploitation, with no serious thought for the real value of things, their significance for persons and cultures, or the concerns and needs of the poor.

191. Whenever these questions are raised, some react by accusing others of irrationally attempting to stand in the way of progress and human development. But we need to grow in the conviction that a decrease in the pace of production and consumption can at times give rise to another form of progress and development. Efforts to promote a sustainable use of natural resources are not a waste of money, but rather an investment capable of providing other economic benefits in the medium term. If we look at the larger picture, we can see that more diversified and innovative forms of production which impact less on the environment can prove very profitable. It is a matter of openness to different possibilities which do not involve stifling human creativity and its ideals of progress, but rather directing that energy along new channels.

192. For example, a path of productive development, which is more creative and better directed, could correct the present disparity between excessive technological investment in consumption and insufficient investment in resolving urgent problems facing the human family. It could generate intelligent and profitable ways of reusing, revamping and recycling, and it could also improve the energy efficiency of cities. Productive diversification offers the fullest possibilities to human ingenuity to create and innovate, while at the same time protecting the environment and creating more sources of employment. Such creativity would be a worthy expression of our most noble human qualities, for we would be striving intelligently, boldly and responsibly to promote a sustainable and equitable development within the context of a broader concept of quality of life. On the other hand, to find ever new ways of despoiling nature, purely for the sake of new consumer items and quick profit, would be, in human terms, less worthy and creative, and more superficial.

193. In any event, if in some cases sustainable development were to involve new forms of growth, then in other cases, given the insatiable and irresponsible growth produced over many decades, we need also to think of containing growth by setting some reasonable limits and even retracing our steps before it is too late. We know how unsustainable is the behaviour of those who constantly consume and destroy, while others are not yet able to live in a way worthy of their human dignity. That is why the time has come to accept decreased growth in some parts of the world, in order to provide resources for other places to experience healthy growth. Benedict XVI has said that "technologically advanced societies must be prepared to encourage more sober lifestyles, while reducing their energy consumption and improving its efficiency".[135]

194. For new models of progress to arise, there is a need to change "models of global development";[136] this will entail a responsible reflection on "the meaning of the economy and its goals with an eye to correcting its malfunctions and misapplications".[137] It is not enough to balance, in the medium term, the protection of nature with financial gain, or the preservation of the environment with progress. Halfway measures simply delay the inevitable disaster. Put simply, it is a matter of redefining our notion of progress. A technological and economic development which does not leave in its wake a better world and an integrally higher quality of life cannot be considered progress. Frequently, in fact, people's quality of life actually diminishes—by the deterioration of the environment, the low quality of food or the depletion of resources—in the midst of economic growth. In this context, talk of sustainable growth usually becomes a way of distracting attention and offering excuses. It absorbs the language and values of ecology into the categories of finance and technocracy, and the social and environmental responsibility of businesses often gets reduced to a series of marketing and image-enhancing measures.

---

[135] *Message for the 2010 World Day of Peace*, 9: AAS 102 (2010), 46.
[136] Ibid.
[137] Ibid., 5: p. 43.

195. The principle of the maximization of profits, frequently isolated from other considerations, reflects a misunderstanding of the very concept of the economy. As long as production is increased, little concern is given to whether it is at the cost of future resources or the health of the environment; as long as the clearing of a forest increases production, no one calculates the losses entailed in the desertification of the land, the harm done to biodiversity or the increased pollution. In a word, businesses profit by calculating and paying only a fraction of the costs involved. Yet only when "the economic and social costs of using up shared environmental resources are recognized with transparency and fully borne by those who incur them, not by other peoples or future generations",[138] can those actions be considered ethical. An instrumental way of reasoning, which provides a purely static analysis of realities in the service of present needs, is at work whether resources are allocated by the market or by state central planning.

196. What happens with politics? Let us keep in mind the principle of subsidiarity, which grants freedom to develop the capabilities present at every level of society, while also demanding a greater sense of responsibility for the common good from those who wield greater power. Today, it is the case that some economic sectors exercise more power than states themselves. But economics without politics cannot be justified, since this would make it impossible to favour other ways of handling the various aspects of the present crisis. The mindset which leaves no room for sincere concern for the environment is the same mindset which lacks concern for the inclusion of the most vulnerable members of society. For "the current model, with its emphasis on success and self-reliance, does not appear to favour an investment in efforts to help the slow, the weak or the less talented to find opportunities in life".[139]

---

[138] BENEDICT XVI, Encyclical Letter *Caritas in Veritate* (29 June 2009), 50: AAS 101 (2009), 686.

[139] Apostolic Exhortation *Evangelii Gaudium* (24 November 2013), 209: AAS 105 (2013), 1107.

197. What is needed is a politics which is far-sighted and capable of a new, integral and interdisciplinary approach to handling the different aspects of the crisis. Often, politics itself is responsible for the disrepute in which it is held, on account of corruption and the failure to enact sound public policies. If in a given region the state does not carry out its responsibilities, some business groups can come forward in the guise of benefactors, wield real power, and consider themselves exempt from certain rules, to the point of tolerating different forms of organized crime, human trafficking, the drug trade and violence, all of which become very difficult to eradicate. If politics shows itself incapable of breaking such a perverse logic, and remains caught up in inconsequential discussions, we will continue to avoid facing the major problems of humanity. A strategy for real change calls for rethinking processes in their entirety, for it is not enough to include a few superficial ecological considerations while failing to question the logic which underlies present-day culture. A healthy politics needs to be able to take up this challenge.

198. Politics and the economy tend to blame each other when it comes to poverty and environmental degradation. It is to be hoped that they can acknowledge their own mistakes and find forms of interaction directed to the common good. While some are concerned only with financial gain, and others with holding on to or increasing their power, what we are left with are conflicts or spurious agreements where the last thing either party is concerned about is caring for the environment and protecting those who are most vulnerable. Here too, we see how true it is that "unity is greater than conflict".[140]

V. RELIGIONS IN DIALOGUE WITH SCIENCE

199. It cannot be maintained that empirical science provides a complete explanation of life, the interplay of all creatures and the whole of reality. This would be to breach the limits imposed

---

[140] Ibid., 228: AAS 105 (2013), 1113.

by its own methodology. If we reason only within the confines of the latter, little room would be left for aesthetic sensibility, poetry, or even reason's ability to grasp the ultimate meaning and purpose of things.[141] I would add that "religious classics can prove meaningful in every age; they have an enduring power to open new horizons. . . . Is it reasonable and enlightened to dismiss certain writings simply because they arose in the context of religious belief?"[142] It would be quite simplistic to think that ethical principles present themselves purely in the abstract, detached from any context. Nor does the fact that they may be couched in religious language detract from their value in public debate. The ethical principles capable of being apprehended by reason can always reappear in different guise and find expression in a variety of languages, including religious language.

200. Any technical solution which science claims to offer will be powerless to solve the serious problems of our world if humanity loses its compass, if we lose sight of the great motivations which make it possible for us to live in harmony, to make sacrifices and to treat others well. Believers themselves must constantly feel challenged to live in a way consonant with their faith and not to contradict it by their actions. They need to be encouraged to be ever open to God's grace and to draw constantly from their deepest convictions about love, justice and peace. If a mistaken understanding of our

---

[141] Cf. Encyclical Letter *Lumen Fidei* (29 June 2013), 34: AAS 105 (2013), 577: "Nor is the light of faith, joined to the truth of love, extraneous to the material world, for love is always lived out in body and spirit; the light of faith is an incarnate light radiating from the luminous life of Jesus. It also illumines the material world, trusts its inherent order, and knows that it calls us to an ever widening path of harmony and understanding. The gaze of science thus benefits from faith: faith encourages the scientist to remain constantly open to reality in all its inexhaustible richness. Faith awakens the critical sense by preventing research from being satisfied with its own formulae and helps it to realize that nature is always greater. By stimulating wonder before the profound mystery of creation, faith broadens the horizons of reason to shed greater light on the world which discloses itself to scientific investigation".

[142] Apostolic Exhortation *Evangelii Gaudium* (24 November 2013), 256: AAS 105 (2013), 1123.

own principles has at times led us to justify mistreating nature, to exercise tyranny over creation, to engage in war, injustice and acts of violence, we believers should acknowledge that by so doing we were not faithful to the treasures of wisdom which we have been called to protect and preserve. Cultural limitations in different eras often affected the perception of these ethical and spiritual treasures, yet by constantly returning to their sources, religions will be better equipped to respond to today's needs.

201. The majority of people living on our planet profess to be believers. This should spur religions to dialogue among themselves for the sake of protecting nature, defending the poor, and building networks of respect and fraternity. Dialogue among the various sciences is likewise needed, since each can tend to become enclosed in its own language, while specialization leads to a certain isolation and the absolutization of its own field of knowledge. This prevents us from confronting environmental problems effectively. An open and respectful dialogue is also needed between the various ecological movements, among which ideological conflicts are not infrequently encountered. The gravity of the ecological crisis demands that we all look to the common good, embarking on a path of dialogue which demands patience, self-discipline and generosity, always keeping in mind that "realities are greater than ideas".[143]

CHAPTER SIX

ECOLOGICAL EDUCATION AND SPIRITUALITY

202. Many things have to change course, but it is we human beings above all who need to change. We lack an awareness of our common origin, of our mutual belonging, and of a future to be shared with everyone. This basic awareness would enable the development of new convictions, attitudes and forms of life. A great cultural, spiritual and educational challenge stands before us, and it will demand that we set out on the long path of renewal.

---

[143] Ibid., 231: p. 1114.

I. TOWARDS A NEW LIFESTYLE

203. Since the market tends to promote extreme consumerism in an effort to sell its products, people can easily get caught up in a whirlwind of needless buying and spending. Compulsive consumerism is one example of how the techno-economic paradigm affects individuals. Romano Guardini had already foreseen this: "The gadgets and technics forced upon him by the patterns of machine production and of abstract planning mass man accepts quite simply; they are the forms of life itself. To either a greater or lesser degree mass man is convinced that his conformity is both reasonable and just".[144] This paradigm leads people to believe that they are free as long as they have the supposed freedom to consume. But those really free are the minority who wield economic and financial power. Amid this confusion, postmodern humanity has not yet achieved a new self-awareness capable of offering guidance and direction, and this lack of identity is a source of anxiety. We have too many means and only a few insubstantial ends.

204. The current global situation engenders a feeling of instability and uncertainty, which in turn becomes "a seedbed for collective selfishness".[145] When people become self-centred and self-enclosed, their greed increases. The emptier a person's heart is, the more he or she needs things to buy, own and consume. It becomes almost impossible to accept the limits imposed by reality. In this horizon, a genuine sense of the common good also disappears. As these attitudes become more widespread, social norms are respected only to the extent that they do not clash with personal needs. So our concern cannot be limited merely to the threat of extreme weather events, but must also extend to the catastrophic consequences of social unrest. Obsession with a consumerist lifestyle, above all when few people are capable of maintaining it, can only lead to violence and mutual destruction.

---

[144] ROMANO GUARDINI, *Das Ende der Neuzeit*, 9th edition, Würzburg, 1965, 66-67 (English: *The End of the Modern World*, Wilmington, 1998, 60).

[145] JOHN PAUL II, *Message for the 1990 World Day of Peace,* 1: AAS 82 (1990), 147.

205. Yet all is not lost. Human beings, while capable of the worst, are also capable of rising above themselves, choosing again what is good, and making a new start, despite their mental and social conditioning. We are able to take an honest look at ourselves, to acknowledge our deep dissatisfaction, and to embark on new paths to authentic freedom. No system can completely suppress our openness to what is good, true and beautiful, or our God-given ability to respond to his grace at work deep in our hearts. I appeal to everyone throughout the world not to forget this dignity which is ours. No one has the right to take it from us.

206. A change in lifestyle could bring healthy pressure to bear on those who wield political, economic and social power. This is what consumer movements accomplish by boycotting certain products. They prove successful in changing the way businesses operate, forcing them to consider their environmental footprint and their patterns of production. When social pressure affects their earnings, businesses clearly have to find ways to produce differently. This shows us the great need for a sense of social responsibility on the part of consumers. "Purchasing is always a moral—and not simply economic—act".[146] Today, in a word, "the issue of environmental degradation challenges us to examine our lifestyle".[147]

207. The Earth Charter asked us to leave behind a period of self-destruction and make a new start, but we have not as yet developed a universal awareness needed to achieve this. Here, I would echo that courageous challenge: "As never before in history, common destiny beckons us to seek a new beginning. . . . Let ours be a time remembered for the awakening of a new reverence for life, the firm resolve to achieve sustainability, the quickening of the struggle for justice and peace, and the joyful celebration of life".[148]

---

[146] BENEDICT XVI, Encyclical Letter *Caritas in Veritate* (29 June 2009), 66: AAS 101 (2009), 699.

[147] ID., *Message for the 2010 World Day of Peace*, 11: AAS 102 (2010), 48.

[148] *Earth Charter*, The Hague (29 June 2000).

208. We are always capable of going out of ourselves towards the other. Unless we do this, other creatures will not be recognized for their true worth; we are unconcerned about caring for things for the sake of others; we fail to set limits on ourselves in order to avoid the suffering of others or the deterioration of our surroundings. Disinterested concern for others, and the rejection of every form of self-centeredness and self-absorption, are essential if we truly wish to care for our brothers and sisters and for the natural environment. These attitudes also attune us to the moral imperative of assessing the impact of our every action and personal decision on the world around us. If we can overcome individualism, we will truly be able to develop a different lifestyle and bring about significant changes in society.

II. EDUCATING FOR THE COVENANT BETWEEN HUMANITY AND THE ENVIRONMENT

209. An awareness of the gravity of today's cultural and ecological crisis must be translated into new habits. Many people know that our current progress and the mere amassing of things and pleasures are not enough to give meaning and joy to the human heart, yet they feel unable to give up what the market sets before them. In those countries which should be making the greatest changes in consumer habits, young people have a new ecological sensitivity and a generous spirit, and some of them are making admirable efforts to protect the environment. At the same time, they have grown up in a milieu of extreme consumerism and affluence which makes it difficult to develop other habits. We are faced with an educational challenge.

210. Environmental education has broadened its goals. Whereas in the beginning it was mainly centred on scientific information, consciousness-raising and the prevention of environmental risks, it tends now to include a critique of the "myths" of a modernity grounded in a utilitarian mindset (individualism, unlimited progress, competition, consumerism, the unregulated market). It seeks also to restore the various levels of ecological equilibrium, establishing

harmony within ourselves, with others, with nature and other living creatures, and with God. Environmental education should facilitate making the leap towards the transcendent which gives ecological ethics its deepest meaning. It needs educators capable of developing an ethics of ecology, and helping people, through effective pedagogy, to grow in solidarity, responsibility and compassionate care.

211. Yet this education, aimed at creating an "ecological citizenship", is at times limited to providing information, and fails to instil good habits. The existence of laws and regulations is insufficient in the long run to curb bad conduct, even when effective means of enforcement are present. If the laws are to bring about significant, long-lasting effects, the majority of the members of society must be adequately motivated to accept them, and personally transformed to respond. Only by cultivating sound virtues will people be able to make a selfless ecological commitment. A person who could afford to spend and consume more but regularly uses less heating and wears warmer clothes, shows the kind of convictions and attitudes which help to protect the environment. There is a nobility in the duty to care for creation through little daily actions, and it is wonderful how education can bring about real changes in lifestyle. Education in environmental responsibility can encourage ways of acting which directly and significantly affect the world around us, such as avoiding the use of plastic and paper, reducing water consumption, separating refuse, cooking only what can reasonably be consumed, showing care for other living beings, using public transport or car-pooling, planting trees, turning off unnecessary lights, or any number of other practices. All of these reflect a generous and worthy creativity which brings out the best in human beings. Reusing something instead of immediately discarding it, when done for the right reasons, can be an act of love which expresses our own dignity.

212. We must not think that these efforts are not going to change the world. They benefit society, often unbeknown to us, for they call forth a goodness which, albeit unseen, inevitably tends to spread. Furthermore, such actions can restore our sense of self-esteem;

they can enable us to live more fully and to feel that life on earth is worthwhile.

213. Ecological education can take place in a variety of settings: at school, in families, in the media, in catechesis and elsewhere. Good education plants seeds when we are young, and these continue to bear fruit throughout life. Here, though, I would stress the great importance of the family, which is "the place in which life—the gift of God—can be properly welcomed and protected against the many attacks to which it is exposed, and can develop in accordance with what constitutes authentic human growth. In the face of the so-called culture of death, the family is the heart of the culture of life".[149] In the family we first learn how to show love and respect for life; we are taught the proper use of things, order and cleanliness, respect for the local ecosystem and care for all creatures. In the family we receive an integral education, which enables us to grow harmoniously in personal maturity. In the family we learn to ask without demanding, to say "thank you" as an expression of genuine gratitude for what we have been given, to control our aggressivity and greed, and to ask forgiveness when we have caused harm. These simple gestures of heartfelt courtesy help to create a culture of shared life and respect for our surroundings.

214. Political institutions and various other social groups are also entrusted with helping to raise people's awareness. So too is the Church. All Christian communities have an important role to play in ecological education. It is my hope that our seminaries and houses of formation will provide an education in responsible simplicity of life, in grateful contemplation of God's world, and in concern for the needs of the poor and the protection of the environment. Because the stakes are so high, we need institutions empowered to impose penalties for damage inflicted on the environment. But we also need the personal qualities of self-control and willingness to learn from one another.

---

[149] ID., *Message for the 1990 World Day of Peace*, 14: AAS 82 (1990), 155.

215. In this regard, "the relationship between a good aesthetic education and the maintenance of a healthy environment cannot be overlooked".[150] By learning to see and appreciate beauty, we learn to reject self-interested pragmatism. If someone has not learned to stop and admire something beautiful, we should not be surprised if he or she treats everything as an object to be used and abused without scruple. If we want to bring about deep change, we need to realize that certain mindsets really do influence our behaviour. Our efforts at education will be inadequate and ineffectual unless we strive to promote a new way of thinking about human beings, life, society and our relationship with nature. Otherwise, the paradigm of consumerism will continue to advance, with the help of the media and the highly effective workings of the market.

III. ECOLOGICAL CONVERSION

216. The rich heritage of Christian spirituality, the fruit of twenty centuries of personal and communal experience, has a precious contribution to make to the renewal of humanity. Here, I would like to offer Christians a few suggestions for an ecological spirituality grounded in the convictions of our faith, since the teachings of the Gospel have direct consequences for our way of thinking, feeling and living. More than in ideas or concepts as such, I am interested in how such a spirituality can motivate us to a more passionate concern for the protection of our world. A commitment this lofty cannot be sustained by doctrine alone, without a spirituality capable of inspiring us, without an "interior impulse which encourages, motivates, nourishes and gives meaning to our individual and communal activity".[151] Admittedly, Christians have not always appropriated and developed the spiritual treasures bestowed by God upon the Church, where the life of the spirit is not dissociated from the body or from nature or from worldly realities, but lived in and with them, in communion with all that surrounds us.

---

[150] ID., *Message for the 1990 World Day of Peace*, 14: AAS 82 (1990), 155.
[151] Apostolic Exhortation *Evangelii Gaudium* (24 Nov 2013), 261: AAS 105 (2013), 1124.

217. "The external deserts in the world are growing, because the internal deserts have become so vast".[152] For this reason, the ecological crisis is also a summons to profound interior conversion. It must be said that some committed and prayerful Christians, with the excuse of realism and pragmatism, tend to ridicule expressions of concern for the environment. Others are passive; they choose not to change their habits and thus become inconsistent. So what they all need is an "ecological conversion", whereby the effects of their encounter with Jesus Christ become evident in their relationship with the world around them. Living our vocation to be protectors of God's handiwork is essential to a life of virtue; it is not an optional or a secondary aspect of our Christian experience.

218. In calling to mind the figure of Saint Francis of Assisi, we come to realize that a healthy relationship with creation is one dimension of overall personal conversion, which entails the recognition of our errors, sins, faults and failures, and leads to heartfelt repentance and desire to change. The Australian bishops spoke of the importance of such conversion for achieving reconciliation with creation: "To achieve such reconciliation, we must examine our lives and acknowledge the ways in which we have harmed God's creation through our actions and our failure to act. We need to experience a conversion, or change of heart".[153]

219. Nevertheless, self-improvement on the part of individuals will not by itself remedy the extremely complex situation facing our world today. Isolated individuals can lose their ability and freedom to escape the utilitarian mindset, and end up prey to an unethical consumerism bereft of social or ecological awareness. Social problems must be addressed by community networks and not simply by the sum of individual good deeds. This task "will

---

[152] BENEDICT XVI, *Homily for the Solemn Inauguration of the Petrine Ministry* (24 April 2005): AAS 97 (2005), 710.

[153] AUSTRALIAN CATHOLIC BISHOPS' CONFERENCE, *A New Earth—The Environmental Challenge* (2002).

make such tremendous demands of man that he could never achieve it by individual initiative or even by the united effort of men bred in an individualistic way. The work of dominating the world calls for a union of skills and a unity of achievement that can only grow from quite a different attitude".[154] The ecological conversion needed to bring about lasting change is also a community conversion.

220. This conversion calls for a number of attitudes which together foster a spirit of generous care, full of tenderness. First, it entails gratitude and gratuitousness, a recognition that the world is God's loving gift, and that we are called quietly to imitate his generosity in self-sacrifice and good works: "Do not let your left hand know what your right hand is doing . . . and your Father who sees in secret will reward you" (*Mt* 6:3-4). It also entails a loving awareness that we are not disconnected from the rest of creatures, but joined in a splendid universal communion. As believers, we do not look at the world from without but from within, conscious of the bonds with which the Father has linked us to all beings. By developing our individual, God-given capacities, an ecological conversion can inspire us to greater creativity and enthusiasm in resolving the world's problems and in offering ourselves to God "as a living sacrifice, holy and acceptable" (*Rom* 12:1). We do not understand our superiority as a reason for personal glory or irresponsible dominion, but rather as a different capacity which, in its turn, entails a serious responsibility stemming from our faith.

221. Various convictions of our faith, developed at the beginning of this Encyclical, can help us to enrich the meaning of this conversion. These include the awareness that each creature reflects something of God and has a message to convey to us, and the security that Christ has taken unto himself this material world and now, risen, is intimately present to each being, surrounding

---

[154] ROMANO GUARDINI, *Das Ende der Neuzeit*, 72 (*The End of the Modern World*, 65-66).

it with his affection and penetrating it with his light. Then too, there is the recognition that God created the world, writing into it an order and a dynamism that human beings have no right to ignore. We read in the Gospel that Jesus says of the birds of the air that "not one of them is forgotten before God" (*Lk* 12:6). How then can we possibly mistreat them or cause them harm? I ask all Christians to recognize and to live fully this dimension of their conversion. May the power and the light of the grace we have received also be evident in our relationship to other creatures and to the world around us. In this way, we will help nurture that sublime fraternity with all creation which Saint Francis of Assisi so radiantly embodied.

IV. JOY AND PEACE

222. Christian spirituality proposes an alternative understanding of the quality of life, and encourages a prophetic and contemplative lifestyle, one capable of deep enjoyment free of the obsession with consumption. We need to take up an ancient lesson, found in different religious traditions and also in the Bible. It is the conviction that "less is more". A constant flood of new consumer goods can baffle the heart and prevent us from cherishing each thing and each moment. To be serenely present to each reality, however small it may be, opens us to much greater horizons of understanding and personal fulfilment. Christian spirituality proposes a growth marked by moderation and the capacity to be happy with little. It is a return to that simplicity which allows us to stop and appreciate the small things, to be grateful for the opportunities which life affords us, to be spiritually detached from what we possess, and not to succumb to sadness for what we lack. This implies avoiding the dynamic of dominion and the mere accumulation of pleasures.

223. Such sobriety, when lived freely and consciously, is liberating. It is not a lesser life or one lived with less intensity. On the contrary, it is a way of living life to the full. In reality, those who

enjoy more and live better each moment are those who have given up dipping here and there, always on the look-out for what they do not have. They experience what it means to appreciate each person and each thing, learning familiarity with the simplest things and how to enjoy them. So they are able to shed unsatisfied needs, reducing their obsessiveness and weariness. Even living on little, they can live a lot, above all when they cultivate other pleasures and find satisfaction in fraternal encounters, in service, in developing their gifts, in music and art, in contact with nature, in prayer. Happiness means knowing how to limit some needs which only diminish us, and being open to the many different possibilities which life can offer.

224. Sobriety and humility were not favourably regarded in the last century. And yet, when there is a general breakdown in the exercise of a certain virtue in personal and social life, it ends up causing a number of imbalances, including environmental ones. That is why it is no longer enough to speak only of the integrity of ecosystems. We have to dare to speak of the integrity of human life, of the need to promote and unify all the great values. Once we lose our humility, and become enthralled with the possibility of limitless mastery over everything, we inevitably end up harming society and the environment. It is not easy to promote this kind of healthy humility or happy sobriety when we consider ourselves autonomous, when we exclude God from our lives or replace him with our own ego, and think that our subjective feelings can define what is right and what is wrong.

225. On the other hand, no one can cultivate a sober and satisfying life without being at peace with him or herself. An adequate understanding of spirituality consists in filling out what we mean by peace, which is much more than the absence of war. Inner peace is closely related to care for ecology and for the common good because, lived out authentically, it is reflected in a balanced lifestyle together with a capacity for wonder which takes us to a deeper understanding of life. Nature is filled with

words of love, but how can we listen to them amid constant noise, interminable and nerve-wracking distractions, or the cult of appearances? Many people today sense a profound imbalance which drives them to frenetic activity and makes them feel busy, in a constant hurry which in turn leads them to ride rough-shod over everything around them. This too affects how they treat the environment. An integral ecology includes taking time to recover a serene harmony with creation, reflecting on our lifestyle and our ideals, and contemplating the Creator who lives among us and surrounds us, whose presence "must not be contrived but found, uncovered".[155]

226. We are speaking of an attitude of the heart, one which approaches life with serene attentiveness, which is capable of being fully present to someone without thinking of what comes next, which accepts each moment as a gift from God to be lived to the full. Jesus taught us this attitude when he invited us to contemplate the lilies of the field and the birds of the air, or when seeing the rich young man and knowing his restlessness, "he looked at him with love" (*Mk* 10:21). He was completely present to everyone and to everything, and in this way he showed us the way to overcome that unhealthy anxiety which makes us superficial, aggressive and compulsive consumers.

227. One expression of this attitude is when we stop and give thanks to God before and after meals. I ask all believers to return to this beautiful and meaningful custom. That moment of blessing, however brief, reminds us of our dependence on God for life; it strengthens our feeling of gratitude for the gifts of creation; it acknowledges those who by their labours provide us with these goods; and it reaffirms our solidarity with those in greatest need.

---

[155] Apostolic Exhortation *Evangelii Gaudium* (24 November 2013), 71: AAS 105 (2013), 1050.

V. CIVIC AND POLITICAL LOVE

228. Care for nature is part of a lifestyle which includes the capacity for living together and communion. Jesus reminded us that we have God as our common Father and that this makes us brothers and sisters. Fraternal love can only be gratuitous; it can never be a means of repaying others for what they have done or will do for us. That is why it is possible to love our enemies. This same gratuitousness inspires us to love and accept the wind, the sun and the clouds, even though we cannot control them. In this sense, we can speak of a "universal fraternity".

229. We must regain the conviction that we need one another, that we have a shared responsibility for others and the world, and that being good and decent are worth it. We have had enough of immorality and the mockery of ethics, goodness, faith and honesty. It is time to acknowledge that light-hearted superficiality has done us no good. When the foundations of social life are corroded, what ensues are battles over conflicting interests, new forms of violence and brutality, and obstacles to the growth of a genuine culture of care for the environment.

230. Saint Therese of Lisieux invites us to practise the little way of love, not to miss out on a kind word, a smile or any small gesture which sows peace and friendship. An integral ecology is also made up of simple daily gestures which break with the logic of violence, exploitation and selfishness. In the end, a world of exacerbated consumption is at the same time a world which mistreats life in all its forms.

231. Love, overflowing with small gestures of mutual care, is also civic and political, and it makes itself felt in every action that seeks to build a better world. Love for society and commitment to the common good are outstanding expressions of a charity which affects not only relationships between individuals but also

"macro-relationships, social, economic and political ones".[156] That is why the Church set before the world the ideal of a "civilization of love".[157] Social love is the key to authentic development: "In order to make society more human, more worthy of the human person, love in social life—political, economic and cultural—must be given renewed value, becoming the constant and highest norm for all activity".[158] In this framework, along with the importance of little everyday gestures, social love moves us to devise larger strategies to halt environmental degradation and to encourage a "culture of care" which permeates all of society. When we feel that God is calling us to intervene with others in these social dynamics, we should realize that this too is part of our spirituality, which is an exercise of charity and, as such, matures and sanctifies us.

232. Not everyone is called to engage directly in political life. Society is also enriched by a countless array of organizations which work to promote the common good and to defend the environment, whether natural or urban. Some, for example, show concern for a public place (a building, a fountain, an abandoned monument, a landscape, a square), and strive to protect, restore, improve or beautify it as something belonging to everyone. Around these community actions, relationships develop or are recovered and a new social fabric emerges. Thus, a community can break out of the indifference induced by consumerism. These actions cultivate a shared identity, with a story which can be remembered and handed on. In this way, the world, and the quality of life of the poorest, are cared for, with a sense of solidarity which is at the same time aware that we live in a common home

---

[156] BENEDICT XVI, Encyclical Letter *Caritas in Veritate* (29 June 2009), 2: AAS 101 (2009), 642.

[157] PAUL VI, *Message for the 1977 World Day of Peace*: AAS 68 (1976), 709.

[158] PONTIFICAL COUNCIL FOR JUSTICE AND PEACE, *Compendium of the Social Doctrine of the Church*, 582.

which God has entrusted to us. These community actions, when they express self-giving love, can also become intense spiritual experiences.

VI. SACRAMENTAL SIGNS AND THE CELEBRATION OF REST

233. The universe unfolds in God, who fills it completely. Hence, there is a mystical meaning to be found in a leaf, in a mountain trail, in a dewdrop, in a poor person's face.[159] The ideal is not only to pass from the exterior to the interior to discover the action of God in the soul, but also to discover God in all things. Saint Bonaventure teaches us that "contemplation deepens the more we feel the working of God's grace within our hearts, and the better we learn to encounter God in creatures outside ourselves".[160]

234. Saint John of the Cross taught that all the goodness present in the realities and experiences of this world "is present in God eminently and infinitely, or more properly, in each of these sublime realities is God".[161] This is not because the finite things of this world are really divine, but because the mystic experiences the intimate connection between God and all beings, and thus feels that "all things are God".[162] Standing awestruck before a mountain, he or she cannot separate this experience from God, and perceives

---

[159] The spiritual writer Ali al-Khawas stresses from his own experience the need not to put too much distance between the creatures of the world and the interior experience of God. As he puts it: "Prejudice should not have us criticize those who seek ecstasy in music or poetry. There is a subtle mystery in each of the movements and sounds of this world. The initiate will capture what is being said when the wind blows, the trees sway, water flows, flies buzz, doors creak, birds sing, or in the sound of strings or flutes, the sighs of the sick, the groans of the afflicted . . . " (EVA DE VITRAY-MEYERO-VITCH [ed.], *Anthologie du soufisme,* Paris 1978, 200).

[160] *In II Sent.*, 23, 2, 3.

[161] *Cántico Espiritual*, XIV, 5.

[162] Ibid.

that the interior awe being lived has to be entrusted to the Lord: "Mountains have heights and they are plentiful, vast, beautiful, graceful, bright and fragrant. These mountains are what my Beloved is to me. Lonely valleys are quiet, pleasant, cool, shady and flowing with fresh water; in the variety of their groves and in the sweet song of the birds, they afford abundant recreation and delight to the senses, and in their solitude and silence, they refresh us and give rest. These valleys are what my Beloved is to me".[163]

235. The Sacraments are a privileged way in which nature is taken up by God to become a means of mediating supernatural life. Through our worship of God, we are invited to embrace the world on a different plane. Water, oil, fire and colours are taken up in all their symbolic power and incorporated in our act of praise. The hand that blesses is an instrument of God's love and a reflection of the closeness of Jesus Christ, who came to accompany us on the journey of life. Water poured over the body of a child in Baptism is a sign of new life. Encountering God does not mean fleeing from this world or turning our back on nature. This is especially clear in the spirituality of the Christian East. "Beauty, which in the East is one of the best loved names expressing the divine harmony and the model of humanity transfigured, appears everywhere: in the shape of a church, in the sounds, in the colours, in the lights, in the scents".[164] For Christians, all the creatures of the material universe find their true meaning in the incarnate Word, for the Son of God has incorporated in his person part of the material world, planting in it a seed of definitive transformation. "Christianity does not reject matter. Rather, bodiliness is considered in all its value in the liturgical act, whereby the human body is disclosed in its inner nature as a temple of the Holy Spirit and is united with the Lord Jesus, who himself took a body for the world's salvation".[165]

---

[163] Ibid., XIV, 6-7.

[164] JOHN PAUL II, Apostolic Letter *Orientale Lumen* (2 May 1995), 11: AAS 87 (1995), 757.

[165] Ibid.

236. It is in the Eucharist that all that has been created finds its greatest exaltation. Grace, which tends to manifest itself tangibly, found unsurpassable expression when God himself became man and gave himself as food for his creatures. The Lord, in the culmination of the mystery of the Incarnation, chose to reach our intimate depths through a fragment of matter. He comes not from above, but from within, he comes that we might find him in this world of ours. In the Eucharist, fullness is already achieved; it is the living centre of the universe, the overflowing core of love and of inexhaustible life. Joined to the incarnate Son, present in the Eucharist, the whole cosmos gives thanks to God. Indeed the Eucharist is itself an act of cosmic love: "Yes, cosmic! Because even when it is celebrated on the humble altar of a country church, the Eucharist is always in some way celebrated on the altar of the world".[166] The Eucharist joins heaven and earth; it embraces and penetrates all creation. The world which came forth from God's hands returns to him in blessed and undivided adoration: in the bread of the Eucharist, "creation is projected towards divinization, towards the holy wedding feast, towards unification with the Creator himself".[167] Thus, the Eucharist is also a source of light and motivation for our concerns for the environment, directing us to be stewards of all creation.

237. On Sunday, our participation in the Eucharist has special importance. Sunday, like the Jewish Sabbath, is meant to be a day which heals our relationships with God, with ourselves, with others and with the world. Sunday is the day of the Resurrection, the "first day" of the new creation, whose first fruits are the Lord's risen humanity, the pledge of the final transfiguration of all created reality. It also proclaims "man's eternal rest in God".[168] In this way, Christian spirituality incorporates the value of relaxation

---

[166] ID., Encyclical Letter *Ecclesia de Eucharistia* (17 April 2003), 8: AAS 95 (2003), 438.

[167] BENEDICT XVI, *Homily for the Mass of Corpus Domini* (15 June 2006): AAS 98 (2006), 513.

[168] *Catechism of the Catholic Church*, 2175.

and festivity. We tend to demean contemplative rest as something unproductive and unnecessary, but this is to do away with the very thing which is most important about work: its meaning. We are called to include in our work a dimension of receptivity and gratuity, which is quite different from mere inactivity. Rather, it is another way of working, which forms part of our very essence. It protects human action from becoming empty activism; it also prevents that unfettered greed and sense of isolation which make us seek personal gain to the detriment of all else. The law of weekly rest forbade work on the seventh day, "so that your ox and your donkey may have rest, and the son of your maidservant, and the stranger, may be refreshed" (*Ex* 23:12). Rest opens our eyes to the larger picture and gives us renewed sensitivity to the rights of others. And so the day of rest, centred on the Eucharist, sheds its light on the whole week, and motivates us to greater concern for nature and the poor.

VII. THE TRINITY AND THE RELATIONSHIP BETWEEN CREATURES

238. The Father is the ultimate source of everything, the loving and self-communicating foundation of all that exists. The Son, his reflection, through whom all things were created, united himself to this earth when he was formed in the womb of Mary. The Spirit, infinite bond of love, is intimately present at the very heart of the universe, inspiring and bringing new pathways. The world was created by the three Persons acting as a single divine principle, but each one of them performed this common work in accordance with his own personal property. Consequently, "when we contemplate with wonder the universe in all its grandeur and beauty, we must praise the whole Trinity".[169]

239. For Christians, believing in one God who is trinitarian communion suggests that the Trinity has left its mark on all creation.

---

[169] JOHN PAUL II, *Catechesis* (2 August 2000), 4: *Insegnamenti* 23/2 (2000), 112.

Saint Bonaventure went so far as to say that human beings, before sin, were able to see how each creature "testifies that God is three". The reflection of the Trinity was there to be recognized in nature "when that book was open to man and our eyes had not yet become darkened".[170] The Franciscan saint teaches us that *each creature bears in itself a specifically Trinitarian structure*, so real that it could be readily contemplated if only the human gaze were not so partial, dark and fragile. In this way, he points out to us the challenge of trying to read reality in a Trinitarian key.

240. The divine Persons are subsistent relations, and the world, created according to the divine model, is a web of relationships. Creatures tend towards God, and in turn it is proper to every living being to tend towards other things, so that throughout the universe we can find any number of constant and secretly interwoven relationships.[171] This leads us not only to marvel at the manifold connections existing among creatures, but also to discover a key to our own fulfilment. The human person grows more, matures more and is sanctified more to the extent that he or she enters into relationships, going out from themselves to live in communion with God, with others and with all creatures. In this way, they make their own that trinitarian dynamism which God imprinted in them when they were created. Everything is interconnected, and this invites us to develop a spirituality of that global solidarity which flows from the mystery of the Trinity.

VIII. QUEEN OF ALL CREATION

241. Mary, the Mother who cared for Jesus, now cares with maternal affection and pain for this wounded world. Just as her pierced heart mourned the death of Jesus, so now she grieves for the sufferings of the crucified poor and for the creatures of this world laid waste by human power. Completely transfigured, she

---

[170] *Quaest. Disp. de Myst. Trinitatis*, 1, 2 concl.

[171] Cf. THOMAS AQUINAS, *Summa Theologiae,* I, q. 11, art. 3; q. 21, art. 1, ad 3; q. 47, art. 3.

now lives with Jesus, and all creatures sing of her fairness. She is the Woman, "clothed in the sun, with the moon under her feet, and on her head a crown of twelve stars" (*Rev* 12:1). Carried up into heaven, she is the Mother and Queen of all creation. In her glorified body, together with the Risen Christ, part of creation has reached the fullness of its beauty. She treasures the entire life of Jesus in her heart (cf. *Lk* 2:19, 51), and now understands the meaning of all things. Hence, we can ask her to enable us to look at this world with eyes of wisdom.

242. At her side in the Holy Family of Nazareth stands the figure of Saint Joseph. Through his work and generous presence, he cared for and defended Mary and Jesus, delivering them from the violence of the unjust by bringing them to Egypt. The Gospel presents Joseph as a just man, hard-working and strong. But he also shows great tenderness, which is not a mark of the weak but of those who are genuinely strong, fully aware of reality and ready to love and serve in humility. That is why he was proclaimed custodian of the universal Church. He too can teach us how to show care; he can inspire us to work with generosity and tenderness in protecting this world which God has entrusted to us.

IX. BEYOND THE SUN

243. At the end, we will find ourselves face to face with the infinite beauty of God (cf. *1 Cor* 13:12), and be able to read with admiration and happiness the mystery of the universe, which with us will share in unending plenitude. Even now we are journeying towards the sabbath of eternity, the new Jerusalem, towards our common home in heaven. Jesus says: "I make all things new" (*Rev* 21:5). Eternal life will be a shared experience of awe, in which each creature, resplendently transfigured, will take its rightful place and have something to give those poor men and women who will have been liberated once and for all.

244. In the meantime, we come together to take charge of this home which has been entrusted to us, knowing that all the good

which exists here will be taken up into the heavenly feast. In union with all creatures, we journey through this land seeking God, for "if the world has a beginning and if it has been created, we must enquire who gave it this beginning, and who was its Creator".[172] Let us sing as we go. May our struggles and our concern for this planet never take away the joy of our hope.

245. God, who calls us to generous commitment and to give him our all, offers us the light and the strength needed to continue on our way. In the heart of this world, the Lord of life, who loves us so much, is always present. He does not abandon us, he does not leave us alone, for he has united himself definitively to our earth, and his love constantly impels us to find new ways forward. *Praise be to him*!

* * * * *

246. At the conclusion of this lengthy reflection which has been both joyful and troubling, I propose that we offer two prayers. The first we can share with all who believe in a God who is the all-powerful Creator, while in the other we Christians ask for inspiration to take up the commitment to creation set before us by the Gospel of Jesus.

A prayer for our earth

All-powerful God, you are present in the whole universe
and in the smallest of your creatures.
You embrace with your tenderness all that exists.
Pour out upon us the power of your love,
that we may protect life and beauty.
Fill us with peace, that we may live
as brothers and sisters, harming no one.
O God of the poor,
help us to rescue the abandoned and forgotten of this earth,

---

[172] BASIL THE GREAT, *Hom. in Hexaemeron*, I, 2, 6: PG 29, 8.

so precious in your eyes.
Bring healing to our lives,
that we may protect the world and not prey on it,
that we may sow beauty, not pollution and destruction.
Touch the hearts
of those who look only for gain
at the expense of the poor and the earth.
Teach us to discover the worth of each thing,
to be filled with awe and contemplation,
to recognize that we are profoundly united
with every creature
as we journey towards your infinite light.
We thank you for being with us each day.
Encourage us, we pray, in our struggle
for justice, love and peace.

A Christian prayer in union with creation

Father, we praise you with all your creatures.
They came forth from your all-powerful hand;
they are yours, filled with your presence and your tender love.
Praise be to you!

Son of God, Jesus,
through you all things were made.
You were formed in the womb of Mary our Mother,
you became part of this earth,
and you gazed upon this world with human eyes.
Today you are alive in every creature
in your risen glory.
Praise be to you!

Holy Spirit, by your light
you guide this world towards the Father's love
and accompany creation as it groans in travail.
You also dwell in our hearts

and you inspire us to do what is good.
Praise be to you!

Triune Lord, wondrous community of infinite love,
teach us to contemplate you
in the beauty of the universe,
for all things speak of you.
Awaken our praise and thankfulness
for every being that you have made.
Give us the grace to feel profoundly joined
to everything that is.

God of love, show us our place in this world
as channels of your love
for all the creatures of this earth,
for not one of them is forgotten in your sight.
Enlighten those who possess power and money
that they may avoid the sin of indifference,
that they may love the common good, advance the weak,
and care for this world in which we live.
The poor and the earth are crying out.
O Lord, seize us with your power and light,
help us to protect all life,
to prepare for a better future,
for the coming of your Kingdom
of justice, peace, love and beauty.
Praise be to you!
Amen.

Given in Rome at Saint Peter's on 24 May, the Solemnity of Pentecost, in the year 2015, the third of my Pontificate.

Franciscus

Index

abortion, 204–5
ACEN. *See* Anglican Communion Environmental Network
Adaptation Fund, 45
Africa, climate change in, 18, 25, 28
   global warming in, 169
   population growth in, 64
   water poverty in, 73, 159
agriculture
   enlightened, 113–14
   global warming and, 108–9
   industrial, 106–8, 111–12
   mixed, 114–15
   new model for, 112–15
   urban, 114
agricultural waste, 94–95
al-Khawas, Ali, 257n159
Amazon basin, 163
Anglican Church, 45
Anglican Communion Environmental Network, 45–46
Annan, Kofi, 135
Anthropocene Era, 20
anthropocentrism, xx, 6, 14–15, 18–21, 67, 139, 178–79, 202–13
anthropology, 19, 203
anti-body sentiment, 7–8
anti-creature sentiment, 7–8
Aparecida Document (Latin American and Caribbean bishops), 171
Aquinas, Thomas, 60, 187

Arch Coal, xvii
Aristotle, 12
attentiveness, 254
Australian Catholic Bishops' Conference, 77–78, 250
AXA, investments of, 46–47

Bacon, Francis, 15
Baltic Sea, 88, 95–96
Ban Ki-moon, xv, 70
Bank of England, 46–47
baptism, 83–84
Bartholomew, Ecumenical Patriarch, xix, 6, 138, 148–50
Basel Convention, 227
Basil the Great, 182
Benedict XVI, xviii, 5, 147–48, 221, 230, 239
Benedict of Norcia, 207
Bergoglio, Jorge Mario, xi–xii. *See also* Francis
Berry, Thomas, 137–42
Berry, William Nathan, 137
Bill and Melinda Gates Foundation, 47
bioaccumulation, 155
biocentrism, 19, 204
biodiversity, xv, 149, 157
   convention on, 227
   loss of, 56–57, 65, 160–65
   protection of, 58–59, 227
biofuels, 109
biological corridors, 162